Multinational
Oil

MULTINATIONAL OIL

A Study in Industrial Dynamics

NEIL H. JACOBY

Studies of the Modern Corporation
Graduate School of Business
Columbia University

MACMILLAN PUBLISHING CO., INC.
NEW YORK
COLLIER MACMILLAN PUBLISHERS
LONDON

Macmillan Publishing Co., Inc.
866 Third Avenue, New York, N.Y. 10022

Collier–Macmillan Canada Ltd.

Library of Congress Catalog Card Number: 74–22381

Printed in the United States of America

Paperback printing number

1 2 3 4 5 6 7 8 9 10

Hardbound printing number

1 2 3 4 5 6 7 8 9 10

Library of Congress Cataloging in Publication Data

Jacoby, Neil Herman
    Multinational oil.

    (Studies of the modern corporation)
    Includes bibliographical references and index.
    1. Petroleum industry and trade. 2. Energy policy.
3. Corporations, International. I. Title.
II. Series.
HD9560.5.J26   338.4'7'6655   74-22381
ISBN 0-02-915990-3
ISBN 0-02-915980-6 pbk.

Studies of the Modern Corporation

Columbia University Graduate School of Business

The Program for Studies of the Modern Corporation is devoted to the advancement and dissemination of knowledge about the corporation. Its publications are designed to stimulate inquiry, research, criticism, and reflection. They fall into three categories: works by outstanding businessmen, scholars, and professional men from a variety of backgrounds and academic disciplines; annotated and edited selections of business literature; and business classics that merit republication. The studies are supported by outside grants from private business, professional, and philanthropic institutions interested in the program's objectives.

Richard Eells
Editor of the Studies

Contents

List of Figures

List of Tables

Preface

WORLD ENERGY PROBLEMS entered the headlines during 1973 and 1974 when members of the Organization of Petroleum Exporting Countries (OPEC) unilaterally quadrupled the price of crude oil. Concurrently, members of the Organization of Arab Petroleum Exporting Countries (OAPEC) cut back production and imposed a temporary embargo on shipments to the United States for political reasons. Suddenly, the industrialized nations awoke to their heavy and increasing dependence upon the abundant supplies of oil from Africa, the Middle East, and Latin America.

This oil price "revolution" touched off an intense public debate over national energy policies. The new price structure and the use of oil for political ends changed the economics and the politics of the world oil industry. President Nixon proposed "Project Independence," by which the United States would attain energy self-sufficiency by 1980. Leasing of the U.S. continental shelves for oil exploration was accelerated. Programs of research were launched to achieve the conversion of oil shales, tar sands, and coal into liquid petroleum. Nuclear power development was speeded up. Scientists looked more closely into the possibilities of geothermal, solar, and tidal energy.

It is clear, however, that crude oil and natural gas will continue to supply the preponderance of the world's energy for the rest of this century. Many governmental inquiries have been launched into the workings of the foreign oil industry. An angry and confused public asks whether the new scarcity and high prices of petroleum products result from a conspiracy among the big international oil companies. Does the public interest require that they be nationalized? Regulated like public utilities? Or subjected to permanent price controls? This book offers answers to these questions.

This study has an unusual history. During 1953, the U.S. Department of Justice filed the International Oil Cartel suit against five large U.S.-based international oil companies—Standard Oil of New Jersey (now Exxon), Socony-Vacuum Oil Company (now Mobil), Standard Oil Company of California, The Texas Company (now Texaco), and the Gulf Oil Corporation—charging conspiracy to restrict production, raise prices, and divide markets in the world oil industry. In 1961, Standard Oil Company of California (Socal), one of the defendants, invited me to make a thorough and objective study of the structure and behavior of the foreign oil industry since World War II. The purpose was to determine whether competitive forces were waxing or waning.

Having had an enduring interest in industrial economics, I viewed the invitation as an opportunity to analyze one of the world's most important—and least understood—industries. I agreed at that time to undertake the study, provided that I would have a completely free hand to carry it out and to publish my conclusions. Most of 1961 and 1962 were spent in intensive research and writing.

Upon its completion in 1963, the study was submitted in confidence to the Department of Justice. Given the slowness with which the wheels of bureaucracy grind, epilogues to the study were prepared during 1965 and again during 1968. In the latter year, the Department of Justice dismissed its complaint against Socal. According to the government attorney in charge of the case, the study showed progressive changes in the international petroleum industry which made the government's case too weak to prosecute.

Publication of that study was nevertheless deferred because some of its contents dealt with politically sensitive issues, and I believed that the national security might be involved. This constraint was removed in early 1974 when the Subcommittee on Multinational Corporations of the Senate Foreign Relations Committee arranged for the publication of hitherto secret documents bearing upon the entry of American oil companies into the Middle East and upon the dismissal of the International Oil Cartel case.* The Subcommittee's purpose was to ascertain whether a lack of competition among the major American oil companies was contributing to high prices and short supplies of petroleum. In the preface to the publication, Senator Frank Church, Chairman of the Subcommittee, wrote that previous actions of the U.S. government had "precluded the creation of a competitive international oil industry." In expressing this conclusion, Senator Church went against much evidence submitted to his Subcommittee, as well as other evidence about the behavior of the world oil industry. Although the Subcommittee did include the original study in its official records, it has not published it so far. Yet public information is needed on trends in the structure and behavior of the world oil industry and its current status.

Now, more than twelve years after that study was done, I have felt it necessary to prepare and to publish

* U.S., Congress, Senate, prepared for the use of the Subcommittee on Multinational Corporations of the Committee on Foreign Relations, *The International Petroleum Cartel, the Iranian Consortium and U.S. National Security*, 93d Cong., 2d sess., February 21, 1974.

this study in the public interest. While including materials from the earlier study, this is a fresh analysis of the original and of subsequent data, designed to provide a basis for making current energy policies. This study has afforded an unusual opportunity to examine the accuracy of the forecasts made in the original study. Although subsequent events have not borne out every prediction, by validating most of them, they have added to the credibility of those that appear in this book.

Notwithstanding the plethora of published information about the world petroleum industry, much information needed to understand its development had to be especially assembled from the published reports of oil companies and from petroleum trade publications, as well as from official government publications. New studies have been made of postwar changes in the ownership of concession areas, crude oil reserves, oil produced, refining capacity, oil tankers, and of the market shares of companies. These underlying materials will, I hope, be published separately in two new volumes: *Statistical Studies of the Foreign Oil Industry* and *Entry Data for the Foreign Oil Industry*, which are cited here simply as *Statistical Studies* and *Entry Data*.

Although the foreign petroleum industry is the subject of an immense literature, most of it is topical and journalistic in character. That part which has scholarly value consists, in the main, of studies of particular divisions or aspects of the industry, or of oil activities in certain countries or regions of the world; or it addresses the history, technology, or politics of the world oil industry. In only a few books have scholars attempted systematic economic appraisals of the performance of the whole industry over time. Important and recent among these books are *Crude Oil Prices in the Middle East* (1966) by Helmut J. Frank, *The Large International Firm in the Developing Countries* (1968) by Edith T. Penrose, *Middle Eastern Oil and the Western World* (1971) by Sam H. Schurr and Paul T. Homan, *Oil: The Facts of Life* (1966) by Paul T. Frankel, and *The World Petroleum Market* (1972) by M. A. Adelman.

This book also ventures to make a comprehensive appraisal of the economic performance of the foreign oil industry in order to derive lessons helpful in resolving the energy problems of our times. It differs from preceding studies in the methodology employed and in the scope of the data analyzed. Emphasis is put on those structural and behavioral changes in the industry that have affected the vigor of competition.

Although the conclusions reached here do not diverge sharply from those of preceding studies, in general they do assert more far-reaching changes in the industry during the post–World War II era than have been perceived by most other scholars. This may result from the employment of both more comprehensive and more recent data on the industry. Also, this study has the advantage of having been written after the "oil revolution" of 1973 and 1974. Building upon the knowledge and insights of other scholars, this book aims to advance us toward a more complete understanding of the economic dynamics of the foreign oil industry.

Readers will, I hope, also perceive this study as a contribution to the methodology of industrial analysis as well as a source of information about the dynamics of the foreign oil industry. Because the detection of competition in an industry and the measurement of its vigor are the crux of most antitrust issues, practical methods for performing these tasks are important.

In a world market that was free of all taxes, royalties, or other governmental constraints, and in which competition was effective, the price of oil would be very low. But the real-world market for oil is dominated by high and rising taxation by the oil-exporting nations, and, since 1972, by concerted efforts of the members of the OPEC to raise prices and to restrict output. Because of effective competition in the industry and the power of OPEC, an international oil company today has relatively little influence on the price of oil to consumers. This is the culmination of a long process of rising intervention by governments in the world oil industry—a process traced in the present study.

Although the OPEC countries may later change their oil pricing and production policies, the future is likely to bring new kinds of governmental intervention into world oil affairs, by the oil-consuming as well as the oil-producing countries. The basic problem today is not how to create effective competition among oil enterprises. By every test, such competition now exists. The central issues are how to maintain a world price for crude oil that serves the long-run interests of all nations and how to define a new role for international oil companies that will bring about a productive relationship between them and national governments. Thoughts about these issues are presented in the concluding chapter of this study.

I gratefully acknowledge the contributions of many persons to this book. My colleague, Professor J. F. Weston, Director of the Research Program in Competition and Business Policy at UCLA, read the manuscript and offered valuable comments. So did Edwin W. Eckard, Jr. Professor Charles F. Stewart of Columbia University added useful perspectives. I am grateful to Richard Eells, Director of the Program for Studies of the Modern Corporation in the Graduate School of Business of Columbia University, for urging me strongly to publish this book in the Program. Chauncey G. Olinger, Jr., has given the text his usual careful and thoughtful editing. Mrs. Lynn Hickman, my secretary, patiently supervised the typing of several drafts of the manuscript. Needless to say, I alone take responsibility for the contents of this book.

Neil H. Jacoby
Los Angeles, California
August 1974

1

The Foreign Oil Industry: A Model for Its Analysis

THE AIMS OF THIS STUDY

D URING THE EARLY 1970s the world petroleum industry underwent a revolution which was marked by four important changes. Strategic crude oil pricing and production decisions were taken from the multinational oil companies by the Organization of Petroleum Exporting Countries (OPEC). OPEC members quadrupled the price of crude oil. Some cut back oil production for political as well as for economic purposes. And most progressively nationalized the oil reserves and producing properties of the private oil enterprises.

These actions precipitated an energy "crisis" in the oil-deficient nations, the full dimensions and ultimate consequences of which will take years to unfold. They raised a whole new range of public policy issues in those many nations of the world whose economies depend upon supplies of imported petroleum: Was the "oil revolution" caused by shortcomings in the operation of the market

1

system in which multinational oil companies competed in the sale of petroleum products? Would consumers be better served if the oil industry were in the hands of government-owned companies? Should the private oil enterprises be subjected to public-utility-type control of their prices, outputs, and profits?

Answers to these pressing new problems should be grounded upon a thorough analysis of the performance of the world oil industry. This study provides such an analysis. It describes the technical, economic, and political changes that have shaped the oil industry since World War II.[1] It analyzes their effects upon the structure and behavior of petroleum markets, upon the vigor of competition, and upon the market power of the big multinational oil companies. It lays out the implications of the new world oil order and the kind of relationships between governments and oil enterprises that appear likely to obtain in the future. By assessing the performance of the foreign oil industry, its strengths and weaknesses, lessons can be learned that are useful in resolving the critical energy issues of our times.

THE METHODOLOGY OF THIS STUDY

This is an economic study of the foreign oil industry. Its raw materials are the operating and financial statistics of the industry. Its methodology is analytical, utilizing the tools of economic theory and statistical inference. The basic concern is to measure changes in market structure and behavior in the world oil industry.

The conceptual model used in this study derives from the modern theory of industrial economics. This theory contemplates an "industry" of firms, all competing in the sale of an identifiable "product" to buyers in a "market." It assumes that the *structure of any industry*—the number and size-distribution of enterprises selling in the market, the conditions of entry, and the degree of concentration of business among firms—is normally shaped by the physical and technical conditions of producing and marketing the industry's products, by the characteristics of demand, and by the environment of public law and regulation affecting the industry. If these determinants are known, it then becomes possible to predict the structure of the industry. Industry structure, in this model, is one of several factors that affect market structure and, indirectly, market behavior.

Because a market necessarily involves buyers as well as sellers, its structure is, in part, determined by the number and the sophistication of buyers. As the number of buyers increases, competition tends to become more effective. There are more numerous bids for available supplies of the product and the chances of collusive action among buyers diminishes. Effective competition is also fostered by the sophistication of buyers, that is, their knowledge of the products and terms of sale asked by sellers and of the offers made by other buyers. See the following diagram of the conceptual model of this study.

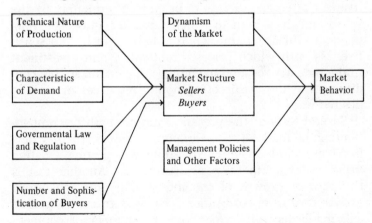

Economic theory also distinguishes several *market structures* on the basis of the number of sellers—including monopoly (one seller), oligopoly (few sellers), and perfect competition (very many sellers)—and the number of buyers—including monopsony (one buyer), oligopsony (few buyers), and perfect competition (very many buyers). The structure of a market—both the selling and buying sides—tends to produce a particular kind of market *behavior,* measured in such terms as price-cost relations, pricing practices, profits, returns on investment, and rate of innovation and technological progress.

Two further factors that affect the behavior of a market are its dynamism (including the growth rate of demand for its products and its technological progress), and the policies and strategies employed by firms trading in the market.

Competition among sellers and buyers is the force that drives a market, and in this study it is viewed as a multi-vectored dynamic process. Its essence is *rivalry* between business enterprises in the independent offering of a complex "mix" of products, services, terms of sales and prices, all of which change through time. The competitive process consists of a continual series of moves and countermoves by individual firms, each seeking to improve or protect its position in the market against rivals. The effectiveness of competition is to be judged ultimately by the speed and the extent to which firms act and react independently in a dynamic environment, and by the sensitiveness with which prices, profit rates, and investment in the industry respond to changes in demand-supply conditions and thus redirect economic resources in socially desired ways.[2]

Several tests of the presence and strength of competition can be made: (1) An important test is whether new firms can and do enter the industry, putting existing firms under competitive pressures. (2) Another test is the pace of growth of the industry, because sustained growth creates opportunities for new entrants as well as existing firms, thus expanding the number of competitors. Change—whether technological, political, social, or economic—also upsets established patterns of business behavior and creates openings for fresh approaches and ideas. In a fast-growing and changing industry, it is very difficult for established firms to gain or to retain monopoly power. (3) The strength of competition can also be tested by the changes over time in the market shares of the leading firms. (4) Yet another test is the trend in concentration of output or sales among the largest firms. If industry concentration declines over long periods of time, many new firms enter, and the market shares of leading firms exhibit considerable instability, one may infer the presence of effective competition.

THE HYPOTHESIS OF THIS STUDY

It is our hypothesis that, when we look at the foreign oil industry in terms of this model, we will be able adequately to measure the vigor of competition and trends in competitive behavior. Viewed in terms of the model, it will be shown that the technical conditions of producing oil in foreign countries, the initially slow growth of demand, and the nature of the governmental controls under which a few American oil companies began foreign oil operations in the 1920s inevitably produced an oligopolistic type of market structure.[3] With seven large United States and foreign companies accounting for nearly all of the foreign output of petroleum products, the pricing and production decisions of each of these firms were sufficiently important to have a discernible bearing upon the total output of the industry and the going prices of crude oil and its products. In the 1930s, the structure of the foreign oil industry became somewhat more pluralistic due to the entrance of several additional American companies. During World War II and the immediate postwar period, the structure of the industry was largely frozen under government controls designed to meet the emergencies of the war and its aftermath.

The rapid evolution of the industry began after the removal of wartime economic controls, between 1945 and 1948. Thereafter, the forces unloosed by the war manifested themselves. The foreign oil industry increased its size by many times, in order to meet a burgeoning demand. Hundreds of new firms entered the industry, which assumed an effectively competitive structure and behavior.

In testing the preceding hypothesis, this study first treats the historical background of the postwar period. It examines the conditions of the original entrance of the major American companies into the foreign oil industry, the impact of World War II on the industry, and the political and economic forces put in motion by that war and its aftermath. Next, the principal postwar technical, political, and economic changes which affected the structure and behavior of the industry are described: the strong postwar growth of demand for petroleum, the even more rapid growth of the world oil supply, the emergence of excess productive capacity, the increase in governmental intervention, and the remarkable penetration of new public and private enterprises, including that of the Soviet Union, into world oil markets. The effects of these changes upon the structure and behavior of the industry, the nature of competition, and the market power of the largest integrated companies are measured in this study. Finally, prospective developments are assessed and their implications for the future are examined.

THE FOREIGN NON-COMMUNIST WORLD OIL MARKET

Although this study has a global frame of reference, it focuses upon the "foreign" oil industry. This is defined to mean all petroleum enterprises doing business in the world outside of the United States, Canada, and the Communist countries. Canada and the United States have been separated from the foreign market by governmental limitations of domestic production, restrictive quotas on the importation of foreign oil, and protection of their own relatively high-cost petroleum production. Neither country is a significant source of petroleum supply to the rest of the world.[4] Information about the American and Canadian oil industries is introduced only to the extent that it is necessary for an understanding of the evolution of the foreign oil industry.

The non-Communist world outside the United States and Canada has constituted a single "market" in the sense that the forces of petroleum demand and supply have played with relative freedom over the whole area. There were strong tendencies for the delivered prices of crude oil and its products, whatever their origin, to be similar at any given point in the area, after allowing for differences in the qualities of products. Of course, this foreign oil market may, for certain purposes, be divided into an *international* market for crude oil and its products and a series of *national* markets, each of which differs from the others according to the particular product-mixes in demand or the type of governmental regulation that is applicable.

The foreign petroleum industry is also defined here to exclude the oil industry of the Communist countries, except for their sales of petroleum to Western nations. The Communist countries are obviously not part of the Western international economy, being separated by high barriers to trade and payments, and being associated within their own organization for mutual economic assistance (COMECON). (The Peoples Republic of China was omitted from this study because reliable data on its petroleum industry were lacking, and its international trade in petroleum was minor.) However, the reentry of the historically important Russian oil industry into Western petroleum markets during the mid-1950s helped to change the anatomy of the foreign oil industry. One of the world's largest oil enterprises—the monolithic Soviet oil trust—entered into competition with Western firms.[5] As a result, the relative importance of private oil companies and the relative concentration of the industry became less. By the 1960s, the Communist bloc exports were exerting important influences upon foreign non-Communist oil markets.

THE 1948–1972 PERIOD AS A
HISTORIC OIL ERA

This study generally encompasses the post–World War II era running from 1948 to the present. By 1948, the majority of foreign wartime economic controls had been dismantled. But World War II had been a watershed in the historic evolution of the world economy. Its aftermath of reconstruction, massive foreign aid by the United States, the breakup of the colonial empires into many new and growing nations, East-West conflict, and the spread of nationalism and industrialism provide a logical basing-point for an inquiry into the dynamics of the petroleum industry. An ancillary reason for studying changes after 1948 is to permit a comparison of data since that time with the data developed by the staff of the Federal Trade Commission regarding the foreign oil industry up to 1948, which was published in the report, *The International Petroleum Cartel,* in 1952.[6] That report was the basis for a long-drawn-out antitrust suit against five American multinational oil companies.[7]

The period from 1953 to 1972 was given the most intensive study. By 1953 the world had completed the initial catching up with war-deferred consumer demands in the United States and the reconstruction of Western Europe and Japan. And 1953 is an important year in the history of the oil industry, because in April of that year the United States Department of Justice filed a complaint against five large American multinational oil companies, charging a worldwide conspiracy to monopolize all phases of the foreign industry. Hence, it is desirable to ascertain whether changes in the industry since 1953 have been substantial.

The years 1973 and 1974 mark the beginning of a new era in the foreign oil industry, because they brought the seizure of control over strategic oil pricing and production decisions by the Organization of Petroleum Exporting Countries (OPEC) and the Organization of Arab Petroleum Exporting Countries (OAPEC), and their actions to quadruple the price of oil. Like World War II, this was another historic watershed, separating the old era of inexpensive oil and enterprise control of industrial strategy from the new era of expensive oil and control of key decisions by the governments of producing countries. The problems and probable actions of governments and oil companies in this new era are examined in the final chapter of this book.

THE "SEVEN LARGEST" AND OTHER FOREIGN OIL ENTERPRISES

Today, the foreign oil industry is composed of a large number of heterogeneous firms. It contains companies with private, governmental, and mixed ownership, integrated and nonintegrated firms, and a vast range of sizes in each category. Some operate throughout the foreign world. Some do business in one or two of the major regions—Latin America, Western Europe, Africa, the Middle East, and the Far East. Some confine their activities to a few nations. And some operate only in their native countries. But all firms in the industry could be divided into the "multinationals," trading across national boundary lines, and the foreign "domestics," each of which typically competes with multinational companies in its home country. Many firms are vertically integrated into all of the major divisions of the industry—exploration, production, transportation, refining, and marketing. Some cover two or three divisions. Still others are specialists in one.

Because the prewar foreign oil industry was characterized by a high concentration of activity in a few very large firms, a special effort has been made to measure postwar changes in concentration. Changes in the proportion of total foreign oil operations accounted for by each group were computed for 1948 and 1972. Following the practice of the Federal Trade Commission, all firms in the industry were divided into the "seven largest" com-

panies and "all others." These seven companies and their
short names (to be used here) are:

The Seven Largest Oil Companies	Short Name
Exxon, formerly Standard Oil Company (New Jersey)	"Exxon"
Mobil, formerly Socony-Vacuum Oil Company	"Mobil"
Gulf Oil Corporation	"Gulf"
Texaco, formerly The Texas Company	"Texaco"
Standard Oil Company of California	"Socal"
British Petroleum Company, Ltd.	"B.P."
Royal Dutch Petroleum Company and Shell Transport and Trading	"Shell"

It should be emphasized that there is no special economic significance to grouping these seven large firms
together, rather than six or eight or some other number.[8]
The dichotomy of seven firms and "others" was made
only for convenience in making comparisons with FTC
concentration ratios in 1949. The only meaningful dis-
tinction that could have been drawn between the seven
firms and the others was that of size in foreign operations. Although they remain the largest in overall magnitude of foreign operations, in no single division of the
industry are all seven today among the "seven largest."
Other firms are referred to here as "entrants," "newcomers," "new multinationals," or simply "others."

So far, we have laid out the aims and the hypothesis of
this study, defined its boundaries, and described the conceptual model proposed for use in analyzing the foreign
oil industry. In the chapters that follow, we shall analyze
the facts about the postwar evolution of the industry in
terms of the conceptual model, and we shall attempt to
draw conclusions useful in the formulation of contemporary energy policies. But first, it is desirable to take account of some salient characteristics of the industry, and

to observe the circumstances that shaped its origin and early history.

NOTES

1. "Technical changes" refer to shifts in the physical, chemical, geological, and mechanical features of the industry and in the technology of its processes; "economic changes" are defined to mean those changes that pertain to the structure and movement of the demand for, the supply of, and the price of crude oil and its products; "political changes" are alterations in the legal and regulatory environment, and in the relations of governments to the petroleum industry.

2. This dynamic concept of competition was first advanced by J. A. Schumpeter in his *Theory of Economic Development*, 1st German ed., 1906 (Cambridge: Harvard University Press, 1936). It was briefly described by the author in "Perspectives on Monopoly," *Journal of Political Economy* 59 (1952): 523–27. Prof. J. M. Clark provided a thorough treatment in his *Competition as a Dynamic Process* (Washington, D.C.: The Brookings Institution, 1961). The author presented a recent statement of the theory in his *Corporate Power and Social Responsibility: A Blueprint for the Future* (New York: Macmillan Co., 1973), chap. 6.

3. "Oligopoly" is a recognized term of economic analysis which simply means a market supplied by a few firms. It does not per se carry any implication of overt or tacit collusion among the supplying firms. An example of an oligopolistic market structure is the U.S. motor vehicle industry. While collusion may be easier among a few rather than among many firms, in fact, a wide variety of forms of behavior is found in oligopolistic markets, including effective competition.

4. Before World War II, the United States was the primary exporter of petroleum to the foreign non-Communist world. Since 1948, however, its exports have become insignificant. Because of import quotas in the United States, the prices of domestic crude oils were substantially higher than foreign non-Communist world crude-oil prices (by as much as $1 per barrel). See *Report to the President by the Petroleum Study Committee*, September 4, 1962, pp. 1–2.

The *Report* was submitted by the Departments of State, Treasury, Defense, Justice, Interior, Commerce, and Labor.

5.   Only Exxon ranks with the Soviet oil trust in size.

6.   U.S., Congress, Senate, Select Committee on Small Business, Subcommittee on Monopoly, *The International Petroleum Cartel*, Staff Report to, and submitted by, the Federal Trade Commission, 82d Cong., 2d sess. (Washington, D.C.: Government Printing Office, 1952). Although this staff study was not formally adopted by the FTC, it received wide attention throughout the world. It has been assumed that the statistics concerning the industry, which were collected by the FTC staff at the beginning of the postwar era, are accurate.

7.   U.S.A. v. Standard Oil Company (New Jersey) et al., Civil Action No. 1779–53, originally filed in the United States District Court for the District of Columbia, April 23, 1953. The case was transferred to the United States District Court in New York City and renumbered Civil Action No. 86–27. Up to the end of 1962, consent decrees had been entered against two of the five defendant companies. In 1963 a third defendant agreed to the entry of a consent decree. In 1968, the Department of Justice dismissed its charges against the two remaining defendants, Standard Oil of California and Mobil.

8.   These seven companies, as will be seen, differed considerably from each other in size, interests, property holdings, and policy. Exxon and Shell were—and are—by far the largest. An eighth important group of companies with early interests in the Middle East and subsequent widespread international operations is the Compagnie Francaise de Petroles, identified as "CFP," and its various subsidiaries and affiliates.

It would be much more logical to follow the well-established practice of other studies of concentration ratios by the FTC, the Bureau of the Census, and other agencies, which group the largest four companies, the largest eight companies, and the largest twenty companies, for comparison with the industry as a whole. See U.S., Congress, Senate, Committee on the Judiciary, Subcommittee on Antitrust and Monopoly, *Concentration Ratios in Manufacturing*, Report prepared by the Bureau of the Census, 87th Cong., 2d sess. (Washington, D.C.: Government Printing Office, 1962).

2

Characteristics of the Foreign Oil Industry

THE ROLE OF ENERGY IN CONTEMPORARY ECONOMIC LIFE

M AN'S PROGRESS from a primitive, hand-to-mouth existence to the complex industrialized society of today has depended upon an increasing use of natural sources of energy. More and more, energy has been used to move machines and vehicles of transportation, and to provide heat and light for daily living. In the contemporary world, the economically significant natural sources of energy are coal, crude oil, natural gas, falling water, and, to some extent, nuclear fuels. Ample supplies of low-cost energy increase the real income of a nation by reducing the costs per unit of output. To achieve economic progress and to attain military security, every nation must progressively supplement and replace human energy with energy derived from these sources.

Nearly all of the world's energy is produced from fossil fuels and they account, in the aggregate, for an important part of the costs of transportation, electrical power generation, metals, fertilizer, and cement production, and the chemical industries. The direct costs of fuel for home heating and cooking, and for the operation of automobiles and domestic appliances, form, in the aggregate, a substantial element of the consumer's cost of living. Petroleum and natural gas also serve, in rapidly increasing amounts, as a feedstock for the gigantic petrochemicals industry that produces a vast range of plastic materials, chemicals, dyestuffs, and pharmaceuticals. For these reasons, more and more nations have formulated national energy policies in recent times; and many have intervened in the petroleum industry in various ways to implement these policies.

Today, the petroleum industry forms a large segment of every developed economy. Its significance in the countries of the world varies according to the degree to which a country is an importer or an exporter of petroleum. Countries like Japan, which produce practically no oil, must acquire large amounts of foreign currencies to pay for their petroleum imports; for them oil imports are an important factor in their balance of international payments. On the other hand, the oil revenues of the five major oil exporting countries in the OPEC group—Iran, Iraq, Kuwait, Libya, and Saudi Arabia—in the mid-1960s, accounted for 70 to 90 percent of foreign exchange earnings and for 60 to 90 percent of government income.[1] During 1974 such revenues covered national budgets and financed huge loans abroad. In the advanced economy of the United States, which in recent years has produced about two-thirds of the crude oil it used, the industry accounted for nearly 6 percent of the nation's tangible assets, provided about 3 percent of its employment, and produced 5.4 percent of its Gross National Product.

THE NATURE OF THE DEMAND FOR ENERGY AND PETROLEUM

Because of its central importance in modern economic life, the demand for energy, *in general,* is relatively *inelastic* with respect to its price over moderate periods of time. That is, a given percentage reduction in the price of energy produces a smaller percentage increase in the quantity purchased, so that, other factors being held constant, total dollar sales of energy will decline. Conversely a given percentage rise in price will produce a smaller percentage decline in the quantity purchased, so that other factors being held constant, total dollar expenditures for energy will rise.

The principal reason for this price-inelasticity of demand is that, in nearly every *particular* use, the cost of energy is a small fraction of the cost of the main product or service demanded. For example, the cost of heating is normally a minor element in the total cost of housing. The cost of gasoline is a relatively small element in the cost of automobile transportation, and the cost of fuel is a small element in the total cost of operating a farm or factory. Changes in the price of energy, within moderate ranges, do not much affect the public's use of energy.

The demand for a *particular* energy source is, however, more elastic with respect to its price because buyers are able to substitute one energy source for another. Thus petroleum competes with coal, natural gas, falling water, and nuclear fuels in the generation of electricity, which is an intermediate form of energy that competes with other fuels in meeting a myriad of needs. In space heating and the generation of industrial power, petroleum competes with electricity, coal, and natural gas. There is the additional competition in space heating of liquified propane and butane. In ship operation, petroleum competes with nuclear fuels; in railroad operation, it competes with coal and electricity. Only in air transportation does petroleum lack a competitor.

All fuels are converted into mechanical power, heat, or light by means of relatively costly and specialized energy-conversion equipment, to which a user is normally committed for considerable periods of time. Households, automobile owners, and business enterprises do not quickly shift to other fuels, requiring substantial investments in new kinds of energy-conversion equipment, unless the long-term savings are substantial.[2] Hence, the demand for crude oil in general, which is derived from the demands for its various products, is quite inelastic in the short run. Consumption is relatively unresponsive to moderate price changes, but reacts to large price movements, such as the fourfold increase during late 1973 and early 1974.[3] While the demand for crude oil, *in general,* is usually price-inelastic, the demand for crude oil from a *particular region* is relatively elastic because of the buyer's ability to substitute oil from one region for that of another in a competitive market. An effective cartel of all oil-exporting countries can, of course, limit such substitution.

STRUCTURAL DETERMINANTS OF THE INDUSTRY

Four fundamental determinants of supply also give the foreign oil industry a distinctive character. They are a high level of risks, a need for continuity of operations, a complex environment of governmental regulation, and relatively difficult conditions of entry, which we now consider in turn.

The first determinant of the oil industry structure is the inherent unpredictability of investments in foreign oil ventures which has always made them highly speculative. Probabilities of large losses have had to be weighed against the possibilities of large gains. The risks that the foreign oil company confronts are technical, economic, and political.

The technical risks in petroleum ventures follow from the fact that petroleum occurs in commercial quantities in traps and porous sands beneath the earth's surface, and its discovery is always fraught with a large element of chance. Increasing use has been made of geological and geophysical methods of locating likely oil-bearing structures. Yet only by the drill bit can the presence, size, and economic value of oil deposits be ascertained. To minimize the risk of catastrophic loss, most oil-producing firms have drilled many wells in a diversity of locations.[4]

To reduce high inherent economic risks, a foreign oil company attempts to diversify its investment among several countries. Operations in a number of countries can reduce the overall risk of expropriation, discrimination, currency devaluation and control, or competition with government-subsidized firms. Hence there are *special* economies of large scale in the foreign oil industry that go beyond those of the domestic industry. This is one reason why concentration of the foreign oil industry historically has been higher than in the United States.[5]

The foreign oil company carries the ever-present political risks that the government of the host country may alter or terminate its concession, impose heavier royalties or taxes, or even nationalize all or part of its investment. Or war, civil disturbances, or economic crises may stop oil production or cause uncompensated loss of its property. And, of course, it must assemble teams of highly skilled geologists, geophysicists, well drillers, pipeline operators, refinery engineers, and other talent under the direction of competent general managers. A study published in 1962 by the Secretary-General of the United Nations emphasized the high degree of uncertainty, the long time, and the large financial resources required in foreign oil exploration.[6]

A second influence upon the organization of the industry is the need for continuity of operations. Crude oil and its products have high costs of storage above ground relative to their values. Consequently, large economies can be achieved by programing operations through the various stages of the industry so as to provide for a steady flow of crude oil from wells to refineries and of products from refineries to distributors to consumers. Oil companies constantly endeavor to operate their expensive facilities at near-capacity rates to minimize the costs of idle productive capacity and above-ground storage. Any one firm normally can do this more efficiently if it participates in all of the major stages of producing, refining, transporting, and marketing. This accounts for the strong drive of oil companies toward *vertical* integration, both in the United States and in foreign countries. However, many specialized firms exist in the international oil business; and no firms—not even the largest ones—have succeeded in maintaining a perfect integration of their operations.[7]

A third influence on the structure of the industry is the complex environment of governmental regulation. A multinational oil company, by definition, operates under the jurisdiction of at least two governments. But it usually deals with dozens of sovereign states, each with its own national aims, policies, and legal systems. The involved tasks of negotiating and renegotiating concessions, of obtaining licenses, of paying royalties, duties, excises and income taxes, and of complying with a host of regulations regarding exports, imports, foreign currencies, prices, and production rates are costly and time consuming.

Relatively high barriers to entry are a fourth structural determinant. An entrant into foreign oil exploration and development must be prepared to spend many millions of dollars and several years in obtaining concessions from a foreign government, in geological and geophysical surveys, and in drilling exploratory wells, often in remote and hostile environments.[8] He must accept the high risk that commercial quantities of oil may not be discovered for years—if at all—and that by the time his oil is available for market other, lower-cost discoveries may have been made which will reduce the value of his own investment. Even if a commercially valuable strike is made, pipelines and marine terminals must usually be installed to bring the crude oil to market, perhaps a continent away; and then refiners must be found to buy it.

Entrance into the refining stage of the foreign oil industry usually has not entailed so large a risk as entry into the exploration and production stages; but its capital requirements are large. The costs of building and putting on stream a modern refinery of 100,000 barrels per day capacity—the minimum size to attain most economies of scale—are upward of $250 million.

Because of the exceptionally high risks and large capital requirements, oil companies often use joint ventures to ease the difficult conditions of entrance into the industry. They are a means of reducing the exposure of any one firm to catastrophic losses and of assembling the funds required to establish operations on an efficient basis. By participating in a series of joint ventures, each firm can disperse its investments geographically and functionally. A joint venture of one company having marketing facilities with a second firm having crude oil reserves has been an especially fruitful combination, creating a new integrated competitor to established, integrated firms.[9]

CHARACTERISTICS OF FOREIGN OIL COMPANIES

The economic features of foreign oil companies have reflected a natural adaptation to their technical and political environments. With some exceptions, the industry is characterized by large, capital-intensive, multinational, vertically integrated firms, operated according to long-range plans.

Large-scale plants dominate the industry. Oil fields, pipelines, tankers, refineries, and distribution systems each require large size, and hence large investments of capital, for an efficient scale of operation. Whereas economies of large scale are mainly confined to refining and transportation in the domestic oil industry, they extend to production and exploration in the foreign industry. The technological problems of foreign development are much increased by the inaccessibility of most oil-bearing lands. Concession areas are larger in size. The lack of geological data makes the risks of drilling much greater and calls for more diversification to limit the average risk of failure.[10] In the United States, a field producing a hundred barrels a day may be quite profitable, particularly if it is close to refineries or markets. But in the remote deserts or offshore areas of Africa or the Middle East, a field one hundred times as large may be "noncommercial"—not worth developing because of the excessive cost of getting the oil to market. If an overland pipeline or special terminal is required, a field may have to produce 20,000 barrels per day or more to make it commercially significant. As Mikesell and Chenery observed, "In foreign production, then, financial, technical and risk-reducing economies all favor large firms."[11] Yet many firms of medium size have entered the arena.

Each stage of the industry is capital-intensive and requires an exceptionally large investment of capital per worker. Gross investment per employee in the United States in petroleum companies was calculated at $567,000 during 1973, over fifteen times the average of $36,000 per employee in all manufacturing businesses.[12] Capital intensivity is likely to be about the same abroad.

Geographical diversification, not only of production but also of refining and marketing operations, has been a means of limiting the risk of large losses, and has produced a considerable measure of horizontal expansion by oil companies. Other forces tending to make for geographic expansion are the need to be able to draw upon diversified sources in order to have continuity of supply in the event that military or political action closes some sources; the flexibility afforded by access to crude oils of different nations or regions; the effort to maintain a competitive position in many markets against rival firms which may benefit from new discoveries of low-cost or strategically located oil; and the ability to spread the overhead costs of management and finance over a larger output so as to reduce these costs per barrel.

Important cost advantages also flow from vertical integration. Concurrent engagement of a firm in production, refining, and marketing (and, to a lesser degree, in transportation), can assure favorable market outlets for production in times of crude oil surpluses and reliable supplies of crude oil in times of shortage. Vertical integration tends to reduce instability in returns on investment and, thus, lowers the costs of capital.

Because of heavy fixed investment, the *average cost* per barrel of crude oil or refined products, including depreciation and normal return on investment, is normally much larger than the *marginal* (incremental) cost of producing an additional barrel of output.[13] If all firms priced their products only at marginal cost, there would be widespread bankruptcy, because none would recover its costs of fixed investment and be able to finance the development of new reserves. Indeed, the tendency to calculate profit on additional sales on the basis of marginal costs has, since 1957, accounted for a considerable instability of crude-oil prices and subnormal profits, as will be seen.

Because of the environment in which they operate, multinational oil companies tend to emphasize continuity of investment activities over fairly long periods of time. They are obliged to program their investments several years in advance; and once a program is adopted, it is not quickly changed. Managements of large integrated foreign oil companies have less flexibility to adapt their investment programs to unexpected changes in demand or in costs than do the managers of firms in most other industries.

CONCENTRATION IN THE INDUSTRY

The technical and political conditions of foreign oil supply have historically produced an industry with strong tendencies toward concentration. Large firms, with a considerable degree of vertical as well as geographical integration, undoubtedly have enjoyed a larger measure of stability and a lower overall level of risk than have smaller, nonintegrated firms. At the end of World War II, no more than a handful of very large companies supplied the preponderance of the foreign non-Communist world's oil. Only a few firms were willing and able to "pay the price of admission" to the industry. While such a high degree of concentration was not desirable—and has since been much reduced—it is clear, on the other hand, that "atomistic" competition among very large numbers of small firms is not a feasible or desirable alternative. It would have meant sacrificing the real economies of large-scale operation, thus raising the average costs of petroleum products and their prices to consumers.

As will be shown, however, during the quarter-century after World War II, the explosive growth of demand and easier conditions of entry induced hundreds of smaller, less diversified, and less integrated firms to enter the industry. It thereby achieved a pluralistic and heterogeneous structure.

NOTES

1.   Sam H. Schurr and Paul T. Homan, *Middle Eastern Oil and the Western World* (New York: American Elsevier Publishing Company, Inc., 1971), p. xi. Even in 1961, direct oil revenues constituted not less than 55 percent of the national income and covered about 81 percent of the governmental expenditures of Saudi Arabia. Abdul Hudy Hassan Taher, "Cost Accounting as a Means of Managerial and Financial Control of the Petroleum Industry," *Proceedings of the Third Arab Petroleum Congress,* October 16–21, 1961, Alexandria, Egypt.

2.   Stone calculated the price elasticity of demand for gasoline in the United States to be −0.44 over the period from 1929 to 1941, indicating that a 10 percent rise in price would produce only a 4.4 percent decline in the quantity sold. See Richard Stone, *The Role of Measurement in Economics* (New York: Macmillan Co., 1951), p. 79. R. F. Mikesell and H. B. Chenery also found the demand for gasoline to be relatively inelastic. See *Arabian Oil* (Chapel Hill: University of North Carolina Press, 1949), p. 158.

3.   This has also been found to be true of the demand for electrical energy. See Franklin M. Fisher and Carl Kaysen, *A Study in Econometrics: The Demand for Electricity in the United States* (Amsterdam: North Holland Publishing Company, 1962). The authors found very low price elasticities for household demand and elasticities close to unity for industrial demand.

4.   Of course, this strategy also reduces the probability of very large returns on overall operations because costs of dry holes and meager producers offset revenues from large strikes. See *Economics of Petroleum Exploration, Development and Property Evaluation,* Conference of the International Oil and Gas Educational Center, March, 1961, Dallas, Texas (Englewood Cliffs: Prentice Hall, 1961). See also C. Jackson Grayson, Jr., *Decisions Under Uncertainty: Drilling Decisions by Oil and Gas Operators* (Boston: Division of Research, Graduate School of Business Administration, Harvard University, 1960).

5.   See Melvin de Chazeau and Alfred Kahn, *Integration and Competition in the Petroleum Industry* (New Haven: Yale University Press, 1959), p. 19, for a discussion of the reasons for the vertical integration in the U.S. petroleum industry.

6.   See United Nations, Secretariat, *Capital Requirements of Petroleum Exploration and Methods of Financing,* Study Prepared by the Secretary-General (U.N. Document No. E/3580, E/C.5/20., Rev. 1, 1962). Over $90 million was spent, beginning in 1953, in Australia without encouraging results until 1961. In West New Guinea, $112 million was spent over a twenty-five-year period, resulting in the discovery of only minor oil deposits.

7.   Because there are enormous differences in the qualities and refinery yields of different crude oils, no oil company is ever able to attain within itself a perfect balance between the crude oils it requires to meet demand in product markets and those it produces near those markets. Inter-company trading of crude oils has developed to supplement geographic diversification and to minimize transportation costs.

8.   Fanning, in 1954, cited numerous examples of U.S. oil companies, each of which spent between $2 million and $25 million in totally unsuccessful searches for oil in foreign countries. Leonard M. Fanning, *Foreign Oil and the Free World* (New York: McGraw-Hill Book Co., 1954), p. 16.

9.   Thus, Amerada, an experienced producer, merged with Hess, an aggressive marketer.

10.   See M. Allais, "Method of Appraising Economic Prospects of Mining Exploration over Large Territories," in

Management Science, vol. 3, no. 4 (July, 1957), pp. 285–347.

11. Mikesell and Chenery, *Arabian Oil,* p. 148. Economists have discussed widely the effects of the integration of the U.S. oil industry upon competition. See Eugene Rostow, *A National Policy for the Oil Industry* (New Haven: Yale University Press, 1948), pp. 139–44. See J. S. Bain, *Economics of the Pacific Coast Petroleum Industry,* Part III (Berkeley and Los Angeles: University of California Press, 1947), p. 18. More recent studies of vertical integration have found that it has produced important reductions of risk and of costs, and is not inherently inconsistent with effective competition. See John G. McLean and Robert W. Haigh, *The Growth of Integrated Oil Companies* (Boston: Graduate School of Business Administration, Harvard University, 1954), especially chap. 24, and de Chazeau and Kahn, *Integration and Competition in the Petroleum Industry,* p. 35.

12. Data are taken from FTC and SEC financial reports and from reports of the Bureau of Labor Statistics of the U.S. Department of Labor.

13. Defining marginal cost as the out-of-pocket expense of lifting another barrel of oil from the well into the pipeline, it is necessarily below average cost. However, the incremental cost of producing another barrel of oil, *including the cost of replacement of that barrel,* may be either higher or lower than its average cost. It appears to be higher for most wells in the United States and lower for most wells in the lush fields of the Middle East.

3

The American Entry into the Foreign Oil Industry

B ECAUSE THE FABULOUS MIDDLE EAST—which by 1972 contained 68 percent of the foreign non-Communist world's proven reserves and accounted for nearly 60 percent of its daily oil output—has played the stellar role in the postwar evolution of the world oil industry, an investigation of the American entry into the foreign oil industry must focus on this region. How did it come about that only a few international oil companies held concessions to all of this region at the end of World War II? The answer lies in the bitter struggle of the United States government to gain an entrance for its nationals into the British-dominated Middle East, a struggle which very significantly shaped the structure of the industry as it emerged from World War II.

THE WORLD OIL INDUSTRY
PRIOR TO WORLD WAR I

At the turn of this century, the United States and Russia together dominated the world petroleum industry, producing more than 90 percent of the world's oil. United

States production exceeded its consumption, and many American firms marketed petroleum products abroad, supplying about one-quarter of foreign consumption. However, American firms had no foreign oil production before 1900. Even by 1914, United States companies had acquired producing properties only in Mexico and Rumania, and foreign production by United States nationals accounted for only 15 percent of the total crude oil output outside of the United States.

The present status of Great Britain, struggling for economic survival, stands in sharp contrast to its powerful position before World War I, when it was the strong and proud defender of a far-flung empire. Its mighty fleets enforced a Pax Britannica throughout the world. Britain had long had a pervasive interest in the Middle East, recognizing it as the strategic gateway to India and the Orient. Its government also recognized early the military and economic significance of petroleum, and had aided a British group in obtaining an exclusive exploration concession to most of Persia in 1901. After several years of search, oil was struck in 1908, and a year later the Anglo-Persian Oil Company (now the British Petroleum Company) was formed.[1]

In 1913, a mission dispatched to Persia by Winston Churchill, then First Lord of the Admiralty, recommended that the British government should provide financial support for the expansion of the Anglo-Persian Oil Company and have "a voice in the direction of the Company's general policy." With characteristic determination, Churchill pursued this recommendation, and, on May 30, 1914, signed a contract with Anglo-Persian under which the company's capital was doubled by a new issue of shares, purchased entirely by the British government.[2] Motivated partly by the decision to convert its navy from coal to oil, the British government ultimately acquired a major interest in what was then the only oil-producing company in the Middle East.

Along with the Dutch, the British had also become dominant in the oil industry of the Far East. The Royal

Dutch Company, organized in the Netherlands in 1890 for the purpose of developing a petroleum industry in the Dutch East Indies, was the most important factor in Far Eastern petroleum production. In 1907, it affiliated with Shell Transport & Trading Company (Ltd.), which originally had carried mother-of-pearl shells in the Far East but had since become an important oil trader. The joint enterprise, Royal Dutch Shell, of which 60 percent was held by the Dutch interests and 40 percent by the British, dominated Far East production for many years.

AMERICAN EFFORTS IN THE 1920s TO OBTAIN FOREIGN OIL CONCESSIONS

Lord Curzon, a member of the British War Cabinet, said at the close of World War I: "The Allies floated to victory on a wave of oil." But an oil shortage had been averted by the narrowest of margins and only by the immense contribution of the American petroleum industry.[3] The United States emerged from the war as the world's largest oil producer, with nearly two-thirds of world crude oil output, and exports which supplied 30 percent of foreign oil consumption. But the United States passed during the war years from complacency to frightened doubt concerning the adequacy of its reserves. These anxieties were heightened by the fact that United States oil companies then held limited participation in only one major foreign oil-producing country, Mexico, where the future was clouded by the hostile attitude of the government. Authorities forecast the exhaustion of domestic reserves within a very short time.[4]

In the years immediately following World War I, the federal government formulated a variety of proposals to encourage foreign exploration by United States nationals.[5] The Executive branch strongly expressed the need to encourage private companies to engage in a worldwide search for oil abroad, safeguarded by United States government protection.[6] The Minerals Leasing Act was amended to deny mineral leases on public land to nationals of countries denying oil exploration rights to United States citizens.[7]

Fear that the United States would rapidly become dependent upon foreign oil was coupled with the anxiety that other countries were acquiring dominant or exclusive control over the most promising foreign deposits. The exclusionary policies of the British government in the Middle East fell under particularly heavy attack.[8] In the years 1919 and 1920, the Senate began an investigation of the steps to be taken to remove the restrictions imposed by foreign governments. In May of 1920, President Wilson submitted to the Senate the Secretary of State's report on the discrimination practiced against American citizens in exploring for oil abroad.[9] The Secretary of the Interior informed Senator Henry Cabot Lodge in 1921 that Great Britain had either prevented Americans from operating in any British-controlled oil field or had placed heavy burdens upon them. Senator Lodge declaimed that "England is taking possession of the oil supply of the world."[10]

The American government launched a determined fight to break the exclusionary policies of foreign governments. An "open door" policy—the doctrine of commercial equality for American enterprise abroad—was strongly advanced by the Department of State in support of American petroleum enterprise in foreign nations.[11]

AMERICAN ENTRY INTO THE MIDDLE EAST

The most significant action by the United States government to give effect to the "open door" policy was to secure participation by American companies in the development of the oil resources of Iraq. The American government, by 1919, had already viewed the situation with sufficient concern to declare that the British administration in these areas "had created the unfortunate impression in the minds of the American public . . . that Great Britain had been preparing quietly for exclusive control of the oil resources in this region."[12] And American resentment was significantly increased by the San Remo agreement between Britain and France in 1920, by which the oil resources of Mesopotamia and South Russia were divided between themselves without any regard for the United States.[13] In July of 1920, the U.S. State Department observed: "It is not clear to the Government of the United States how such an agreement can be consistent with the principles of equality of treatment understood and accepted during the peace negotiations at Paris."[14]

As diplomatic and political discussions continued, attention focused upon the Turkish Petroleum Company (TPC). This company had been formed with the help of the British Foreign Office in 1912. After reorganization in 1914, it was owned by the Deutsche Bank (25 percent), Royal Dutch (22.5 percent), Anglo-Persian (47.5 percent), and one individual, Calouste S. Gulbenkian (5 percent). Pursuant to the San Remo agreement, the 25 percent interest of the Deutsche Bank had been allotted to the French. The State Department indicated to several interested American companies that it would not object to private negotiations to secure rights in the Turkish Petroleum Company, provided that no reputable American company was excluded. Thereafter, direct negotiations began between TPC and a consortium of seven American companies.[15] These negotiations continued for a number of years, and, in 1928, the parties ultimately arrived at an agreement whereby the French, Royal Dutch, Anglo-Persian, and American groups would each have a 23.75 percent interest in TPC, and Gulbenkian would retain his 5 percent share.

At the insistence of the British, however, the American participants were compelled to agree not to seek concessions within an area circled by a bold red line, including the former Ottoman Territory beyond the bounds of Mesopotamia, *except* through TPC. As early as 1922, the United States Department of State had indicated to the American group that this provision would not affect the attitude of the United States government in the diplomatic protection of the American interests.[16] When negotiations ended, the American group again asked the State Department whether this "Red-Line" clause was in conformity with American policy. The State Department again replied in the affirmative.[17]

Thus, in 1928, after six years, American companies finally were able to break through the stubborn resistance of the British, Dutch, and French to secure their first substantial interest in the potential oil resources in the Middle East.[18] Of the seven American companies which began efforts to obtain interests in TPC, only five companies remained at the end (Atlantic, Exxon, Gulf, Standard Oil of Indiana, and Mobil); Sinclair and Texaco had withdrawn during the long negotiations. The Turkish Petroleum Company, whose name was later changed to Iraq Petroleum Company (IPC), then began to search for oil in Iraq. But oil was not developed in any substantial quantity until 1934. By then Gulf, Atlantic, and Standard Oil of Indiana had sold their interests in IPC to Exxon and Mobil, who became the sole owners of the American 23.75 percent interest.

By the later 1920s, fears of a world shortage had been allayed as a result of new discoveries in Venezuela, a revival of Soviet Union exports, and the buildup of production in the United States. Also, by 1928, an economic recession had begun in Western Europe, and this led to a weakening of petroleum markets and culminated in the worldwide depression. It was in this setting that three IPC participants—Shell, B.P., and Exxon—reportedly entered into a cartel agreement (the so-called "Achnacarry" or "As Is" agreements) to share markets outside the United States and to coordinate facilities in an effort to stabilize prices.[19] Viewing the matter in purely economic terms, restraints upon markets and efforts to maintain prices during an economic depression are not improbable consequences of an oligopolistic industrial structure. Such behavior may ensue from a recognition of interdependence as well as from an overt agreement. The structure of the foreign oil industry at that time was oligopolistic, due primarily to national barriers to entrance.

With the rise of a pluralistic and heterogeneous industrial structure after World War II, an effective cartel became highly improbable, as will be seen.[20]

AMERICAN ENTRY INTO THE FAR EAST

During the 1920s, the United States also continued negotiations for American participation in developing the oil fields of the Dutch East Indies.[21] In 1920 a bill was introduced into the Netherlands legislature granting oil exploration rights to a new Dutch Company for the entire petroleum area in Djambi, "the most valuable mineral oil fields in the whole Colony."[22] Sinclair's formal application to the Dutch minister of the colonies for participation in the Djambi fields had been rejected in September of 1920. Other American companies were also interested in Djambi. Secretary of State Hughes pointed out to the Dutch government that their proposals proved that "responsible American concerns are ready and desirous of assisting the Dutch Government in the development of the oil industry."[23] But arguments were unavailing and the Djambi bill became law in July of 1921. The United States retaliated by refusing to grant Shell a permit to prospect in certain United States public lands until the Netherlands was declared a "reciprocating country" under the Mineral Leasing Act.[24] Only in 1928, after seven years of continuing United States government intercession, did the Dutch government finally sign contracts permitting Exxon to develop a concession in the Dutch East Indies.

AMERICAN ENTRY INTO LATIN AMERICA

In view of the exclusionary policies of the British and the Dutch in the Middle East and the Dutch East Indies, it was to be expected that American companies made greater headway in Central and South America. Mexican production, largely controlled by American companies, had been greatly expanded during World War I. After 1921, however, production in Mexico declined and by 1926 had been reduced over 50 percent.[25] American firms began commercial development in Venezuela about 1923; and after 1925, American-owned production rose rapidly. By 1928 more than 35 American companies had acquired concessions, and Americans controlled over 50 percent of Venezuelan production. Venezuela had moved to second place among the oil-producing countries of the world. Exploration also began during this period in other South and Central American countries. Up to fifty United States firms were active in the Western Hemisphere.[26] However, during the depression of the 1930s, American activity in Latin America diminished. Only about a dozen firms weathered the depression and remained.

THE CHANGING ROLE OF AMERICAN OIL COMPANIES ABROAD

Significant changes occurred in the foreign position of American oil companies during the 1920s. Foreign crude oil production doubled between 1920 and 1929, but foreign output by American firms increased only 15 percent, reducing United States participation in foreign production to under 30 percent. This declining share was largely attributable to the fact that United States companies had, as yet, virtually no participation in the expanded crude oil production of the Eastern Hemisphere (including Europe, Africa, and Asia).[27]

Important changes also took place in the composition of foreign oil supply. Foreign consumption, while still quite small in relation to consumption in the United States, more than doubled between 1920 and 1929. During this period, foreign crude oil production reached about two-thirds of foreign consumption. Foreign refining capacity was built up adjacent to expanding sources of foreign crude oil; but a large gap remained between foreign refinery output and foreign consumption. This presented a growing export market for United States refined products, exports of which nearly doubled over the decade. The United States emerged from the 1920s as a net exporter once again. However, it was now mainly an exporter of products rather than of crude oil (see Table 3.1).

THE GREAT DEPRESSION AND THE WORLD OIL SURPLUS

By the early 1930s, world oil production capacity had come full circle from the fears of depletion in the early 1920s. By 1929 large domestic surpluses had developed in the United States. With the outpouring of oil from the new East Texas fields in 1931, domestic crude oil prices fell as low as 5 cents a barrel! By 1933 United States exports of refined products had dropped by nearly half from their 1929 level, and the American export share of foreign

TABLE 3.1

Relation of U.S. Oil Exports to Domestic Production and to
Foreign Oil Consumption, 1920, 1924, 1929

(Amounts in Thousands of Barrels per Day)

| | | | | Ratio of U.S. Exports to | |
Year	U.S. Crude Oil Production	Foreign Crude Oil Consumption	U.S. Exports of Petroleum	U.S. Production (Percent)	Foreign Consumption (Percent)
1920	1,211	619	217	17.9	35.1
1924	1,952	900	321	16.4	35.7
1929	2,760	1,476	446	16.2	30.2

Source: U.S., Congress, Senate, Special Subcommittee Investigating Petroleum Resources, *American Petroleum Interests in Foreign Countries,* Hearings, 79th Cong., 1st sess., June, 1945.

consumption had fallen from 30 to 17.5 percent. Indeed, a clamor arose for protection against foreign *imports*, and, in 1931, the President imposed voluntary restrictions on imports. Legislation was adopted, in 1932, imposing a tax upon imported crude oil and its products. Import quotas were officially established in June of 1933, under the National Industrial Recovery Act Petroleum Code.[28]

Intensified competition also emerged for the limited foreign markets. Latin American crude oils, which could no longer find a market in the United States, went to outlets abroad. But, between 1929 and 1934, total crude oil output in the Eastern Hemisphere rose 50 percent to nearly a million barrels a day. And because of the slump in foreign oil demand during the early 1930s, other countries also restricted marketing opportunities. United States companies with foreign production therefore found foreign sales prospects equally poor. A number of substantial U.S. companies withdrew from foreign operations, including Standard Oil of Indiana which was beset with management problems.[29]

NEWCOMERS BREAK INTO THE MIDDLE EAST

The participants in the TPC had, after years of negotiations, gotten their company into operation in 1925 and were endeavoring to consolidate their holdings throughout the old Ottoman Empire. They were, no doubt, hoping to develop the entire Middle East by themselves. But in 1930 a newcomer broke into exploration in the Middle East.

Despite extensive effort, Standard Oil of California's search for foreign production in the period following World War I had not been crowned with success.[30] On the tiny island of Bahrain, however, in the Persian Gulf offshore from the mainland of Saudi Arabia, Socal proved to be more fortunate. Its Bahrain concession, although within IPC's "Red Line," was not originally considered to be a choice property. Gulf had been assigned an option to the concession by a British syndicate, but because of its "Red Line" commitment Gulf was prevented from exercising the option. A transfer of the option to Socal was arranged. Although the British Colonial Office at first opposed the transfer, because of the prompt intervention of the United States Department of State, Socal gained a concession in 1930, thereby initiating a successful Middle East entry by a venture controlled by American interests.[31] Exploration commenced in 1931, oil was found in 1932, and commercial export was begun in 1934.[32]

The intrusion of this new American oil company into the IPC "sphere of influence" was no doubt a rude shock to the established companies. But it was followed by an earthquake. The discovery of oil on Bahrain generated great interest in the oil prospects of Saudi Arabia.[33] Negotiations for a concession were begun by Socal in February of 1933—a month before the United States closed its banks and revised the gold standard. The Saudi concession was won only after fierce opposition from IPC.

Stephen H. Longrigg, the IPC representative, has written that the deciding factor was an offer of gold to the Saudi king by Socal, whereas IPC offered only paper rupees. However, King Saud may also have feared British political designs on the Middle East. On May 29, 1933, an agreement was signed for a sixty-year concession to Socal of the al-Hasa province.[34]

Gulf Oil Company, smarting under the constraint of the Red Line agreement which had obliged it to surrender the Bahrain concession to Socal, turned its attention to the Sheikdom of Kuwait, which lay outside the Red Line. Prolonged negotiations, carried on in competition with the Anglo-Persian Oil Company (now B.P.), followed. The British Foreign Office sought to bar Gulf from Kuwait, but Gulf obtained from the U.S. Department of State a strong affirmation of the "open door" policy. Ultimately, the two rivals joined in forming the Kuwait Oil Company in which each had equal ownership; and in December of 1934 the Kuwaiti ruler granted a concession to the new company.

An American company thus acquired a half-interest in what was to become the second largest oil-producing concession in the Middle East.

Oil was not quickly found in Arabia. Although initial reconnaissance took place in 1933 and test drilling commenced in 1934, a series of wells were drilled without encountering oil. Success finally came in 1938. The Arabian concession proved to be the world's richest, although that was not appreciated until after World War II.[35]

The Bahrain and Arabian discoveries had a dual impact upon the shareholders of IPC. Socal had no organization to market its potential production abroad. In the midst of a worldwide depression, it could not readily generate the capital necessary to develop production in this remote land as well as to build a marketing system. In the interim, IPC might have prevailed. Socal sought a solution to this formidable problem by negotiating an agreement with The Texas Company in 1936, granting it a 50 percent interest in Socal's two Middle East concessions in return for a 50 percent interest in Texaco's Far Eastern marketing facilities. Texaco, in turn, had long been a marketer in the Eastern Hemisphere. Because it had to rely on United States exports for supply, it was losing its position to its competitors. Both Texaco and Socal solved their problems by creating the joint marketing company, Caltex.[36] IPC's owners, therefore, suddenly found that both their crude oil domains in the Middle East had been invaded by a new concessionaire and that their traditional marketing positions were being challenged by a new, integrated competitor armed with ample Middle East oil supplies. The basic premise of exclusivity underlying the "Red Line" agreement had been deeply undercut.

During the 1930s, foreign oil operations were marked by the increasing importance of Venezuela and the Middle East as world export centers. The United States was being converted from a primary source of supply to a balance wheel for world requirements. Before the potential of the Middle East could be developed, however, the fires of war had begun to burn in Europe. In 1938 Hitler invaded Austria and in September Chamberlain went to Munich. The oil industry turned to the task of preparing for war.

THE IMPACT OF WORLD WAR II UPON THE INDUSTRY

The foreign oil industry was radically affected by World War II. The burden of meeting Allied military requirements fell largely on the United States.[37] Between December of 1941 and August of 1945, nearly 7 billion barrels of oil were produced to meet the requirements of the United States and its allies, almost 6 billion barrels of which came from the United States. The organization of this prodigious undertaking began even before the declaration of war by the United States.[38] By December of 1942, the Petroleum Administration for War assumed control of the entire United States industry, both in its operations at home and abroad.

As the strain of supplying the bulk of Allied oil requirements became apparent, the United States government became apprehensive over the domestic supply situation.[39] A special technical mission which had been assigned by the Secretary of the Interior to study the oil prospects of the Middle East reported: "The center of gravity of world oil production is shifting from the Gulf-Caribbean area to the Middle East—to the Persian Gulf area—and is likely to continue to shift until it is firmly established in that area."[40]

Special attention was, therefore, paid to preserving the American position in Saudi Arabia. Since Saudi Arabia was not originally eligible for Lend Lease, the United States had arranged for aid to be advanced indirectly through the British government. But it began to appear that Great Britain was using this aid to enhance *its* prestige. There was serious concern about increasing British activity in Saudi Arabia that was potentially prejudicial to United States interests there. In 1944, Secretary of State Hull stated in a memorandum to the President of the United States that:

> If Saudi Arabia is permitted to lean too heavily upon the British, there is always the danger that the British will request a *quid pro quo* in oil. To obviate this danger, it is recommended that this Government share the subsidy on an overall equal basis with the British.[41]

Secretary Hull records that the President wrote his "O.K." on this memorandum, and the United States entered into negotiations with the British.[42] The Saudi Arabian government was made eligible for Lend Lease assistance.

During the war years, the United States government gave serious thought to acquiring a direct interest in Arabian reserves. A committee set up within the State Department rendered a report to Secretary Hull on March 22, 1943, recommending the establishment of a government-owned Petroleum Reserves Corporation. This was done.[43] Taking a leaf from Winston Churchill's book, Secretary Ickes was delegated to negotiate for stock in the Arabian American Oil Company (ARAMCO), then a jointly owned subsidiary of Socal and Texaco which produced oil in Saudi Arabia, "in the interest of national defense and the economic needs of the Nation."[44]

This plan to acquire ARAMCO never materialized. But it was followed by another proposal to construct a U.S.-owned pipeline from Kuwait and Saudi Arabia to the Mediterranean, sponsored by the Petroleum Reserves Corporation under a proposed agreement with ARAMCO and Gulf.[45] Under the proposed agreement the U.S. government would construct and own the pipeline system; the oil companies would operate it; and, in return, a reserve of one billion barrels of oil would be set aside for U.S. government purchase at any time for military or naval use at 25 percent below the market price in the Persian Gulf. This proposal, too, was dropped during 1944.

The United States government continued its efforts to

consolidate American interests in ARAMCO. Its proposal to construct a pipeline from Saudi Arabia to the Mediterranean had recognized the need for *financing* the greatly expanded production of oil that the Saudi Arabian king sought in order to increase his revenues. It was becoming evident that the Arabian oil fields were physically able to sustain large production; but Socal and Texaco had only limited marketing outlets. Only by construction of a thousand-mile pipeline could Arabian oil be brought in volume and at reasonable costs to Western European markets. Without such increased outlets, it was feared that the American companies might lose the concession. In 1945, therefore, officials of the State Department suggested to ARAMCO that the American companies in IPC (i.e., Exxon and Mobil) might undertake either to purchase large quantities of Arabian oil or to become part owners of ARAMCO. Negotiations between the parties followed during 1946 and 1947, at the same time that Exxon and Mobil were attempting to terminate the "Red Line" agreement with their IPC partners in London.[46] In the end, they concluded that the "Red Line" agreement was no longer binding, and, in 1948, they became 40 percent owners of ARAMCO. (Exxon acquired 30 percent and Mobil 10 percent of ARAMCO.)[47] The French government lodged official protests with the British and American governments. However, the State Department rejected these protests, and the American companies declared the "Red Line" agreement dissolved. A major structural change was thus achieved, bringing four American companies into the Arabian concession. These companies provided ARAMCO the marketing outlets it needed to expand production, enabled it to finance the pipeline to a Mediterranean port, and thus assured continued American participation in the new center of the petroleum world.

Thus, the foreign oil industry at the end of World War II consisted, essentially, of seven international firms with interests in the rich Middle East fields, plus CFP (which at that time utilized its share of Iraqi oil mainly to serve the French market), and a number of governmental oil companies in Latin America.[48] Middle East production, which had dropped during the war, began to rise very rapidly. With this phenomenal increase, companies which had a historical position in the Middle East necessarily became *the* major international oil companies. What the situation might have been had Standard Oil of Indiana, Sinclair, Atlantic, and Gulf chosen to hold on to their interests in Iraq, and had Sinclair held its concession in Persia, can only be surmised. *The technical and governmental forces which conditioned the structure of the industry had, at the end of World War II, placed seven companies in a position to supply the overwhelming bulk of the foreign non-Communist world's petroleum requirements.*

TABLE 3.2

Chronology of Some Major Events in the Foreign Oil Industry up to 1949

Year	Event
1880	Britain obtains control of the foreign relations of Bahrain.
1888	Ottoman Empire grants oil rights to a group controlled by Deutsche Bank.
1890	Shell Transport and Trading Company starts sales of kerosene. Royal Dutch Company formed to explore the East Indies.
1899	Britain acquires control of the foreign relations of Kuwait.
1901	Charles D'Arcy, a British entrepreneur, obtains a sixty-year concession in Persia.
1907	Royal Dutch Shell alliance formed: 60 percent—Dutch, 40 percent—British.
1908	Oil discovered in Persia.
1912	Turkish Petroleum Company formed: 35 percent—National Bank of Turkey, 25 percent—Deutsche Bank, 25 percent—Royal Dutch Shell, 15 percent—Gulbenkian.
1914	British government buys control of Anglo-Persian Oil Company. Anglo-Persian Oil Company acquires the shares of the National Bank of Turkey in Turkish Petroleum Company, as a part of the reorganization of the ownership of TPC.

TABLE 3.2 (Continued)

Year	Event
	TPC participants agree to joint action within the "Red Line" area (old Ottoman Empire).
	World War I begins.
1916	Britain acquires control of the foreign relations of Qatar.
1918	Venezuelan oil production begins.
	World War I ends.
	Bolshevik revolution in Russia ends.
1920	France and Britain enter into the San Remo Agreement.
	Iraq becomes a British mandate.
	France obtains Deutsche Bank shares in TPC; United States protests.
1922	United States oil companies begin negotiations with TPC for participation in Iraqi oil.
1925	Iraq grants seventy-five year concession to TPC.
1927	Gulf acquires Bahrain rights from Eastern and General.
	Major oil discovery in Iraq at Kirkuk.
1928	American oil companies admitted to TPC and sign the "Red Line" agreement.
	Gulf sells its Bahrain rights to Socal.
1929	Name of TPC changed to IPC.
1930	Bahrain grants exclusive concession to Socal.
1932	Bahrain Petroleum Company, Socal subsidiary, discovers oil in Bahrain.
1933	Socal obtains Saudi Arabian concession.
1934	Anglo-Iranian and Gulf granted seventy-five year concession by Kuwait. Iraq-Mediterranean pipeline system put into operation.
1935	Anglo-Iranian acquires seventy-five year concession from Qatar (which was subsequently transferred to IPC).
1936	Texaco acquires from Socal 50 percent interest in Bahrain Petroleum Company and Saudi Arabian concession.
	Caltex formed by Socal and Texaco.
1937	Mexico nationalizes its oil industry.
1938	Commercial oil discovered in Saudi Arabia and Kuwait.
1939	Commercial oil discovered in Qatar.
	Hitler invades Poland.
	World War II begins.
1941	Japan bombs Pearl Harbor.
	United States enters World War II.
1942	United States Petroleum Administration for War created.
1945	World War II ends.
	Arab League formed in Cairo.

TABLE 3.2 (Continued)

Year	Event
1946	United States companies declare the "Red Line" agreement dissolved.
1948	Exxon and Mobil become partners in the expansion of ARAMCO. Aminoil (Phillips, Signal, and eight other United States companies) obtains sixty-year concession to Kuwait's interest in the Neutral Zone.
1949	Getty obtains sixty-year concession to Saudi Arabia's interest in the Neutral Zone.

NOTES

1. See L. P. Elwell-Sutton, *Persian Oil* (London: Lawrence & Wishart, Ltd., 1955), p. 20.

2. Elwell-Sutton, *Persian Oil,* pp. 22–23.

3. ". . . [C]ritical shortages . . . had been met by American supplies poured into Europe in response to Clemenceau's and Balfour's appeals to President Wilson and to the oil companies." Herbert Feis, *Petroleum and American Foreign Policy*, Commodity Policy Studies, No. 3, Food Research Institute (Stanford: Stanford University Press, 1944), p. 5.

4. ". . . [W]ithin the next 2 to 5 years the oil fields of this country will reach their maximum production, and from that time on we will face an ever increasing decline. . . ." *National Petroleum News*, October 29, 1919, p. 51.

5. For example, Senator Phelan proposed that the United States establish a government corporation for the purpose of developing the oil resources of foreign countries (S. 4396, 66th Cong., 2d sess.). See also a statement by the Secretary of the Interior, *The Oil & Gas Journal*, June 18, 1920, p. 76.

6. In February of 1920, the Director of the Geological Survey stated that the United States should support ". . . every effort of American business to expand its circle of activity in oil production. . . ." See U.S., Congress, Senate, Special Subcommittee Investigating Petroleum Resources, *American Petroleum Interests in Foreign Countries*, Hearings, 79th Cong., 1st sess., June, 1945, p. 299. U.S., Department of State, Bureau of Mines, and Geological Survey, *Joint Report of the Fuel Administration*, May, 1919; U.S., Secretary of the

Interior, *Annual Report, 1919;* Release by the Bureau of Mines, May 16, 1920, *National Petroleum News,* May 26, 1920, pp. 104–106.

7.   Public Law 146, 66th Cong., 1920. A bill was also introduced providing for mandatory embargoes on oil exports to countries refusing to grant oil concessions to American companies (S. 4747, 67th Cong., 2d sess., 1922). See also S. 4866, 67th Cong., 1st sess., 1921, introduced by Senator Phelan.

8.   "Practically all the visible future production of the world is under the control of Great Britain." Statement by Director of Operations, United States Shipping Board, April 21, 1920. See U.S., Congress, Senate, Special Subcommittee Investigating Petroleum Resources, *American Petroleum Interests in Foreign Countries,* p. 302. See also "Report by the Geological Survey," *The Oil & Gas Journal,* June 18, 1920; *Report by the Department of State to the United States Senate,* May 17, 1920.

9.   *Report by the Department of State to the United States Senate,* May 17, 1920; Senate Document 272, 66th Cong., 2d sess., 1920, p. 4. See also Senate Document 11, 67th Cong., 1st sess., 1921; Senate Document 97, 68th Cong., 1st sess., 1924.

10.   The statement by Sir Edward McKay Edgar in September, 1919, did nothing to allay American concern: ". . . [A]ll the known . . . likely or probable oil fields outside the United States itself, are . . . under British management or control, or financed by British capital. . . ." Gibson and Knowlton, *History of Standard Oil Company (New Jersey): The Resurgent Years, 1911–1927* (New York: Harper, 1940), pp. 262–63.

11.   See the message from President Coolidge, in response to Senate Resolution No. 149 of February 13, 1924; *Oil Concessions in Foreign Countries,* Senate Document 97, 68th Cong., 1st sess., 1924; *Diplomatic Protection of American Petroleum Interests in Mesopotamia, Netherlands East Indies and Mexico,* Study for the Special Subcommittee Investigating Petroleum Resources, Senate Document 43, 79th Cong., 1st sess., 1945.

12.   U.S., Department of State, *Papers Relating to the Foreign Relations of the United States, 1920* (Washington, D.C.: Government Printing Office, 1936), vol. 2, p. 652.

13. Great Britain acquired the oil rights of Persia for herself in similar manner. U.S., Department of State, *Foreign Relations of the United States, 1920*, vol. 2, pp. 655–58.

14. Great Britain, *Correspondence between His Majesty's Government and the United States Ambassador Respecting Economic Rights in Mandated Territories* (Cmd. 1226, 1921), p. 4.

15. This group included Exxon, Mobil, Atlantic, Gulf, Texaco, Mexican Petroleum Co. (later, a part of Standard Oil of Indiana), and Sinclair.

16. U.S., Congress, Senate, *Diplomatic Protection of American Petroleum Interests in Mesopotamia, Netherlands East Indies and Mexico*, Study Prepared for the Special Subcommittee Investigating Petroleum Resources, Senate Document No. 43, 79th Cong., 1st sess., 1945, p. 21.

17. See letter of the Secretary of State to the Associate General Counsel (Wellman) of Standard Oil Company (New Jersey), April 9, 1927, U.S., Department of State, *Foreign Relations, 1927*, vol. 2, p. 822 et seq.

18. In 1923 Sinclair had obtained a concession in Northern Persia (over the protests of the British Government), but the concession was abandoned within a year. See Elwell-Sutton, *Persian Oil*, pp. 36–41.

19. U.S., Congress, Senate, Select Committee on Small Business, Subcommittee on Monopoly, *The International Petroleum Cartel*, Staff Report to, and submitted by, the Federal Trade Commission, 82nd Cong., 2d sess. (Washington, D.C.: Government Printing Office, 1952), pp. 199–205.

20. See Chapters 9 and 10.

21. Some of the correspondence is referred to in U.S., Congress, Senate, *Oil Concessions in Foreign Countries*, Senate Document 97, 68th Cong., 1st sess. See also, Wetter, "Diplomatic Assistance to Private Investment—A Study of the Theory and Practice of the United States during the Twentieth Century," 29, *University of Chicago Law Review*, p. 275 et seq. (1962).

22. Wetter, "Diplomatic Assistance to Private Investment," 29, *University of Chicago Law Review*, p. 34 (1962); U.S., Department of State, *Foreign Relations, 1920*, vol. 3, p. 262.

23.   Letters of the Secretary of State to the Minister in the Netherlands, April 12, 1921, p. 40; U.S., Department of State, *Foreign Relations, 1921*, vol. 2, pp. 534–35.

24.   U.S., Federal Trade Commission, Report, *Foreign Ownership in the Petroleum Industry* (Washington, D.C.: Government Printing Office, 1923), pp. 37–38; Herbert Feis, *Petroleum and American Foreign Policy*, p. 10.

25.   U.S., Congress, Senate, Special Subcommittee Investigating Petroleum Resources, *American Petroleum Interests in Foreign Countries*, pp. 335, 336.

26.   U.S., Congress, Senate, Special Subcommittee Investigating Petroleum Resources, *American Petroleum Interests in Foreign Countries*, pp. 67, 81, 248, 333–39.

27.   American companies controlled 60 percent of the oil in the Western Hemisphere. Throughout Europe, Africa, and the Near East, however, American companies controlled only 3 percent of production. U.S., Congress, Senate, Special Subcommittee Investigating Petroleum Resources, *American Petroleum Interests in Foreign Countries*, pp. 189–91.

28.   *NRA Petroleum Code*, August 19, 1933, Sec. 1, Art. 3.

29.   *Oil & Gas Journal*, April 28, 1932, p. 18.

30.   At the time of World War I, Socal had no foreign production. By 1930 it had carried out exploration in more than a dozen countries, without any commercial production to show for the effort. *Handbook for American Employees* (New York: Arabian American Oil Company, 1952 ed., vol. 1), p. 23; Gerald T. White, *Standard Oil Company of California, Formative Years in the Far West* (New York: Appleton-Century-Crofts, 1962), pp. 558–59.

31.   U.S., Congress, Senate, Committee Investigating the National Defense Program, *Report of the State Department*, February 10, 1944. Report No. 10, Part 15, 78th Cong., 2d sess., 1944, p. 70; see also U.S., Department of State, *Foreign Relations, 1929*, vol. 3, pp. 80–82.

32.   See *Middle East Oil Development* (New York: Arabian American Oil Company, 4th ed., 1956).

33.   Richard Sanger, *The Arabian Peninsula* (Ithaca: Cornell University Press, 1954), p. 100.

34. Brigadier Stephen Hemsley Longrigg [the IPC nego-
tiator], *Oil in the Middle East* (Oxford: Oxford University
Press, 2d ed., 1961), pp. 107–108. See also *Aramco and
World Oil*, Arabian American Oil Company Handbook for
American Employees (New York: Arabian American Oil
Company, 1952), vol. 1, pp. 23–26.

35. Oil in commercial quantities was not discovered until
1938, and the first tanker of Arabian crude oil was not
loaded until May of 1939, six years after the concession was
granted.

36. Socal also obtained an option to buy a 50 percent
interest in the Texaco marketing facilities in Europe. It
purchased this half-interest shortly after World War II.
Subsequently, in 1967, the joint operations of Caltex, west
of the Suez Canal, were dissolved.

37. The relative importance of Russia, Rumania, and
Mexico as exporters declined. U.S., Congress, Senate, Special
Subcommittee Investigating Petroleum Resources, *American
Petroleum Interests in Foreign Countries*, pp. 354 et seq.
Important exporting sources in the Eastern Hemisphere were
lost to the Allies, and Middle East oil supplies were restricted
until the African campaign was completed. The brunt of the
responsibility for fueling the Allied war effort thus fell on the
Western Hemisphere.

38. Immediately after the President's declaration of the
unlimited national emergency on May 27, 1941, the mobiliza-
tion of the industry began under the Petroleum Coordinator.
*A History of the Petroleum Administration for War, 1941–
1945* (Washington, D.C.: Government Printing Office,
1946), Appendix 7, Exhibits 9, 10, 11, and 12.

39. See, e.g., U.S., Congress, Senate, Committee Investigating the National Defense Program, *Report of the Committee*, Report No. 10, Part 15, 78th Cong., 2d sess., 1944.

40. Address by the Secretary of Interior, March 16, 1944.
Statement by the Deputy Director of the PAW, Nov. 28,
1945; U.S., Congress, Senate, Special Committee Investigating
Petroleum Resources, *Wartime Petroleum Policies Under the
Petroleum Administration for War*, Hearings before the Com-
mittee, 79th Cong., 1st sess., November 28–30, 1945, pp. 6,
10; Minutes of the Meeting of the Special Interdepartmental
Committee on Petroleum, July 27, 1943; *Investigation of the*

National Defense Program, Additional Report of the Special Interdepartmental Committee on Petroleum, July 27, 1943; U.S., Congress, Senate, Special Committee Investigating the National Defense Program, *Investigation of the National Defense Program,* Additional Report of the Special Committee Investigating National Defense Program, Senate Report No. 440, Part 5, 80th Cong., 2d sess., April 28, 1948, pp. 49–50.

41.   Cordell Hull, *Memoirs of Cordell Hull,* vol. 2 (New York: Macmillan Co., 1948), pp. 1514–15.

42.   U.S., Congress, Senate, Special Subcommittee Investigating Petroleum Resources, *American Petroleum Interests in Foreign Countries,* p. 321; U.S., Congress, Senate, Committee on Foreign Relations, *Hearings on Executive H.,* 80th Cong., 1st sess., June, 1947.

43.   Cordell Hull, *Memoirs of Cordell Hull,* pp. 1517–18. See also U.S., Congress, Senate, Special Subcommittee Investigating Petroleum Resources, *American Petroleum Interests in Foreign Countries,* p. 320. See also the Report presented by Senator Harry S. Truman, Senate Document No. 109, 78th Cong., 1st sess., 1943, pp. 32–33; Senate Report No. 440, Part 5, 80th Cong., 2d sess., 1948, p. 13.

44.   See the Report of Senator Truman, p. 44. In announcing the formation of the Petroleum Reserves Corporation, Secretary of the Interior Ickes said that American oil companies "have established themselves in the foreign oil business . . . entirely as a result of proved initiative, with the Government simply extending its good offices . . . [However,] the other principal nations, or most of them, have conducted their foreign oil business through corporations or agencies entirely or partly owned or in effect controlled by the Government itself." U.S., Congress, Senate, Special Subcommittee Investigating Petroleum Resources, *American Petroleum Interests in Foreign Countries,* p. 320.

45.   The text of the proposed agreement is contained in U.S., Congress, Senate, Committee Investigating the National Defense Program, *Report of the Committee,* Report No. 10, Part 15, 78th Cong., 2d sess., 1944, pp. 77–79. See also Announcement by the Secretary of the Interior, *Middle East Pipeline Proposal,* Feb. 9, 1944, *United States Foreign Oil Policy and Petroleum Reserves Corporation,* a Report of the Petroleum Industry War Counsel, March 1, 1944, p. 14.

46. See *Oil & Gas Journal,* December 21, 1946, pp. 42–44. The U.S. Department of State sent "unofficial observers" to the London meetings.

47. See *Oil & Gas Journal,* January 18, 1947, p. 44.

48. For a detailed and lively narrative of the evolution of oil enterprise in the Middle East, focusing upon the colorful personalities involved, see Leonard Mosely, *Power Play: Oil in the Middle East* (New York: Random House, 1973), especially chaps. I–IV.

4

The Postwar Explosion
of Foreign Oil
Consumption

THE POSTWAR YEARS witnessed an explosive growth in the foreign consumption of fuels—particularly of petroleum—with a slower, but still substantial, increase in the use of petroleum for energy by the United States and Canada. We now examine these changes in the patterns of fuel consumption, the growth in demand for petroleum, and the shifts in the international petroleum trade that resulted.

THE SHIFT FROM COAL
TO OIL AND GAS

According to the United Nations, annual world energy consumption more than tripled between 1949 and 1971, rising from 2.3 to 7.1 billion metric tons of coal-equivalent. Even more remarkable than this enormous increase in total energy consumption was the shift in the energy consumption pattern, in every region of the world, from

49

coal to oil and natural gas. In 1949 coal met nearly two-thirds of the world's energy needs, oil less than one-quarter, and natural gas about one-tenth, with water power a residual 2 percent. By 1971 the use of coal had dropped to one-third of world energy consumption, while the use of oil had risen to 43 percent and natural gas to 21 percent. Petroleum and natural gas combined had replaced coal as the source of two-thirds of man's energy consumption by 1971. In the foreign non-Communist world, consumption of oil increased from 37 to 59 percent of total energy usage between 1960 and 1971 (see Table 4.1).

There were marked differences, however, in the energy consumption patterns of the major regions of the world by 1971. The energy consumption pattern of the United States and Canada, economically the most advanced nations with the highest per capita incomes, showed a far heavier reliance upon natural gas (37 percent) than was true of the foreign non-Communist world as a whole (10 percent).[1] The Communist countries had an energy consumption pattern more heavily committed to coal (59 percent).

For many years, it appeared that the energy consumption pattern of the economically developed nations of the world would gradually approach that of the United States and that oil and natural gas together would ultimately meet about three-quarters of energy consumption, and coal one-quarter, with nuclear fuels playing a minor—but rapidly expanding—role. The prospect was that Western Europe and the Communist countries would probably meet most of their growing energy requirements from oil and natural gas.[2] However, the quadrupling of oil prices during 1973 and 1974, striking advances in the technology of coal production, and the development of coal gasification may combine to stop the encroachment of oil and gas on coal.

TABLE 4.1

Percentage of World Energy Consumption Accounted for by
Oil, Coal, Natural Gas, and Water and Nuclear Power
in Major Regions, 1949, 1960, and 1971

Year and Major Region	Oil (Percent)	Coal (Percent)	Natural Gas (Percent)	Water and Nuclear Power (Percent)
1949				
World	24	64	10	2
1960				
United States and Canada	42	24	32	2
Western Europe	30	65	2	3
Other Non-Communist World	48	43	6	3
Foreign Non-Communist World	37	57	3	3
Communist Bloc	14	80	5	1
World	31	52	15	2
1971				
United States and Canada	42	19	37	2
Western Europe	57	30	10	3
Other Non-Communist World	62	26	9	3
Foreign Non-Communist World	59	28	10	3
Communist Bloc	24	59	16	1
World	43	34	21	2

Sources: United Nations, *Statistical Yearbook,* 1960 ed., pp. 270–73; 1961 ed., pp. 275–77; and *World Energy Supplies,* 1968–1971; 1973 ed., pp. 10–33.

Note: Total consumption was 2,316 million metric tons of coal-equivalent in 1949, 4,236 million in 1960, and 7,096 million in 1971.

WESTERN NATIONS DEVELOP
ENERGY-INTENSIVE SOCIETIES

The huge increase in energy consumption and the progressive substitution of petroleum for coal combined to bring about an almost explosive growth in foreign non-Communist world consumption of petroleum after World War II. Oil-burning equipment was installed in millions of new homes, commercial establishments, and factories, and older buildings were converted from coal to oil. The number of motor vehicles in use in the world outside the United States multiplied eight times between 1949 and 1971, rising from 17.3 million to 146.3 million cars, trucks, and buses.[3] Millions of farmers began using petroleum products, as foreign agriculture began to mechanize and to use chemical fertilizers. Thousands of factories and electrical generating stations became petroleum users, as Western Europe and the Far East underwent an industrial renaissance.

In the foreign non-Communist world, consumption of petroleum increased elevenfold in the twenty-four year period from 1948 to 1972, rising from 2.4 to 26.2 million barrels per day to establish an average compound growth rate of nearly 11 percent per annum. (The remarkable speed of this growth may be appreciated by noting that it involved a doubling of oil consumption every six and a half years!) In the Communist countries, the growth rate was only slightly lower, although their total consumption in 1972 was only one-fourth as much as in the non-Communist world. In the United States and Canada, however, consumption only tripled, rising from 6 to 18 million barrels per day, an average compound yearly growth of 4.5 percent. Looking at the matter in another way, the foreign market rose from under 30 to over 50 percent of aggregate world petroleum consumption between 1948 and 1972, adding 23.8 million barrels per day to its usage, while the United States and Canada added 12.0 million barrels per day to their usage. A milestone was passed in 1964, when foreign non-Communist world consumption

FIGURE 4.1

World Energy Consumption, by Sources, in 1949, 1960, and 1971

(WIDTH OF BARS PROPORTIONAL TO CONSUMPTION)

TOTAL WORLD

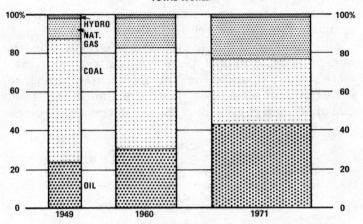

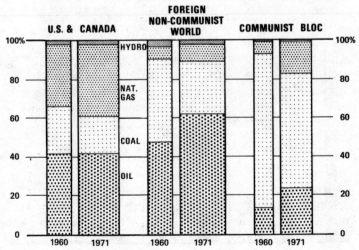

Source: Table 4.1

surpassed that of North America. Countries having the most rapid growth in consumption included Germany and Italy in Europe, and Japan in the Far East. Clearly, the foreign market was by far the most dynamic segment of the non-Communist petroleum industry after World War II (see Figure 4.1, Figure 4.2, and Table 4.2).

Analysis of the year-to-year percentage changes in consumption reveals how well sustained the growth was. In addition to a much higher average rate of expansion, the foreign non-Communist petroleum markets also grew more steadily than did the American market, which revealed cyclical tendencies. Thus, the United States and Canadian market grew little during the general business

FIGURE 4.2
Non-Communist World Oil Consumption, by Region, in 1948, 1962, and 1972

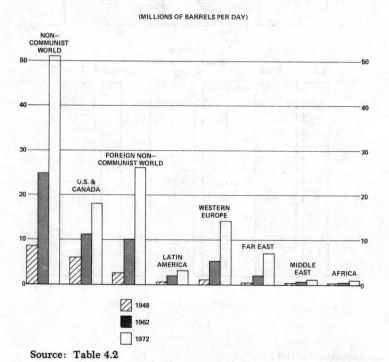

(MILLIONS OF BARRELS PER DAY)

Source: Table 4.2

TABLE 4.2

Petroleum Consumption in the Principal Consuming Countries
and Regions of the World, 1948, 1962, and 1972

(*Amounts in Thousands of Barrels per Day*)

Countries and Regions	1948	1962	1972	Change 1962–1972 Amount	Percent
United States and Canada	6,008	11,151	18,032	6,881	61.7
Argentina	136	319	444	125	39.2
Brazil	61	315	655	340	107.9
Mexico	126	300	560	260	86.7
Venezuela	34	159	229	70	44.0
Other Latin America	283	784	1,192	408	52.0
Latin America	640	1,877	3,080	1,203	64.1
France	167	727	2,241	1,514	208.3
West Germany	42	997	2,769	1,772	177.7
Italy	75	669	2,079	1,410	210.8
United Kingdom	357	1,122	2,242	1,120	99.8
Other Western Europe	326	1,665	4,761	3,096	186.0
Western Europe	967	5,180	14,092	8,912	172.1
Australia	80	247	541	294	119.0
India	50	182	424	242	133.0
Indonesia	72	110	145	35	31.8
Japan	32	934	4,376	3,442	368.5
Other Far East	96	491	1,572	1,081	220.2
Far East	330	1,964	7,058	5,094	259.4
Middle East	247	610	1,073	463	75.9
Africa	207	431	876	445	103.3
Foreign Non-Communist World	2,391	10,062	26,179	16,117	160.2
Communist Bloc	727	3,546	7,144	3,598	101.5
Total World	9,126	24,759	51,355	26,596	107.4

Source: United States Bureau of Mines.

recession years of 1954 and 1961, and actually declined in 1957. Because the economies of the foreign non-Communist world were freer of periodic business recessions, in no year did they fail to show an appreciable gain in the usage of petroleum and its products. Nor is there evidence of a substantial decline in the annual growth rate of foreign non-Communist world consumption until the 1970s (see Table 4.3).

The steady—as well as fast—postwar growth of foreign non-Communist world oil consumption had a twofold significance. For existing oil companies it provided a basis upon which they could plan and execute long-term programs of expansion in their supplies of petroleum products, confident that an expanding market would soon absorb their output. It also attracted scores of new entrants into the industry, each eager to capture a position in a booming market and to reap the profits that normally accompany growth. It was in the countries of fastest growth in oil consumption that these entrants into the foreign oil industry made their deepest market penetration.

CHANGES IN PETROLEUM
PRODUCTS CONSUMED

Changes also occurred in the structure of consumption of different petroleum products. A barrel of crude oil may be refined into more than a hundred distinct end products, which are customarily grouped into five major categories: gasoline, kerosenes, distillate fuels, residual fuels, and lubricating oils.[4] In 1953 gasoline accounted for 43 percent of the aggregate consumption of petroleum products in the non-Communist world: kerosene for 6 percent, distillate fuels for 20 percent, residual fuels for 29 percent, and lubricating oils for 2 percent. However, in the *foreign* non-Communist countries gasoline was 30 percent of aggregate consumption, whereas it was 50 percent in the United States and Canada.[5] But the proportion of

TABLE 4.3

Annual Percentage Changes in Consumption of Petroleum
Products by Regions of the Non-Communist World,
1951–1972

Year	United States and Canada (Percent)	Western Europe (Percent)	Other Non-Communist World (Percent)	Foreign Non-Communist World (Percent)	Total Non-Communist World (Percent)
1951	8.4	20.4	17.3	18.7	11.3
1952	4.1	9.5	7.6	8.4	5.4
1953	4.5	9.1	6.2	7.5	5.4
1954	0.4	16.9	11.7	14.1	4.7
1955	7.4	11.0	5.0	7.8	7.6
1956	4.6	17.1	9.5	13.1	7.5
1957	−0.2	0.5	11.7	6.2	2.1
1958	1.8	16.2	15.3	15.7	7.0
1959	7.0	9.0	5.3	7.0	7.0
1960	3.0	14.6	10.3	12.4	6.8
1961	0.5	14.3	12.3	11.0	6.0
1962	4.5	15.2	9.0	12.1	8.0
1963	3.4	14.9	10.3	12.6	7.8
1964	3.1	13.9	10.1	12.0	7.5
1965	4.6	12.2	8.0	10.2	7.5
1966	4.9	11.1	8.6	9.9	7.6
1967	5.8	6.9	6.8	6.9	6.4
1968	7.0	11.7	14.2	12.8	10.2
1969	5.1	13.9	12.2	13.1	9.6
1970	4.2	8.7	10.0	9.3	7.1
1971	3.5	4.4	9.3	6.7	5.4
1972	7.6	7.5	5.6	6.6	7.0

Source: United States Bureau of Mines.

aggregate consumption accounted for by residual fuels, used mainly for heating and power, was sharply higher (44 percent) in the foreign non-Communist world than in the United States and Canada (23 percent).

By 1972 these consumption patterns had changed somewhat. The relative importance of gasoline for the non-Communist world as a whole had declined from 43 percent to 30 percent, despite a large absolute increase in motor fuel usage. The huge *relative* expansion in the use of residual fuels and distillates for heat and power in Western Europe and Japan meant that, by 1972, foreign non-Communist countries consumed only 30 percent of petroleum products in the form of gasoline.

CHANGES IN INTERNATIONAL TRADE

In recent years crude oil and its products have accounted for over half of the tonnage of all water-borne international commerce in the world. International trade in petroleum is vast both because of its intrinsic economic importance and because great distances separate major consuming regions from major producing regions.

Prior to World War II, international trade occurred primarily in the products of petroleum; transoceanic movements of crude oil formed only one-third of the total volume. After World War II, the amount of this trade expanded and its composition shifted radically. Between 1950 and 1972, the volume of international trade in crude oil and petroleum products rose about tenfold, from 2.9 to 30 million barrels per day. As a result of the postwar tendency to locate refineries in the consuming markets, however, for both economic and political reasons, international commerce in crude oil had risen, by 1950, to over one-half of the total international petroleum trade, and, by 1972, crude oil constituted 83 percent of the total commerce, as petroleum products declined to 17 percent (see Table 4.4).

In 1950 the primary flows of petroleum were from South America into the United States and Europe, and

TABLE 4.4

Major International Flows of Crude Oil and Petroleum Products,
1950, 1961, and 1972

(*Amounts in Thousands of Barrels per Day*)

Commodity	1950		1961		1972	
	Amount	Percent	Amount	Percent	Amount	Percent
Crude Oil	1,568	54	6,470	69	24,909	83
Petroleum Products	1,326	46	2,895	31	4,977	17
Total	2,894	100	9,365	100	29,886	100

Sources: 1950 data from Petroleum Administration for Defense; 1961 data from United States Office of Oil and Gas; and 1972 data from *1972 Petroleum Supply and Demand in the Non-Communist World*, Federal Energy Administration.

from the Middle East into Europe and the Orient. Eleven years later, in 1961, in addition to a great expansion in volume, the following new international movements had appeared: a very significant movement of Middle East oil into the United States and Canada had developed; North African oil was moving into Western Europe; the Soviet Union was shipping oil into many markets; petroleum was moving from Indonesia into Australia and Japan; and Middle East output was going in large quantities to Southeast Asia and Japan.

What stands out when flows during 1972 are depicted on a map of the world is the rise of the Persian Gulf from a minor position to a posture of surpassing world importance as a source of oil exports (see Figure 4.3). The great expansibility of their oil production endows the nations of this region with vast bargaining power. The growth of North Africa as an oil exporter is also apparent.[6] Important new foreign sources of petroleum exports were developed which gave rise to a greater diversity of petroleum movements between countries. Oil-importing countries had a wider range of alternative sources of supply, thereby increasing the geographical scope of competition among foreign oil companies.

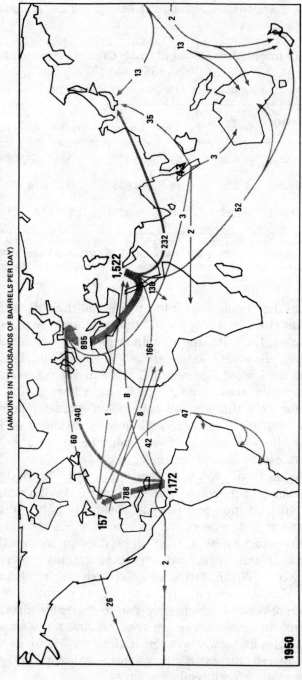

Figure 4.3

Major International Oceanic Flows of Petroleum, 1950 and 1972

(AMOUNTS IN THOUSANDS OF BARRELS PER DAY)

1950

Source: Data from *Petroleum Administration for Defense.*

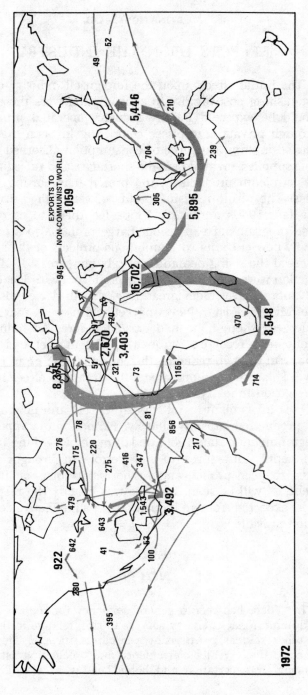

EXPORTS TO
NON-COMMUNIST WORLD
1,059

1972

Source: Data from *1972 Petroleum Supply and Demand in the Non-Communist World*, Federal Energy Administration.

EFFECTS UPON THE INDUSTRY

The initial effects upon the foreign oil industry of the astonishing postwar rise in consumption were those that would be expected in any industry operated primarily through private enterprises competing in open markets. The strong upward surge of consumption absorbed available supplies, created periodic shortages, and raised prices of petroleum products in the principal importing countries. The resulting rising profits of established firms in the late 1940s and early 1950s led them to carry out bold programs of expansion. Large profits also attracted many new entrants with ambitious projects of their own. To feed the rising demand, entirely new areas of oil production were opened up by new producers with locational advantages over older areas (e.g., North Africa vis-à-vis the Middle East). New markets with new marketers emerged where none had existed before. As industrial economists recognize, growth of the market can be a powerful force in reducing the concentration of an industry.[7] This principle operated with dramatic effect in the foreign oil industry.

Vast investment by oil companies, old and new, raised oil production capacity sharply. Periodic gluts appeared. Beginning in the late 1950s and through most of the 1960s, competitive pressures to sell petroleum brought price cuts, reduced profits, and subnormal returns on investment, as will be seen. But this was exactly the response to be expected from an industry in which effective competition prevailed.

NOTES

1.   There has been a general tendency for the use of oil and natural gas as energy sources to rise, relative to the use of other sources, with rising per capita income. This has reflected their greater convenience and broadening usage in personal transportation and home heating as standards of

living rose. Natural gas experienced a relatively greater rise than petroleum as a result of its cleanliness and low cost, and enhanced its share of the U.S. and USSR energy markets. It may be expected to increase its share of Western Europe's energy market as a result of the important postwar gas discoveries in the Groningen reservoir in Holland and the British sector of the North Sea.

2. Coal consumption in the United States and Canada actually declined between 1953 and 1960. In Western Europe, coal consumption was virtually unchanged. On the other hand, striking recent advances in the technology of coal production and a quadrupled price of crude oil may retard the future encroachment of oil on coal. See Chapter 11.

3. American Petroleum Institute, *Petroleum Facts and Figures,* 1949 ed. (Washington, D.C.: American Petroleum Institute), p. 453, and U.S., Bureau of the Census, *Statistical Abstract of the United States 1973* (Washington, D.C.: Government Printing Office, 1973), p. 825.

4. Gasolines are used primarily for automotive transportation; kerosenes for jet aircraft transportation; distillate fuels for space heating, farm, industrial, and transportation equipment; residual fuels for steam generation; and lubricating oils for reducing friction in the operation of machinery.

5. This reflected the immensely greater per capita usage of automobile transportation in North America.

6. North African exports rose from almost nothing in 1958 to a rate of 800,000 barrels a day by the end of 1962, and to 3.4 million barrels per day during 1972.

7. Nelson has observed that concentration *declines* in rapidly growing industries, offsetting the increasing concentration in slowly growing or declining industries. Ralph Z. Nelson, *Concentration in the Manufacturing Industries of the United States* (New Haven and London: Yale University Press, 1963), p. 10.

5

The Rising Tide of the Foreign Oil Supply

STIMULATED by the powerful upsurge of postwar demand and by the relatively high returns on investment, foreign oil companies began, during the 1950s, to build up their capacity to supply petroleum products. This expansion gained such momentum that, notwithstanding the maintenance of a very high rate of growth in demand, substantial excess capacity appeared by the late 1950s in all divisions of the industry. The course of this growth can be traced clearly in the rise of crude oil reserves and annual production rates, of transportation and refining capacity, and of marketing facilities and gross investment in the industry.

THE EXPANSION OF FOREIGN CRUDE OIL RESERVES

Proven crude oil reserves in the foreign non-Communist world were estimated to be just under 41 billion barrels at the end of 1948; they had increased sixfold to 250 billion barrels by 1962 and then more than doubled this amount to 522 billion barrels by 1972. This increase over a twenty-four-year period was equivalent to an average annual compound growth rate of 11.2 percent—a spectacular expansion of the non-Communist world's oil stock outside the United States and Canada.

This rate of expansion about equalled that of the Communist countries, which, in raising their reserves from 6.5 billion to 98 billion barrels, established an average annual compound growth rate of 12 percent. Both contrasted sharply with the record of the United States and Canada, which little more than doubled their reserves (from 21.5 billion to 47 billion barrels), achieving, despite heavy investments in domestic exploration, an annual growth rate of only 3.5 percent. In 1972 the foreign non-Communist world held in reserve enough oil to supply its needs for almost 55 years at the 1972 rate of consumption —without discovering another barrel—whereas the United States and Canada had little more than seven years' supply within their own boundaries (see Figure 5.1 and Table 5.1).

The growth of reserves proceeded at a fast rate in Africa, from virtually nothing in 1948 to 106 billion barrels in 1972, primarily as a consequence of the huge discoveries in Algeria, Libya, and Nigeria. The Far East showed a large gain, primarily in Indonesia. Reserves in the Middle East multiplied twelvefold. In Latin America, a relatively small rise occurred, primarily because Venezuelan reserves had declined in recent years. Even Western Europe, long thought to be almost barren of hydrocarbons, benefited by the discovery of the Groningen natural gas field in The Netherlands—the world's largest —and from huge oil fields under the North Sea.

In absolute quantities, the 327 billion barrel increase in the oil reserves of the Middle East far outweighed that of the rest of the world. The Middle East accounted for about seven of every ten barrels of the total increase in non-Communist world reserves during the years from 1948 to 1972.

FIGURE 5.1
World Crude Oil Proven Reserves, by Region, 1948, 1962, and 1972

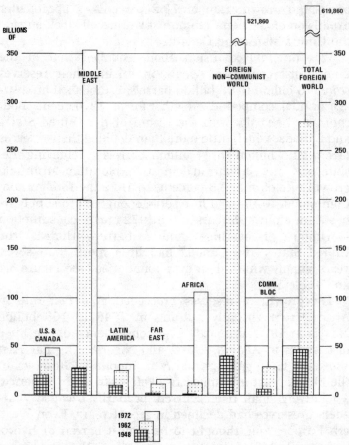

Source: Table 5.1

In general, fields with prolific reserves enjoy the lowest costs in the production of oil. There are immense differences, both between countries and between oil fields within each country, in the average costs per barrel of crude oil delivered to refineries in consuming markets. In general, these differences derive from disparities of three kinds: variations in physical productivities, that is, in the discovery, development, and lifting costs per barrel; variations in the concession bonuses, royalties, and income taxes per barrel collected by the national governments; and variations in the outlays per barrel for transporting crude oil from producing wells to refineries in the consuming markets.

The wide differences in average physical productivities of oil wells in different countries and areas are suggested by the following figures (for 1972): in the United States, 526,000 producing wells yielded an average output of 18 barrels per day; in Venezuela, 11,000 wells had an average daily output of 285 barrels per day; in the Middle East, 3,000 wells each produced an average of 5,530 barrels per day.[1] Other things being equal, high physical productivity of wells would mean low-cost oil. However, the amounts collected by the governments of the Middle East and Venezuela in the form of royalties and income taxes alone were, in 1974, more than $7.00 per barrel (as compared with less than $1.00 per barrel in the United States), and the more remote location of Middle East oil from consuming markets called for relatively high transport costs. Hence, the differences in *delivered* costs per barrel were very much less than were suggested by variations in the physical productivity of wells, although they were still substantial. In effect, the oil-exporting nations charged high economic "rents," which offset the low production costs of their oil.

ARE CURRENT RESERVES ADEQUATE?

Are the crude oil reserves in the non-Communist world presently adequate, deficient, or redundant? This question provokes active debate; and it cannot be answered categorically. Neo-Malthusians, who believe that increasing world population and industrialization are putting severe pressures on a planet with limited resources, consider present reserves dangerously small. They call for a radical reduction in the use of petroleum.

Technological optimists, who hold that rising energy prices will slow the growth of consumption and that ad-

TABLE 5.1

World Crude Oil Proven Reserves, by Region and Principal Producing Country, 1948, 1962, and 1972

(Amounts in Millions of Barrels)

Regions and Countries	1948 Amount	1948 Percent of Total Foreign	1962 Amount	1962 Percent of Total Foreign	1972 Amount	1972 Percent of Total Foreign	Change 1962–1972 Amount	Change 1962–1972 Percent of Change
United States and Canada	21,470	45.3	39,900	14.3	47,023	7.6	7,123	17.9
Argentina	200	0.4	2,400	0.9	4,900	0.8	2,500	104.2
Mexico	1,200	2.5	2,500	0.9	2,800	0.5	300	12.0
Venezuela	8,500	18.0	18,487	6.6	13,700	2.2	(4,787)	−25.9
Other Latin America	950	2.0	2,326	0.8	11,200	1.8	8,874	381.5
Latin America	10,850	22.9	25,713	9.2	32,600	5.3	6,887	26.8
Western Europe	50	0.1	1,891	0.7	12,632	2.0	10,741	568.0
Africa	100	0.2	12,420	4.4	106,402	17.2	93,982	756.7
Iran	9,500	20.1	38,200	13.6	65,000	10.5	26,800	70.2
Iraq	7,500	15.8	26,000	9.3	29,000	4.6	3,000	11.5
Kuwait	5,000	10.6	63,000	22.5	64,900	10.5	1,900	3.0

Neutral Zone	....	....	11,000	3.9	16,000	2.6	5,000	45.5
Saudi Arabia	6,000	12.7	52,000	18.6	138,000	22.3	86,000	165.4
Other Middle East	550	1.2	8,375	3.0	42,402	6.8	34,027	406.3
Middle East	28,550	60.3	198,575	70.9	355,302	57.3	156,727	78.9
Indonesia	800	1.7	10,000	3.6	10,005	1.6	5	0.1
Other Far East	500	1.1	1,330	0.5	4,917	0.8	3,587	269.7
Far East	1,300	2.7	11,330	4.0	14,922	2.4	3,592	31.7
Foreign Non-Communist World	40,850	86.3	249,929	89.3	521,860	84.2	271,931	108.8
Communist Bloc	6,500	13.7	29,976	10.7	98,000	15.8	68,024	226.9
Foreign World	47,350	100.0	279,905	100.0	619,860	100.0	339,955	121.5
Total World	68,820	145.3	319,805	114.3	666,883	107.6	347,078	108.5

Source: *Oil and Gas Journal.* Figures apply to ends of years.
Note: Turkey is included in Western Europe total.

69

vancing technology will make possible the discovery of additional crude oil and other sources of energy, regard the current reserves as adequate. They note that the reserve/consumption ratio has risen—not fallen—during the past quarter-century. Thus, in 1948, the 62 billion barrels of proven reserves would have lasted about twenty years at the then-current annual rate of consumption of 3 billion barrels. By 1972 the 569 billion barrels of reserves would have lasted about thirty-five years at the 1972 rate of 16 billion barrels a year. They point out that the United States lived through periods of anxiety about energy shortages after World Wars I and II, and yet large new petroleum deposits were discovered later. If the world runs out of petroleum by the end of this century, they believe that technologies for the conversion of plentiful coal and oil shales into oil and synthetic gas will have been developed, and nuclear—or even fusion—energy will have come into extensive use. Bearing in mind that the *present value* of crude oil reserves in the ground diminishes rapidly as the date of sale recedes into the future, especially when the rate of discount (or interest) is relatively high, the optimists conclude that present reserves are at a comfortable level.

Without taking sides in this debate, it should be noted that there has been a historically strong tendency toward *aggregate* overinvestment in oil exploration and development. The pressures of national security and competition tend to drive each country and each oil company to try to expand *its own reserves*, even though *reserves in the aggregate* appear to be ample. These pressures include the following factors:

1. Most countries seek a reliable energy base by encouraging the development of indigenous resources and by giving diplomatic and financial support to the foreign operations of locally based petroleum companies.

2. The concession agreements of host governments press oil companies to search for oil, under penalty of the forced relinquishment or nationalization of their concessions.

3. The tax systems of the United States and many other countries encourage oil investments by treating intangible drilling costs as business expenses, granting percentage depletion allowances, and permitting an American oil company to reduce its American income taxes by offsetting against profits earned on domestic operations many of the expenses of carrying on exploratory activities abroad.

4. Companies with ample reserves in current producing areas nevertheless explore new areas in order to diversify their sources of crude oil for political, locational, or quality advantages. They seek to protect themselves against the possibility that rivals may discover large reserves of low-cost crude oil. Few, if any, of the more than four hundred firms in the foreign oil industry possess *all* of the reserves they desire, of the *types* and in the *locations* needed.

5. The "bonanza effect" operates in the oil industry, as it does in other human activities in which there is a wide dispersion of individual returns around the average. As national lotteries, the Irish Sweepstakes, and the casinos of Las Vegas testify, men eagerly "invest" in activities in which there is a small chance of a big prize, even when they know in advance that the average return (i.e., the mathematical expectation) is *negative!* The lure of the "big strike" is powerful.

For all these reasons, the worldwide search for crude oil will continue, notwithstanding large proven reserves and a high reserve/consumption ratio. While oil investment *is* responsive to the rate of return, as will be shown, there is a bias toward overinvestment.

THE GROWTH OF FOREIGN CRUDE OIL PRODUCTION

Foreign non-Communist crude oil production, which stood at 3.1 million barrels per day in 1948, rose tenfold during the next twenty-four years to reach 31 million barrels per day in 1972. This represented an average annual compound growth rate of 10 percent; the difference between this and the 11 percent annual compound growth of consumption in the foreign non-Communist world was supplied by Communist bloc exports to the non-Communist world after 1953.[2] In the United States and Canada, by contrast, the increase in crude oil production from 5.6 million to 11 million barrels per day over the same period represented an average annual compound growth of only 2.6 percent. By far the largest absolute gains in foreign output were recorded in Venezuela, the Middle East, North Africa, and Indonesia (see Figure 5.2 and Table 5.2).

In absolute volume, the vast increase of just under 17 million barrels per day in Middle East production dwarfed that in any other region and accounted for 51 percent of the total postwar expansion in non-Communist world output. Middle East production maintained an average annual compound growth rate of more than 10 percent per annum—double that of Latin America and more than that of the Communist countries. This was a remarkable achievement, considering the substantial production base on which the gain was measured. The expanding role of Middle East oil in the world's consuming markets was certainly inconsistent with the allegation of the U.S. government, in 1953, that there was in existence an effective scheme for restricting production in order to maintain prices. While each of the largest companies had an interest in gearing its production to its anticipated sales, the many new firms that came into the region were interested only in raising their output to commercial levels and carving out markets for their newly found crude oil. There were, in fact, strong competitive pressures on all oil companies to expand production and sales.[3]

Year-to-year growth of foreign non-Communist world production was well maintained throughout the postwar period and up to the end of 1972. In the United States and Canada, the postwar trend of oil output rose moderately, but year-to-year changes were very marked, reflecting the

FIGURE 5.2
World Crude Oil Production, by Region, 1948, 1962, and 1972

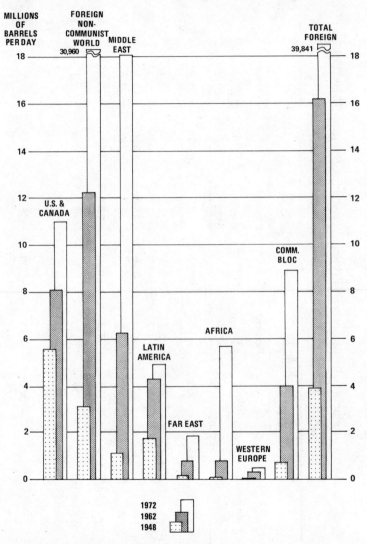

Source: Table 5.2

TABLE 5.2

World Crude Oil Production, by Region and Principal Producing Country, 1948, 1962, and 1972

(Amounts in Thousands of Barrels per Day)

Regions and Countries	1948		1962		1972		Change 1962–1972	
	Amount	Percent of Foreign World	Amount	Percent of Foreign World	Amount	Percent of Foreign World	Amount	Percent of Change
United States and Canada	5,554	145.2	8,005	49.6	10,973	27.5	2,968	37.1
Argentina	65	1.7	267	1.7	433	1.1	166	62.2
Mexico	160	4.2	305	1.9	505	1.3	200	65.6
Venezuela	1,339	35.0	3,196	19.8	3,220	8.1	24	0.8
Other Latin America	167	4.4	478	3.0	727	1.8	249	52.1
Latin America	1,713	45.2	4,246	26.3	4,885	12.3	639	15.1
Western Europe	39	1.0	329	2.0	444	1.1	115	35.0
Africa	37	1.0	794	4.9	5,680	14.3	4,886	615.4
Iran	520	13.6	1,300	8.1	5,038	12.7	3,738	287.5
Iraq	71	1.9	1,005	6.2	1,446	3.6	441	43.9

Kuwait	127	3.3	1,860	11.5	2,999	7.5	1,139	61.2
Neutral Zone	...	...	238	1.5	566	1.4	328	137.8
Saudi Arabia	390	10.2	1,523	9.4	5,733	14.4	4,210	276.4
Other Middle East	31	0.8	276	1.7	2,281	5.7	2,005	726.5
Middle East	1,139	29.8	6,202	38.4	18,063	45.3	11,861	191.2
Indonesia	87	2.3	458	2.8	1,081	2.7	623	136.0
Other Far East	66	1.7	123	0.8	807	2.0	684	556.0
Far East	153	4.0	581	3.6	1,888	4.7	1,307	225.0
Foreign Non-Communist World	3,099	81.0	12,152	75.3	30,960	77.7	18,808	154.7
Communist Bloc	727	19.0	3,992	24.7	8,881	22.3	4,889	122.5
Foreign World	3,826	100.0	16,144	100.0	39,841	100.0	23,697	146.8
Total World	9,380	245.2	24,149	149.6	50,814	127.5	26,665	110.4

Source: United States Bureau of Mines.

impact of business cycles and annual changes in oil consumption.

THE BOOM IN TANKER AND PIPELINE CONSTRUCTION

A large increase in transportation facilities was essential to accommodate the rising flood of crude oil production. Such an increase took place, both in major trunk pipelines and in the non-Communist world tanker fleet.

At the end of 1948, there were no more than thirteen major oil trunk pipelines in operation in the foreign non-Communist world, with an aggregate length of about 1,800 miles. So rapid was the expansion of trunk pipeline facilities that, at the end of 1972, there were 111 major crude oil pipelines in operation in the non-Communist world, having an aggregate length of over 15,000 miles. (Petroleum product pipelines were also expanding rapidly.) The rate of growth of oil pipeline transportation outstripped that of oil production because of the steady encroachment of the pipeline upon such other modes of land transport as the rail tank car and the tank truck. There was a growing tendency to build refineries inland near consuming centers and to pipe crude oil to them, instead of refining it at marine terminals and then shipping the products inland by truck or rail. The rise of transnational pipelines in Europe was one of the major competitive and technological developments of the 1960s.

The growth of marine transportation capacity for crude oil and for petroleum products nearly matched that of pipeline capacity between 1949 and the end of 1972. In 1949 the total capacity of the non-Communist world tanker fleet, including governmental as well as private vessels and ships owned by non-oil, as well as by oil, companies, was 26.2 million deadweight tons. The fleet then comprised some 2,781 ships, of which only 18 (with an aggregate capacity of 500,000 deadweight tons) were the then "supertankers" (i.e, ships with a capacity of at least

25,000 deadweight tons). By 1972 the non-Communist world tanker fleet had risen to 3,750 vessels with 219 million deadweight tons of capacity. Of this aggregate fleet, 2,350 were larger than 25,000 deadweight tons and 287 were larger than 200,000 deadweight tons. And the greater speed of these ships meant, of course, that the growth in the number of ton-miles of oil transportation which the 1972 fleet was capable of providing was much more than proportionate to the growth in the tonnage of the fleet (see Table 5.3).

THE EXPANSION OF FOREIGN REFINING CAPACITY

The rise in foreign non-Communist capacity to refine crude oil between 1948 and 1972 matched the increase in consumption, soaring from 2.8 to 35.1 million barrels per day, and establishing an average compound growth rate of about 11 percent a year. The growth rate of refining capacity in the Communist countries was slower—about 10 percent—so that total foreign refining capacity rose twelvefold from 3.7 million to 43.3 million barrels per day. In sharp contrast was the relatively sluggish twofold expansion of United States and Canadian refining capacity over the same period. These countries had almost three times as much refining capacity as the rest of the non-Communist world in 1948—7.3 versus 2.8 million barrels per day. But because foreign non-Communist world capacity increased much faster than North American capacity, it had far outweighed domestic capacity by 1972—35.1 versus 14.8 million barrels per day.

Most of the new foreign non-Communist refining capacity was constructed in the Western European countries, especially in the United Kingdom, France, Italy, and West Germany. Yet, more capacity was built in Japan than in any other single country. Africa, which contained virtually no oil refining activities in 1948, had a signifi-

TABLE 5.3

Non-Communist World Tanker Deadweight Capacity, 1949, 1953, and 1972

(Amounts in Thousands of Deadweight Tons)

Categories of Companies	1949		1953		1972		Change 1949–1972	
	Amount	Percent	Amount	Percent	Amount	Percent	Amount	Percent
"Seven Largest" Oil Companies	9,108	34.8	9,842	28.5	41,609	19.0	32,501	356.8
Other Oil Companies								
Government	557	2.1	1,168	3.4	3,787	1.7	3,230	579.9
Private	2,447	9.3	2,642	7.7	13,786	6.3	11,339	463.4
Non-Oil Companies								
Government	3,087	11.8	2,994	8.7	} 159,708	} 73.0	} 145,631	} 1,034.5
Private	10,990	42.0	17,877	51.8				
Total—Other than the "Seven Largest" Oil Companies	17,081	65.2	24,681	71.5	177,281	81.0	160,200	937.9
Total—Non-Communist World Companies	26,189	100.0	34,523	100.0	218,890	100.0	192,701	735.8

Sources: Statistical Studies; Clarkson's Tanker Register; and Skinner's Oil and Gas International Yearbook-1973.

78

cant refining industry in 1972. Latin America also had additions to its refining capabilities, particularly in Argentina, Brazil, Venezuela, and Mexico. The smallest percentage gains were recorded in the Middle East, as a result of the strong tendency to locate the new refineries near consumption centers rather than oil-producing fields.[4] (See Table 5.4.)

The postwar era brought important changes in the location and technology of refineries. After World War II, the Organization for European Economic Cooperation (OEEC), working with U.S. officials to coordinate Marshall Plan aid, adopted a master plan for increasing Western European refining capacity in order to eliminate major imports of petroleum products. Under the OEEC plan, Western European refining growth proceeded at a truly heroic rate. By 1962 refining capacity there had reached 4.84 million barrels per day (20 times the 1946 capacity), and, by 1972, it was 17.2 million barrels per day. It had far outstripped even the burgeoning rise in European consumption, and Europe had become substantially self-sufficient in refinery capacity.

The same transformation occurred in the large oil-consuming nations in other regions throughout the non-Communist world. In 1953, refining capacity was located in forty-one nations, but, by 1972, 104 nations had refineries. These remarkable changes have had far-reaching competitive implications, as will be seen.

The shift from resource-oriented to market-oriented refinery locations was attributable to a number of factors, political as well as economic. One political influence was the Marshall Plan, which put pressure on European consuming countries to build local refining capacity to conserve scarce foreign exchange by importing lower-valued crude oil instead of higher-valued products. Other political factors included the security of supplies of petroleum products as well as national prestige. The economic factors included the ability of the new refineries to adapt more flexibly to the needs of their local markets by tailoring outputs to requirements. The development of the high-

TABLE 5.4

World Crude Oil Refining Capacity, by Region, 1949, 1962, and 1972

(Amounts in Thousands of Barrels per Day)

Regions	1948		1962		1972		Change 1962–1972	
	Amount	Percent of Foreign World	Amount	Percent of Foreign World	Amount	Percent of Foreign World	Amount	Percent of Change
United States and Canada	7,302	199.1	10,992	72.6	14,812	34.2	3,820	34.8
Latin America	1,253	34.2	3,559	23.5	6,544	15.1	2,985	83.9
Western Europe	458	12.5	4,837	31.9	17,210	39.7	12,373	255.8
Africa	42	1.1	325	2.1	994	2.3	669	205.9
Middle East	872	23.8	1,403	9.3	2,484	5.7	1,081	77.1
Far East	210	5.7	2,088	13.8	7,916	18.3	5,828	279.1
Foreign Non-Communist World	2,835	77.4	12,212	80.6	35,148	81.2	22,936	187.8
Communist Bloc	833	22.7	2,934	19.4	8,159	18.8	5,225	178.1
Foreign World	3,668	100.0	15,146	100.0	43,307	100.0	28,161	185.9
Total World	10,970	299.1	26,138	172.6	58,119	134.2	31,981	122.4

Sources: World Petroleum; World Petroleum Report; Oil and Gas Journal.

capacity pipelines and the larger tankers enormously reduced the costs of transporting crude oil, making it increasingly more advantageous to import crude oil rather than petroleum products.

Other factors which helped to shift refining to consuming markets were: the growth of national markets to levels that justified construction of refineries of efficient scale; the proximity of markets for petrochemicals, which were coming to form an important source of revenue for oil companies; and the huge increase in demand for middle distillate and heavy fuel oils, which could readily be produced by smaller refineries lacking cracking capacity.[5]

These locational and technological changes created many opportunities for new firms, illustrating a principle long ago noted by Schumpeter. Many of the entering refiners, who accounted for a rising proportion of the additions to refining capacity after 1948, had locational advantages over older international oil companies, who were to a greater degree committed to older plants in less desirable locations.

THE RISE OF FOREIGN MARKETING FACILITIES

Comprehensive information about the postwar growth of foreign petroleum marketing facilities is not available. However, the great upsurge of petroleum product consumption since 1948 obviously required a parallel enlargement of the marketing apparatus for moving products from refineries to consumers. But, some relevant facts are known. Between 1953 and 1962, the number of primary marketing firms in a sample of non-Communist nations increased by almost 25 percent; the number of retail service stations all but doubled; and the volume of estimated product sales almost tripled. The marketing facilities added during this period were of larger average capacity than earlier facilities, because the volume of products sold rose at a much higher rate than did the number of facilities.

Gross investment in marketing facilities increased fourteenfold between the end of 1946 and the end of 1972, rising by $20 billion, from $1.5 billion to $21.6 billion (see Table 5.5). Especially in the industrialized countries of Western Europe and the Far East, in which petroleum consumption rose most rapidly, huge investments were made in marine and inland oil terminals, in bulk storage stations, in railroad tank cars and tank trucks, in underground storage facilities, and in systems of retail service stations and outlets.

The enlargement of product markets also created opportunities for new firms in every country. As in other divisions of the industry, marketing became less concentrated, with a consequent enlivenment of competition.

THE SURGE OF INVESTMENT IN FOREIGN OIL

The remarkable postwar growth in the physical operations of the foreign oil industry naturally called for prodigious amounts of capital; and financing requirements were further swollen by rising price levels, which inflated the cost of acquiring real assets. In fact, oil formed the backbone of U.S. postwar foreign direct investment. Gross investment in the fixed assets of the foreign non-Communist world petroleum industry (including Canada for this purpose) multiplied nearly twenty times between the end of 1946 and the end of 1972, rising from $6.9 billion to $134.5 billion.[6] Investment proceeded at especially fast rates in pipelines, refineries, and petrochemical plants. At the end of the period, production assets accounted for about one-quarter of total investment, transportation for about one-quarter, refineries and related installations for more than a quarter, and marketing and other facilities for the balance (see Figure 5.3 and Table 5.5).

Geographically, there was a wide dispersion of this

FIGURE 5.3

Gross Investment in Fixed Assets of the Foreign Non-Communist Petroleum Industry, by Division, 1961 and 1972

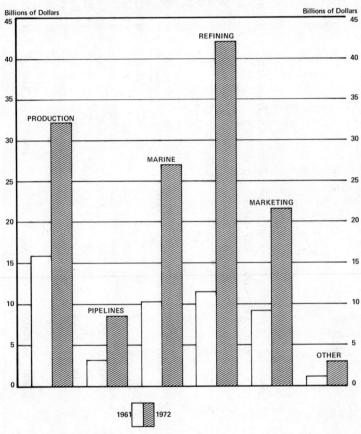

Source: Table 5.5

petroleum investment throughout the non-Communist world. By far the largest dollar increases occurred in Latin America and Western Europe, which jointly accounted for almost half of the total rise. In terms of percentage increases, the growth was much the greatest in Africa, the major area of new oil development. Considering that more than 327 billion barrels of proven reserves were added in the Middle East, against less than 180 billion

TABLE 5.5

Gross Investment in Fixed Assets of the Foreign Non-Communist Petroleum Industry, by Division and by Region, Year-end, 1946, 1961, and 1972

(Amounts in Millions of Dollars)

Division	1946 Amount	1946 Percent	1961 Amount	1961 Percent	1972 Amount	1972 Percent	Change 1961–1972 Amount	Change 1961–1972 Percent
Production	$2,410	34.9	$15,810	31.0	$ 32,220	24.0	$16,410	103.8
Pipelines	255	3.7	3,095	6.1	8,590	6.4	5,495	177.5
Marine	1,325	19.2	10,170	20.0	26,950	20.0	16,780	165.0
Refineries and Chemical	1,220	17.7	11,390	22.4	42,030	31.3	30,640	269.0
Marketing	1,545	22.4	9,225	18.1	21,615	16.1	12,390	134.3
Others	145	2.1	1,210	2.4	3,045	2.2	1,835	151.7
Total–Foreign Non-Communist World*	$6,900	100.0	$50,900	100.0	$134,450	100.0	$83,550	164.1

Region

Latin America	$2,400	34.8	$12,525	24.6	$ 21,775	16.2	$ 9,250	73.9
Western Europe	1,125	16.3	10,825	21.3	36,600	27.2	25,775	238.1
Africa	175	2.5	2,950	5.8	8,650	6.4	5,700	193.2
Middle East	900	13.0	4,500	8.8	9,350	7.0	4,850	107.8
Far East	550	8.0	4,475	8.8	18,050	13.4	13,575	303.4
Others†	1,750	25.4	15,625	30.7	40,025	29.8	24,400	156.2
Total–Foreign Non-Communist World	$6,900	100.0	$50,900	100.0	$134,450	100.0	$83,550	164.1

Sources: Chase Manhattan Bank, *Investment Patterns in the World Petroleum Industry* (New York: December, 1956), p. 8; and *Capital Investments by the World Petroleum Industry* (New York: November, 1962), pp. 9–10; and *Capital Investments of the Petroleum Industry* (New York: December, 1973), pp. 20–21.

* Includes Canada in Foreign Non-Communist World.

† Unallocated, including foreign flag tankers and Canadian investment.

barrels in the balance of the non-Communist world, it might appear that the $8.4 billion additional investment in the Middle East had a much larger potential return than investment elsewhere. However, it must be remembered that oil in the ground is given value only by huge investments in transportation, refining, and marketing facilities necessary to develop and supply a market for that oil.

How was the $134.5 billion of gross investment in the fixed assets of the foreign non-Communist oil industry at the end of 1972 divided as between American and foreign ownership?[7] U.S.-based companies owned an estimated $49.1 billion, or 36 percent, of these assets: foreign-based private corporations and governments owned the balance of $85.3 billion, or 64 percent. The relative position of U.S. companies has declined in recent years, notwithstanding the fact that a rising fraction of total United States investment in petroleum was made abroad. American companies have been especially heavy investors in non-Communist world oil producing facilities and owned 50 percent of them at the end of 1972.

According to the United Nations, the preponderance of exploration and development funds came from private sources in the non-Communist world. Governmental funds were important in a dozen countries and played a minor role in a dozen more. However, more than 94 percent of the postwar funds supplied for exploration and development was private. Even if British Petroleum were considered a government company, less than 15 percent of 1961 oil production was governmental in ownership; but the percentage rose sharply during the 1970s.[8]

A CONSPECTUS OF THE INDUSTRY'S GROWTH

The explosive postwar growth of the foreign oil industry is recapitulated in Table 5.6, which gives the average annual compound growth rates maintained over the post-

TABLE 5.6

Postwar Growth in Petroleum Consumption, Reserves, Production, Refining Capacity, Investment in Fixed Assets, and Tanker Tonnage

(Average Annual Compound Rates)

Regions	Consumption 1948–1972 (Percent)	Reserves 1948–1972 (Percent)	Production 1948–1972 (Percent)	Refining Capacity 1948–1972 (Percent)	Fixed Assets 1946–1972 (Percent)	Tanker Tonnage 1949–1972 (Percent)
Latin America	6.8	4.7	4.4	7.1	8.9	…
Western Europe	11.8	25.9	10.7	16.3	14.3	…
Far East	13.6	10.7	11.0	16.3	14.4	…
Middle East	6.3	11.1	12.2	4.5	9.4	…
Africa	6.2	33.7	23.3	14.1	16.2	…
Foreign Non-Communist World	10.5	11.2	10.1	11.1	11.8[a]	…
United States and Canada	4.7	3.3	2.9	3.0	7.2[b]	…
Non-Communist World	7.2	9.7	6.8	6.9	9.2	9.7
Communist Bloc	10.0	12.0	11.0	10.0	n. a.	n. a.
World	7.5	9.9	7.3	7.2	n. a.	n. a.

Source: Previous tables.
[a] Includes Canada in Foreign Non-Communist World.
[b] United States only.

war period from 1948 to 1972 in petroleum consumption, crude oil reserves, crude oil production, refining capacity, tanker capacity, and investment in fixed assets. Annual compound growth rates for the foreign non-Communist world were maintained at the extraordinarily high levels of around 10 percent for production and around 11 percent for crude oil reserves, refining capacity, and consumption. They reached nearly 12 percent a year for dollar investments in fixed assets.[9] In general, the foreign petroleum industry grew about three times as fast as the United States and Canadian oil industries. In North America, oil consumption rose at a compound rate of 4.7 percent a year; reserves, 3.3 percent; production, 2.9 percent; and refining, 3.0 percent, even though investment in fixed assets grew 7.2 percent a year. The growth of the petroleum industry in the Communist countries was generally parallel to that in other foreign countries, although the growth rate of their oil production was somewhat higher and that of their refinery capacity somewhat lower. This reflected the Soviet drive to expand crude oil output and exports to the non-Communist world, while controlling the growth of domestic demand.

THE EMERGENCE OF SURPLUS CAPACITY

As a result of sustained high postwar rates of investment, there existed, during the late 1950s and the 1960s, a large margin of unutilized productive capacity in every stage of the foreign oil industry. "Surplus capacity," broadly defined, means the margin of expansibility in the current rate of output of a plant (oil field, pipeline, tanker, refinery) without incurring any additional fixed costs. Narrowly defined, "surplus capacity" is that part of unused productive capacity which is *in excess* of that which the managements of firms *prefer* to keep idle in order to meet emergencies or to seize unusual profit opportunities. This is apparently about 10 percent of total capacity in U.S. manufacturing industries. It does *not* include inefficient, obsolete plants held in reserve and called into operation only when demand is so strong that their relatively high operating costs can be covered.

The ratio of surplus capacity to crude oil output rose during the 1950s and the 1960s, as a consequence of the huge fields discovered and developed in the Middle East and Africa. It would have been possible greatly to increase foreign crude oil production at little, if any, higher average costs of replacement per barrel. The Director of the United States Office of Oil and Gas estimated that the unused oil-producing capacity of the non-Communist world during 1960 was about 42 percent more than actual output.[10] The Chase Manhattan Bank put "potential" non-Communist world crude oil output at 50 percent in excess of actual production during 1961. Even making allowances for a reasonable margin of efficient capacity to meet emergencies, it is clear that the non-Communist world possessed a substantial *surplus* capacity to produce crude oil—leaving the Soviet Union's supply entirely aside. The basic cause of this condition was overinvestment in foreign oil exploration and development, the reasons for which have been previously described.

The unused margin of efficient capacity to transport oil to points of processing and consumption was less than the unused capacity to lift it from wells; but it was still considerable. The Director of the United States Office of Oil and Gas estimated in 1962 that existing, efficient, non-Communist world capacity to deliver crude oil to refineries or deep-water ports by marine transportation was about 14 percent above the level of current movements; and the prospect was that this margin would be maintained through 1965.[11] He estimated further that unused tanker capacity, in 1961, was about 10 percent of utilized capacity and that the construction of supertankers under way or planned would raise unutilized capacity to 11 percent and maintain this margin through 1965.

In regard to refining, the Director stated that unused non-Communist world crude oil refining capacity in 1961 was about 15 percent in excess of the current rate of usage; and that refinery construction programs planned and under way would maintain this margin at least until 1965.[12] For the OECD countries as a group, a comparison of refinery throughputs with refinery capacities shows that the margin of unused capacity averaged 22.6 percent of utilized capacity during the four-year period from 1955 to 1959.[13] And, in Japan, unused capacity was almost 33 percent of utilized capacity during 1962. A comparison of non-Communist world consumption of petroleum with its refining capacity, in 1962, suggests that the percentage of unutilized to used capacity was about 20 percent. Perhaps half of this excess capacity was "surplus" in the strict sense.

Powerful competitive forces caused oil companies to anticipate future demands and to overbuild refineries. Building a refinery was the key to entry into the product markets of many a country. Governments often made it a condition of entry. Oil companies acceded to these pressures in the hope that future growth of a national market would justify the investment, or in order to avoid losing a national market to a competitor who agreed—or would agree—to build a refinery in the country. In some countries refineries were built as joint ventures, with the governments or local enterprises as partners with multinational oil companies.

To sum up the situation in the early 1960s: the evidence amply supports the conclusions of the Director of the United States Office of Oil and Gas: "This progressive imbalance between world consumption of petroleum products and ability to produce is generating intensive, sometimes disruptive, competition in oil marketing. It is creating instability in the entire world petroleum price structure." A similar evaluation was made in the 1961 report of the OECD, representing the largest oil-importing countries in the world.[14]

Surplus oil producing capacity persisted throughout the 1960s. But the decade of the 1970s brought a sharp change. Beginning in 1970, oil production in the United

States and Canada began to reach the limits of capacity, and a similar condition prevailed in Venezuela. More and more, spare production capacity was concentrated in Libya and the Persian Gulf. This endowed the oil-exporting nations of that region with new economic power and laid the groundwork for the revolution in the world oil industry described in Chapter 11.

NOTES

1. *Within* each country, of course, there were enormous differences in the physical productivities of individual wells, pools, and fields, which were concealed by national averages.

2. Statistics on non-Communist world production of petroleum in a given year will differ from those on non-Communist world consumption in that year. The two figures are reconciled by this calculation: Crude oil production *plus* other raw materials (e.g., natural gasoline) *plus* net imports from the Communist bloc *minus* net exports to the United States and Canada *minus* net increases in stocks on hand *equals* petroleum consumption.

3. These pressures were augmented by the Middle East governments, whose revenues were dependent upon the volume of production. See Chapters 5, 6, and 9.

4. In 1939, 63 percent of non-Communist world capacity was located at crude oil production sites. By 1960, the ratio had declined to 30 percent.

5. See M. E. Hubbard, "The Economics of Oil Transport and Refining Operations," *Interregional Seminar on Techniques of Petroleum Development,* January 23–February 21, 1962 (New York: United Nations, 1962).

6. These are estimates, based on an extensive sample of U.S. oil companies by the Petroleum Department of the Chase Manhattan Bank. In contrast, gross investment in fixed assets of the United States petroleum industry less than tripled over the fourteen-year period, rising from $17.7 billion to $57.8 billion. "Gross investment" *includes* all drilling costs, including dry holes, but *excludes* costs of geophysical searches and amounts paid for leases.

7. See *Capital Investments of the World Petroleum Industry—1972* (New York: Chase Manhattan Bank, 1973), pp. 20–24 and Chart on p. 19.

8. Secretary-General of the United Nations, *Capital Requirements of Petroleum Exploration and Development*, United Nations Document No. E/3580, E/C 5/20, March 15, 1962.

9. The truly remarkable size of these growth rates may be better appreciated by observing that $1 left at 10 percent compound interest would yield $6.73 at the end of twenty years.

10. Jerome J. O'Brien, Address to the Annual Convention of the Texas Oil and Gas Association, April 9, 1962, page 2 of the Annex. Mr. O'Brien measured unused capacity as a percentage of total capacity.

11. Jerome J. O'Brien, *op. cit.*

12. Jerome J. O'Brien, *op. cit.*

13. See Organization for European Economic Cooperation, *Oil—Recent Developments in the OEEC Area* (Paris: OEEC, January, 1961), p. 47.

14. Organization for European Economic Cooperation, *Oil—Recent Developments in the OEEC Area*, pp. 11–14.

6

Rising Governmental Intervention in the Industry

GOVERNMENTAL POLICY toward an industry may assume one or a combination of three basic forms: *first*, a government may own and operate all enterprises in an industry, as is the case in Communist countries. *Second*, a government may treat the firms in an industry as "public utilities" and regulate their prices, outputs, and rates of return on investment, while leaving ownership and operation in private hands. *Third*, a government may enforce a competitive structure and behavior upon an industry, requiring its private enterprises to be "regulated" impersonally by competition in the market.

These three types of industrial policy are rarely found in their pure form. The policies of the non-Communist governments toward most industries—including the petroleum industry—have been a mixture of these forms, varying from country to country, with many joint ventures of governments and private firms. However, the public policy of the great majority of countries toward the oil industry traditionally has been based primarily on the concept of competitive private enterprise.

During the era that followed World War II, the structure and behavior of the foreign oil industry was progressively shaped by rising governmental intervention in its affairs. This intervention involved changed regulation of private oil enterprises, as well as wider governmental participation in the petroleum business. There was a distinct postwar movement toward more government ownership. But the outstanding postwar development was a series of governmental actions whose effect was to multiply the number of private firms, to reduce the industry's concentration, and to reduce the economic power of the largest international oil companies.

Toward the end of the 1950s and into the 1960s, as oil production capacity surpassed consumption, *supranational* regulation of the industry emerged. Coalitions of national governments were established for the purposes of defining and executing collective energy policies. The most prominent of these were the Organization of Petroleum Exporting Countries (OPEC), established in 1960, the Organization of Arab Petroleum Exporting Countries (OAPEC), established in 1968, and the European Economic Community (EEC), established in 1958, whose proposed Common Market for energy was actively discussed for many years. The OPEC coalition of the large oil suppliers steadily consolidated its economic power, and, by the early 1970s, it was operating as a full-fledged cartel, dictating prices and outputs. At the same time, the United Nations began to increase its interests in the world oil industry. Because exporting and importing nations have conflicting goals, and the interests of individual countries within each group are not identical, United Nations efforts to regulate the industry have not been successful. However, the success of the OPEC members in quadrupling oil prices and of the OAPEC members in cutting back production during 1973 and 1974, and the drive of the oil-producing nations for majority ownership of oil properties within their boundaries, has created a totally new government-business relationship in the industry.

WHY GOVERNMENTS INTERVENED

The underlying cause of rising governmental intervention in the petroleum industry following World War II was the many political-economic changes spawned by that holocaust. The breakup of the British, Dutch, and French colonial empires resulted in the creation of dozens of new nations, each with its own goals, interests, policies, and problems.[1] The rise of the Soviet Union to global power and as a contender for the support of the uncommitted nations, brought a powerful sponsor of statism on to the world scene. The grouping of countries into economic blocs brought shifts in petroleum policies. And, dramatic advances in popular education, travel, and communications spread an awareness of the fruits of economic progress among the peoples of the less-developed regions of Asia, Africa, and Latin America, which contain most of the world's oil reserves. They generated an impatience to attain higher living standards quickly.

Given the crucial role of petroleum in national security and economic growth, these factors motivated many foreign governments to adopt national oil policies. Some entered the oil industry directly. Still other governments relied upon direct controls rather than upon market competition to safeguard the public interest. Protection of local energy producers, particularly in coal mining, was a strong motivating force in Western Europe. International balance of payments problems caused petroleum import regulation in many instances. Governments of some new countries were moved by considerations of national prestige, mistrust of foreign corporations, or sheer xenophobia, to set up national oil companies or to introduce controls of private firms in order to prevent "exploitation" of their resources.

The postwar oil policy goals of foreign countries were determined by the interaction of three main variables: the relation between a country's domestic production and its consumption of oil, the extent of the ownership of foreign oil by its nationals, and the role of domestic coal as a

competitive energy source. The oil-surplus countries of
Venezuela and the Middle East naturally sought higher
oil prices, wider markets, and a maximum share of the
gross income from their exports. Oil-deficient countries
with large coal deposits but without a large stake in foreign oil, like Belgium and West Germany, sought low-
priced oil while expanding their foreign petroleum investments and moderating the replacement of coal with excise
taxes on petroleum products. Oil-deficient countries with
only modest coal or foreign oil interests, such as Italy and
Japan, encouraged tough bargaining for low-priced oil
while seeking to acquire a stake in foreign oil deposits.
Oil-importing countries with substantial investments in
both foreign oil and domestic coal, like the United Kingdom and France, took measures to accommodate conflicting energy interests. The Soviet Union, which had no
foreign petroleum investments, but which provided much
technical assistance, had an interest in penetrating foreign markets with its oil.

These postwar petroleum policy goals of foreign countries were pursued by a variety of means. They included
the expropriation and nationalization of private oil properties; the regulation of private oil exploration and development; the control of the refining and marketing of
products; the relaxation of international trade barriers;
the enforcement of antimonopoly laws; increased taxation; and increasing governmental intrusion into petroleum pricing and production decisions.

EXPROPRIATION AND
NATIONALIZATION

Foreign oil companies suffered major expropriations of
their property during the postwar period, usually without
payment of full compensation to the private owners.
These episodes—the most significant were in Algeria,
Ceylon, Cuba, Egypt, Iran, Libya, and Peru—followed by
many years the first major oil industry expropriation by
the Bolshevik government of Russia in 1918 and a second

major expropriation of foreign oil properties by the Mexican government in 1938. All illustrated the great latent power of governments over the international oil companies and the reality of the political risks inherent in the industry. Implicit threats of expropriation stood behind many less extreme forms of regulation; and the nationalization of foreign oil company assets was an "easy" way to build up the assets and operations of a government-owned oil enterprise.

The most prominent expropriation of the 1950s was that of the properties of the Anglo-Iranian Oil Company (now B.P.) by the government of Iran in 1951. An agreement was reached in 1954 between the government of Iran, the National Iranian Oil Company (its newly organized oil monopoly), and a consortium of eight oil companies. The consortium was to conduct oil exploration and production in Southern Iran and to operate the Abadan refinery, but NIOC was to be the legal owner of the assets.[2] Ownership of the consortium was initially distributed 40 percent to B.P., 14 percent to Shell, 6 percent to CFP, and 40 percent (8 percent each) to five American companies, i.e., Exxon, Mobil, Gulf, Socal, and Texaco. Subsequently, the five original American members of the consortium transferred 5 percent of their part in the consortium (1 percent each) to IRICON, a group of nine American oil companies. The bulk of the compensation to B.P. for its properties was to be paid by the consortium members. The settlement increased competition by bringing in smaller American operators who had not theretofore had any foreign production.

In 1960 the Cuban government served notice on Exxon, Texaco, and Shell that, in the furtherance of a new Cuban-Soviet Trade Pact, each of them would be required to purchase stipulated quantities of Soviet crude oil for their Cuban refineries. When the companies refused to refine the Soviet crude oil, their refineries were seized and operated by the Cuban Petroleum Institute, with the help of foreign technicians. Up to the present, the Cuban government has not paid any compensation to the American oil companies for the seized properties.

The Ceylon Petroleum Corporation Act of 1961 created a government corporation (CPC) to engage in the petroleum business and to acquire any private oil property for this purpose. Government expropriations began in the spring of 1962, ultimately giving CPC one-half of the internal business of Ceylon. The bulk of the oil products handled by CPC were provided by the Soviet Union, Rumania, and Egypt under bilateral trade agreements. In 1963 the government ordered the companies to terminate their activities in Ceylon and to assign their remaining assets to CPC by the year's end. The governments of the United Kingdom and the United States protested these expropriations and called for compensation, which the new government of Ceylon, in 1965, agreed to pay.[3]

In 1961 the Iraq government expropriated 99.56 percent of the IPC concession area owned by B.P., CFP, Exxon, Mobil, and Shell. Only about 750 square miles were left to IPC, less than one percent of its previous concession area. The government of Iraq had previously made drastic demands on IPC. IPC called upon the government to enter arbitration in accordance with the provisions of its concession agreement, but it did not heed the request. The seized areas were to constitute a concession owned by a newly formed Iraq National Oil Company (INOC) and to be developed by INOC alone or in conjunction with other firms. (All of the Iraqi properties of American oil companies were nationalized in 1973.)

Beginning in 1963, Algeria began to reduce the role of foreign oil companies and to increase governmental control of the industry. It established SONATRACH as a national oil company and put pressure upon France to convert the French companies in Algeria into minority partners of SONATRACH. In 1967 Algeria nationalized an Exxon exploration company, and Exxon and Mobil refining and marketing companies. In 1970 AMIF, Elwerath, Mobil, Phillips, and Shell were compelled to turn their production operations over to SONATRACH.

Under a 1961 decree, Shell and B.P. were required to cut their shareholdings in Anglo Egyptian Oil Company from 31 percent each to 15.5 percent each. Other private shareholdings of British and Egyptian nationals were also decreased by one half, in order to increase the government's 9.5 percent interest to more than 50 percent. Subsequently, all government-controlled oil enterprises in Egypt were coordinated under what is now the Egyptian General Petroleum Corporation (EGPC). By 1974, however, the Egyptian government was again hospitable to private oil enterprises.

While there had been no expropriation of oil properties in Indonesia through 1972, a 1960 decree excluded all foreign firms from direct exploration and development of Indonesian oil fields and required companies with pre-existing concessions to surrender their rights. A 1961 decree permitted them to operate their developed fields as "contractors" for the government, provided, however, that they enter into contractors' agreements under which the government would, from then on, receive 60 percent of the profits instead of the 50 percent it had received before.

The Soviet Union, as might be expected, conducted a ceaseless campaign to persuade the less-developed countries to nationalize their petroleum industries, by deprecating the record of private oil enterprise and extolling the virtues of governmental petroleum monopolies.[4]

Throughout the 1960s, political forces favoring the nationalization of petroleum resources were gathering strength in the OPEC countries, and nationalization actions became more frequent. Not until the 1970s, however, did the drive for control of indigenous oil production operations become nearly universal. It formed an important aspect of the world oil revolution described in Chapter 11.

THE REGULATION OF OIL
EXPLORATION AND DEVELOPMENT

Among the important oil endowed nations of the world, the United States is unusual in vesting legal ownership of underground petroleum resources in the owner of the land surface. Most other nations retain such rights in the state or in the ruler. Thus, the process of searching for oil abroad must begin by obtaining a concession from a ruler or a sovereign state. Petroleum concession agreements prior to World War II were specially negotiated, covered large areas, were of very long duration, and vested the development of a country's oil resources in one or a few oil companies with established marketing organizations. Concessionaires were given wide latitude to explore for, develop, produce, and market petroleum. In return for these privileges, the companies paid royalties and taxes to the host governments. The prewar concessions to the large international oil companies in Iran, Iraq, Kuwait, Qatar, Saudi Arabia, and Venezuela all conformed to this pattern, which naturally promoted a relatively high concentration of the industry.[5]

After World War II, national regulation of oil exploration and development activity proliferated rapidly and changed its nature. General petroleum laws were enacted by most countries to regularize the terms of all exploration and development concessions. Areas conceded to any one firm were sharply limited both in space and in time. The duration of new concessions was reduced and local partners were often required.[6] In consequence, the number of concessionaires rose in nearly every oil-producing country.

Under these general petroleum laws, separate grants of rights to oil companies are often required for the successive stages of operation. Thus, a reconnaissance permit authorizes preliminary exploration, often on a nonexclusive basis; an exploration license will next afford the holder exploration rights in a described area; and a development lease may subsequently be granted to develop all or part of an area previously explored, with the state retaining either a percentage of the area or "checkerboarded" blocks of land therein. Relinquishments were far more frequent than before the war.

Beyond his general obligations, the concessionaire may be required to meet very specific requirements. Examples are: to refine specified amounts of crude oil domestically;

to deliver to a government company a pro rata share of oil for domestic consumption; to acquire local partners; to begin operations within a specified number of months and to expend specified amounts; or to cooperate in unitized development. By incorporating such requirements in concession agreements, governments closely controlled the subsequent activities of their concessionaires and the development of the industry.

General petroleum laws in the postwar era have commonly set maximum limits to the areas granted to foreign concessionaires; these areas were much smaller than those covered by prewar agreements. The result was to multiply the number of firms holding concessions and, subsequently, to increase competitive pressures to find and produce oil. Relinquishment of concession areas to the state has been pressed even beyond the requirements of law. Thus government pressure caused "voluntary" relinquishments of half the entire area of their Kuwait concession by Gulf and B.P., one-third of the Qatar concession by the IPC group, and three-quarters of ARAMCO's original concession in Saudi Arabia. The purpose of these provisions manifestly was to induce a larger number of firms to engage in the rapid development of the oil resources of a country, thereby speeding up the flow of revenues to public treasuries.[7]

A powerful trend in governmental regulation is to engage foreign firms to explore for and develop oil production as *government contractors*, rather than to grant them concessions to work as principals. Mexico engaged in this practice as a result of the mediocre record of Pemex (its government monopoly) in finding oil after nationalization of the industry in 1938. Egypt's EGPC invited contractors to do offshore drilling and development in the Gulf of Suez in return for payment in crude oil. Contractor agreements were also initiated by Argentina in 1958 and by Indonesia after 1960. In both of these countries, the oil companies were to receive a share in the oil produced or in the profits from its sale.[8] Venezuela, following establishment of its state oil company (CVP) in 1960, also announced that no new concessions would be granted to private firms except as contractors for CVP.

An allied form of governmental intervention by the oil-exporting nations was to establish government-owned corporations to serve as instruments of national petroleum policy. Examples are Saudi Arabia's Petromin, the Abu Dhabi National Oil Company, Kuwait National Oil Company, and SONATRACH in Algeria. Oil-importing nations also established or strengthened their national-interest companies in order to gain better bargaining positions. Thus, France amalgamated several of its companies into one organization; Germany formed Deminex; and Japan organized the Japan Development Company. Such companies undertook participation in several oil exploration ventures.

NEW CONTROLS ON REFINING AND MARKETING

Governmental regulation of the refining and marketing of petroleum products has gone far beyond the traditional licensing of new refineries and distributing facilities. Some countries have sought to assure adequate local refining capacity, or to favor and protect a domestic refining industry. Others have sought to give preference to indigenous crude oils in local refining. Still others aimed to influence the domestic prices of petroleum products— either upward or downward.

We have noted the profound impact of Marshall Plan aid and the OEEC upon the evolution of local refineries in Western Europe. Because more and smaller refineries were built, more firms entered the business as nonintegrated refiners. This generated intense competition among suppliers of crude oil. In addition, *government* refining and/or marketing companies were set up, or greatly expanded, in many nations to offer competition to international oil companies. In India, private refiners were under government pressure during the early 1960s to reduce import prices of crude oil and domestic prices of refined products. This pressure took the form of threats by the Indian government to import low-priced Soviet petroleum products and to limit foreign exchange made available to the companies to pay for their own crude oils. Moreover, its Ministry of Mines and Fuels announced a policy of reserving more than 50 percent of the country's refining capacity to the public sector.

Seeking to stabilize its oil supply and to minimize its foreign exchange requirements, Japan during the 1950s also controlled crude oil imports by restricting the foreign exchange it would permit to be used for this purpose. The government put strong downward pressures on oil prices because, with a given exchange allotment, an importer could increase its volume of imports by buying at a lower f.o.b. price per barrel. When foreign exchange was decontrolled in 1962, Japan enacted another instrument to maintain control. A comprehensive petroleum law authorized the Ministry of International Trade and Industry (MITI) to lay down annually a five-year petroleum supply plan that specified quantities of petroleum products to be imported and *locally* refined. MITI was empowered to fix the standard selling prices of petroleum products, and it has done so.[9]

THE RELAXATION OF BARRIERS TO INTERNATIONAL TRADE

After World War II, there was a progressive relaxation of governmental controls on international trade, with favorable consequences for the growth of competition in the petroleum industry. With some notable exceptions, currency controls, tariff barriers, and quantitative restrictions on trade (e.g., import quotas) were either reduced or eliminated.

The principal impediments to the world oil trade immediately after the end of World War II were currency controls growing out of the acute "dollar shortage" that obtained up to 1950. European countries discriminated against U.S. imports in order to save dollars. The United Kingdom proposed, in 1949, to curtail, by 25 percent, dollar outlays on oil to be used in the sterling area.[10] The step-up of Marshall Plan economic aid and United States military assistance gradually obviated the problem. Later, the large trade surpluses developed during the 1950s by Western European countries enabled them to build up their monetary reserves and progressively relax their currency controls. This progressive freeing of international payments also occurred outside Europe.[11]

Tariffs levied against imports of crude oil usually have been relatively low because foreign countries with large oil imports have not had a substantial domestic oil-producing industry to protect. Most countries have imposed higher tariffs on refined products for the purpose of encouraging the development of domestic refining capacity. There was little change in these tariff policies during the postwar years. The evolution of the European Common Market ultimately erased all barriers to trade in petroleum among the Common Market countries, but imposed a common external tariff on imported products (see Table 6.1).

TABLE 6.1
Import Duties of EEC Countries, 1972

(*Percent of Import Value*)

Product	Percent
Motor Gasoline	6.0
Illuminating Kerosene	6.0
Heating Gas Oil	3.5
Residual Fuel Oil	3.5
Finished Lubricants	6.0

Source: The European Economic Community.

Quotas have, from time to time, been used by various governments to control the aggregate quantities of imports, or the amounts that importers could bring into a country from a particular source. For example, the French quota system reserves a major share of imports to French-controlled companies. But there was a general relaxation of quota systems by most governments after the war.

The most conspicuous example of a quota system on oil imports after World War II was that imposed by the U.S. government, first (in 1957) on a "voluntary" basis and later (in 1959) on a mandatory basis. During the 1950s, growing imports of lower-priced foreign crude oils had threatened to nullify the operation of the prorationing laws under which the American states endeavored to maintain higher domestic petroleum prices by restricting oil production to estimated market "demand." The federal government instituted the import quota system in order to protect the domestic producer and to reinforce the operation of the state prorationing laws.[12] Here, we are not concerned with the wisdom of this quota system nor with its anticompetitive effects in the domestic petroleum market, but rather with its profound repercussions upon foreign nations. By limiting the growth of imports, quotas, in effect, separated the U.S. oil market from the rest of the world. A major result of these restrictions against the entry of foreign crude oil into the United States was to add significantly to the amount of crude oil available to the rest of the non-Communist world, thereby intensifying competition in foreign markets and depressing foreign prices. Unable to sell foreign crude oil in the huge U.S. market, oil companies—both American and foreign—were obliged to dispose of it abroad. To no small degree, the rising tempo of competition in the foreign oil industry after 1957 was a significant—if unintended—consequence of U.S. import quotas.

The American oil import quotas continued in effect through the 1960s, although they were gradually relaxed to permit rising imports. After U.S. oil production topped out at the end of 1970, imports rose rapidly. In April of

1973, President Nixon removed import quotas altogether. Their disservice to the national interest had become apparent.

THE ENFORCEMENT OF ANTIMONOPOLY LAWS

The postwar years witnessed a type of foreign government regulation of the oil industry which had theretofore largely been confined to the United States. This was the control of industrial structure and behavior through antimonopoly laws. By the 1960s, such laws were being enforced in most of the developed nations of the non-Communist world.[13] They were a direct product of the postwar revival of competitive market policies, encouraged by the military occupation and economic aid programs of the U.S. government.

While these laws differed considerably among countries, most required that agreements among firms be registered with a government agency, and they prohibited agreements which had anticompetitive purposes or effects. They authorized public authorities to inquire into business practices and to terminate those found contrary to the public interest. Of especially great significance were the antimonopoly provisions of the Treaty of Rome, which prohibited any business practices likely to affect commerce between the Common Market countries adversely, or to distort or restrict competition within a substantial part of the Common Market. Violators were made subject to heavy fines. The Common Market Commission, as administrator, was given broad powers. Another new supranational agency concerned with antimonopoly practices is the Organization for Economic Cooperation and Development (OECD), formed in 1961 by the North Atlantic countries as an enlarged successor to the OEEC.

Pervasive antimonopoly regulation in the industrially advanced countries placed new constraints upon the managements of foreign oil companies. Most importantly, they constituted an endorsement of the U.S. competitive market system by European nations, which had not always been defenders of effective competition.

INCREASED TAXATION

After World War II, foreign government levies on the incomes of private oil companies were progressively and substantially increased. This was true of both royalty and income tax rates (see Table 6.2). In Venezuela, immediately prior to the war, private oil companies were required to pay royalties of 15 percent of the value of oil produced. In 1943 the royalty rate was raised to 16.67 percent, and a law instituting a 50 percent income tax was proclaimed.[14] In the Middle East, the 50 percent taxation formula was introduced by Saudi Arabia in 1950, by Kuwait in 1951, by Iraq, Qatar, and Bahrain in 1952, and by Iran in 1954. The new formula later found expression in the laws of other oil-exporting nations.

Later, the 50 percent rate of taxing foreign oil income was materially increased in many nations. In 1958, Venezuela changed its tax rate from 50 to 60 percent. Colombia's oil law of 1962 changed the tax rate to 68 percent of net income from production. Contractor agreements with Indonesia provided that 60 percent of profits should go to the government. Moreover, under governmental pressures oil companies progressively waived allowances and deductions. The trend toward higher taxation of the profits of the international oil companies, based upon rising percentages of successively increased posted prices, reached a crescendo in the early 1970s, as will be seen in Chapter 11.

Rising government income tax rates undoubtedly operated to reduce profits and rates of return on foreign oil investment, both of which sharply declined after 1957. What happened, in essence, was that the oil-owning countries progressively raised the "rents" charged for the use of their resources. The oil companies were unable to pass

TABLE 6.2

Crude Oil Royalties and Income Tax Rates Imposed on Petroleum Companies by the Principal Foreign Oil-Producing Countries, 1948 and 1972

Country and Company	1948		*Country and Company*	1972	
	Royalty	*Income Tax*		*Royalty*	*Income Tax*
Saudi Arabia ARAMCO	Four shillings gold per ton (onshore production) Four shillings gold per ton plus 5¢ per barrel (offshore production)	Exempt	Saudi Arabia ARAMCO	$12\frac{1}{2}$% of posted price	55% of net profits (royalty expensed)
Iran AIOC	Four shillings per ton plus 20% of distribution to ordinary stockholders in excess of £671,250 in any year	Exempt, except for one shilling per ton on first 6,000,000 tons of annual production and nine pence per ton on remainder	Iran Consortium	$12\frac{1}{2}$% of posted price	55% of net profits (royalty expensed)
Iraq IPC and Basrah	Four shillings gold per long ton	Exempt, except for modest tax commutation payments	Iraq IPC[1] and Basrah	$12\frac{1}{2}$% of posted price[2]	55% of net profits (royalty expensed)

Kuwait Kuwait Oil Co.	3¼ rupees per long ton	Exempt, except for commutation payment of 4 annas per ton	12½% of posted price	55% of net profits (royalty expensed)
Kuwait AOC Saudi Arabia AOC			Either: (a) 20% expensed royalty plus 45% tax, whichever is the greater	Or: (b) 62% of net profits,
Algeria	No special legislation	No special legislation	12½% of posted price	55% of profits (royalty expensed)
Venezuela	Production tax of 16⅔% of calculated price based on U.S. Gulf Coast prices	Minimum of 50% of net income	16⅔% of agreed commercial value based on Texas posted prices	60% of net income (production tax expensed)
Indonesia	Production tax of 4% of value of gross production	Graduated scale of 10–30% of net proceeds, but not exceeding 20% of total net proceeds	No royalty per se[3]	60% of earnings (Contract of Work); 65% of production (Production Sharing)

TABLE 6.2 (Continued)

Country and Company	1948		Country and Company	1972	
	Royalty	Income Tax		Royalty	Income Tax
Libya			Libya	12½% of gross production	55% of profit (royalty expensed) & supplemental per barrel payment (approx. $.09/bbl.)
Nigeria			Nigeria	12½% of posted price (onshore) 10% of posted price (offshore)	55% of profits (royalty expensed)

Sources: Copies of original laws, decrees, and concession agreements; Northcutt Ely, *Summary of Mining and Petroleum Laws of the World* (Washington, D.C.: United States Bureau of Mines, 1961); Barrow's *Petroleum Legislation*; and *Petroleum Press Service*, January, 1971.

[1] Nationalized June 1, 1972, but Basrah Petroleum Company continues in operation.

[2] Estimated as there is no recent information.

[3] Requirement for supplying proportional share of local market needs as defined by the ratio of company production to total country production.

on all of the increased costs per barrel to petroleum consumers after 1957, because of the redundancy of supplies.
They were obliged to absorb, in lower profit margins,
whatever additions to unit costs they were unable to offset by cost reductions or operating efficiencies. After
market conditions firmed in the early 1970s, however,
the companies did pass along to buyers more of cost increases.

MULTINATIONAL INTERVENTION
IN OIL PRICING

The postwar tendency of foreign governments to inter-
vene directly in the regulation of petroleum production
and pricing contrasts sharply with the laissez-faire policies followed up to World War II. Formerly, rates of output and prices were almost entirely within the discretion
of the private oil companies. In intervening, foreign governments followed the American example. Beginning in
the 1930s, most oil-producing states of the United States
held down production to "market demand," primarily in
order to prevent sharp declines in prices; when rising oil
imports threatened the domestic crude oil production industry during the late 1950s, the U.S. government imposed quotas to help keep petroleum prices up.[15]

THE UNITED NATIONS

The United Nations has become deeply concerned with
world energy and petroleum problems. Among its 135
members at the end of 1973, the less-developed countries
far outnumbered the industrialized nations. They used
U.N. organizations as forums for airing their views on
the issues of a country's permanent sovereignty over its
natural resources and the use of national law in the settlement of investment disputes between multinational
companies and foreign governments, both issues vitally
important to the international petroleum industry. The

views of these nations found expression in a 1973 resolution of the General Assembly affirming the right of a country, in the event of nationalization, to determine compensation in accordance with its national laws, rather than international law.

In addition, the Economic and Social Council of the U.N. has become active in the conservation of natural resources through its Committee on Natural Resources, established in 1970. This too has affected the oil industry, by exerting pressure upon it to expand the use of conservation measures. And a Group of Eminent Persons to Study the Impact of Multinational Corporations on Development and International Relations was formed in 1973. Its report in 1974 criticized many aspects of multinational company operations.

Finally, the U.N. Committee on the Seabed has been attempting to work out international agreements and organizations to define territorial seas, the breadth of national jurisdiction over the oceans, and regulations of marine technology and environment. All of these activities could affect the international oil industry profoundly, as the search for petroleum extends over the earth's continental shelves.

THE ORGANIZATION OF PETROLEUM
EXPORTING COUNTRIES

By far the most significant postwar efforts of governments to influence petroleum prices on a multinational basis were those of the OPEC, a coalition of important oil-exporting nations. The OPEC was formed in September of 1960 by Iran, Iraq, Kuwait, Saudi Arabia, and Venezuela. It was a direct consequence of the reductions of posted prices of Middle East crude oil made by the international oil companies during 1959 and 1960 in the face of persistent surpluses and vigorous price competition. By 1962, Indonesia, Libya, and Qatar had become members of the OPEC. Abu Dhabi, Nigeria, Algeria, and Ecuador joined later, bringing total membership to twelve nations. This meant that 93 percent of the crude oil exports to the non-Communist world (excluding those of the Soviet Union) and over 75 percent of the world's oil reserves lay within the jurisdiction of the OPEC.

The publicly announced aims of the OPEC were to raise crude oil prices, to secure a larger share of revenues from the private oil companies, and to work out plans to regulate production in order to stabilize prices. At its 1962 meeting, the OPEC adopted resolutions calling upon member countries to negotiate with the oil companies to raise posted prices to levels prevailing in August, 1960; to formulate jointly a "rational price structure" which would possibly tie the price of oil to an index of the prices paid for industrial goods; to establish uniform royalty payments which could not be credited against the income taxes of producing countries; and to create governmental bodies to prevent sales of crude oil at substantial discounts.

Later during the 1960s, the OPEC turned its attention to a system of restricting crude oil production and prorating the total among its members. It had become clear that efforts to raise prices without simultaneously limiting production were unavailing. However, it was difficult to arrive at a mutually agreeable formula for controlling oil production, because the economies of the OPEC members differed so greatly in size, population, stage of development, and capacity to absorb investment. Thus, Iran's interests lay in expansion of its petroleum output, whereas Libya's and Saudi Arabia's interests could be met with oil outputs far under their capacities. It was not until the 1970s that the immense bargaining power of the OPEC was organized into an effective international cartel. It was then that the OPEC succeeded in replacing market determined with politically determined prices of crude oil, as will be seen.

The OPEC was more successful during the 1960s in raising the oil revenues of its members than in restricting oil production. After becoming the bargaining agent of its member countries in 1963, the OPEC succeeded in getting the oil companies to agree, in 1965, that royalty payments should be deducted as an operating expense in computing taxable income, instead of being credited in full against income taxes due. The revenues of the Middle East governments were increased about 9 cents a barrel during 1965 and 1966 by this and other changes. Yet this was a mere pittance in comparison with the vast bonanza realized by the OPEC members when it first began to wield its world monopoly powers in the early 1970s.

At its Sixteenth Conference in June of 1968, the OPEC adopted a major statement of petroleum policy which was a harbinger of things to come. It declared that the oil companies' payments to governments were to be based on a posted (or tax reference) price *to be determined by the OPEC governments*. The crude oil price was to rise proportionally to the rise in prices of manufactured goods. And oil prices were to be consistent among the OPEC countries, taking into account the quality, gravity, and location of the product. Not until surplus oil producing capacity disappeared at the beginning of the 1970s, however, was the OPEC able to implement this bold new "declaration of independence," as is subsequently shown.

THE ORGANIZATION OF ARAB PETROLEUM EXPORTING COUNTRIES

The common interests of Arab petroleum-exporting countries were first represented in the Arab League, founded in 1959. It sponsored annual petroleum congresses concerned with the regulation of oil production. It was succeeded by the OAPEC, organized in 1968, with Kuwait, Libya, and Saudi Arabia, the founding members. Its membership expanded subsequently to include all Arab oil-exporting nations. The OAPEC can engage in commercial ventures, and plans to do so. In 1972 it announced an intention to form a company to own and operate a tanker fleet, and another company to operate a drydock in Bahrain. It was at an OAPEC meeting in

Kuwait, in 1973, that the Arab oil ministers decided to use oil as a weapon in the Arab-Israeli war. After a ministerial conference in July of 1974, the OAPEC members announced their agreement to finance research into alternative energy sources and to establish an Arab Capital Investment Corporation.

THE ORGANIZATION FOR ECONOMIC COOPERATION AND DEVELOPMENT

The European Economic Community (EEC), popularly known as the Common Market, also has had a long, multinational interest in oil. In April, 1962, its Ministerial Council agreed that a common market for energy should be established for the six member nations. Its aims were: cheap and secure energy supplies, a four to six months stockpile of petroleum products, a common external tariff on products with the free admission of crude oil, standardization of internal consumption taxes, and freedom of petroleum trade within the EEC. Proposals were drafted embodying these aims. They touched off a prolonged debate which lasted many years. Just as the conflicting interests of the OPEC members delayed the organization of an effective world oil monopoly until the 1970s, so did the clashing interests of EEC member countries frustrate the efforts to attain a common energy policy among the major oil-importing countries. France's national monopoly of petroleum imports was a persistent stumbling block. Difficulties also arose from the division of energy responsibilities within the EEC, coal coming under the European Coal and Steel Community and nuclear energy under Euratom. Although the EEC Commission endorsed the earlier recommendations in 1966, and a coordination of oil, coal, and nuclear interests was effected in 1967, yet progress continued to be slow. The oil "revolution" of the 1970s found the EEC still lacking a common energy policy.

The early 1970s brought the matter to a head. The OPEC's drastic price-raising and output-limiting actions

during 1973 and 1974 dealt a heavy blow to the EEC
members and to the other industrialized powers, all of
which had formed the Organization for Economic Cooperation and Development in 1961. The group interests of
the OPEC members, on the one hand, and those of the
OECD members, on the other hand, tended to polarize.
In this polarization of group interests lay the startling
possibility of a coalition of the most important oil-importing nations bargaining directly with a monopolistic organization of the most important oil-exporting countries,
each seeking to attain for its members the greatest economic advantage.[16] Even though this result may never
be reached, the international oil companies were, by the
early 1970s, "ground between the upper and nether millstones" of opposing political pressures exerted by importing and exporting countries. Unable to satisfy fully the
claims of either, but vulnerable to the regulatory pressures of both, the power of the international oil companies
over oil prices and production had been sharply reduced.

THE NET RESULT—MORE
COMPETITION AND MORE CONTROL

The combined effects of growing governmental intervention on the structure and behavior of the foreign oil
industry were profound and numerous. In general, non-
Communist governments moved during the postwar years
from a position of laissez faire to one of active participation in or control of the industry. The promulgation of
national energy policies, the organization of government-
owned oil companies, and the regulation of private petroleum enterprises by multinational blocs as well as
individual nations were hallmarks of the times.

Expropriation and nationalization of private oil properties, and the growth of government oil companies, extended public ownership in oil. However, *the primary
result of postwar governmental petroleum policies was
to enhance competition in the industry*. Governments en-

couraged new entrants, which diffused the structure of the industry. The number of competing firms increased, and the market positions of the largest international oil companies declined, reducing concentration. As the entrants developed more concession areas, the growth of petroleum supply relative to demand accelerated, intensifying competition in both crude oil and product markets, and depressing prices and rates of return on investment. The primary impact of the new regulatory environment was naturally borne by the largest international oil companies, whose powers of flexible managerial action were sharply reduced. The vigilant concern of both oil-exporting and oil-importing countries with crude oil output and pricing decisions meant that no private oil company or group of companies could act unless their actions were consistent with national interests and aspirations.

NOTES

1.   There were fifty-one member countries of the United Nations at the time of its organization in 1945. The number had mounted to 135 by the end of 1973.

2.   See Allen W. Ford, *The Anglo-Iranian Oil Dispute of 1951–1952* (Berkeley: University of California Press, 1954). The U.S. companies undertook negotiations at the request of the State Department.

3.   After the government of Ceylon had failed to take appropriate steps for the payment of compensation, the United States invoked the Hickenlooper amendment to the Foreign Assistance Act and cut off foreign aid to Ceylon as of February 10, 1963. Later, compensation was paid and aid was restored.

4.   See, for example, "Some Problems of Development of the Oil and Gas Industry in the Developing Countries," *Symposium on the Development of Petroleum Resources of Asia and the Far East.* This paper was submitted by the USSR representatives to the Symposium, which was held by the Economic Commission on Asia and the Far East of the United Nations, September 1–15, 1962, Teheran, Iran.

5.   An authoritative treatment is given by Stephen H. Longrigg, *Oil in the Middle East* (Oxford: Oxford University Press, 1961).

6.   See United Nations, *The Status of Permanent Sovereignty over Natural Wealth and Resources*, Revised Study by the Secretariat, United Nations Document A/AC.97/5/-Rev. 2, E/3511, A/AC.97/13 (New York: United Nations, 1962), for a review of measures taken by states to serve their economic or political goals.

7.   The Libyan Petroleum Law of 1955 "was enacted in such a manner as to encourage oil companies to search and explore for petroleum in a big way to determine the country's oil potential in the shortest time. The Law largely fulfilled these aims as it led to a fast increasing activity in the search for petroleum." Petroleum Commission of Libya, *Petroleum Development in Libya, 1954 through Mid–1961* (Tripoli: Government Printing Office, 1961).

8.   "Contractor" agreements vary considerably from nation to nation and even within a nation. In some instances, the contractor assumes little risk: he simply performs a specific task for a prescribed fee. In other instances, the contractor is paid in a share of the oil he finds, if any, thus sharing part of the risk. In still other instances, he must sell all the oil he produces to the government. But, in some cases, he has almost all the prerogatives of a concession owner except the name, being free to sell any oil he produces to any customer he desires at any price he can obtain, paying the government a specified percentage of profits.

9.   During November, 1962, price competition had become so keen and profits so low that MITI established *minimum* prices of several key products that were substantially *above* the then-prevailing market levels.

10.   See *Middle East Journal*, vol. 4, no. 4 (October, 1950), p. 484; Horst Mendershausen, "Dollar Shortage and Oil Surpluses in 1949–50," in *Essays in International Finance* 11 (Princeton: Princeton University Press, 1950).

11.   Although exchange controls have not recently formed an important impediment to international *trade* in petroleum, they are still being applied to international *investment* in petroleum in many countries.

12. See Report of the Attorney General, pursuant to section 2 of the Joint Resolution of August 7, 1959, consenting to an Interstate Compact to Conserve Oil and Gas, May 15, 1963; *Report to the President by the Petroleum Study Committee*, September 4, 1962, pp. 1–4. Also William H. Peterson, *The Question of Governmental Oil Import Restrictions* (Washington, D.C.: American Enterprise Association, 1959).

13. See Lee Loevinger, "Antitrust Law in the Modern World," *Antitrust Law Symposium of the New York State Bar Association* (New York: January 25, 1962); *Guide to Legislation on Restrictive Business Practices in Europe and North America*, vols. 1, 2, and 3 (Paris: Organization for European Economic Cooperation, 1960).

14. Royalties differ from income taxes, of course, in that royalties are payable as "rent" for a concession, whether or not it produces a profit from the sale of oil.

15. See Erich W. Zimmerman, *Conservation in the Production of Petroleum* (New Haven: Yale University Press, 1957); pp. 138–39.

16. In economic theory, direct negotiation between the OPEC and the OECD would approach the classical case of bilateral monopoly or *monopoly-monopsony*, in which both rate of production and price of the product are indeterminate within wide ranges, and the outcome depends upon the relative bargaining powers of the adversaries and the skills with which they are used.

7

The Entrance of Firms
into the Industry

O F THE MANY STRIKING CHANGES in the foreign oil
industry since World War II, the most important
was the phenomenal expansion in the number of private
and government-owned petroleum enterprises all over
the world. During the period from 1953 to 1972, more
than *three hundred private companies and more than
fifty different government-owned companies* either entered the foreign oil industry de novo or significantly expanded their participation in it.[1] By the end of 1972, at
least fifty of them were integrated, international oil enterprises, participating in several divisions of the industry
in several nations. Twenty-five to fifty more were inter-
nationally significant in one or another division of the
industry.

The new entrants were extraordinarily diverse in character, involving enterprises of many sizes and nationali-
ties.[2] Some entries were made by petroleum companies
that had previously confined their operations to their own
national markets. In other cases, companies which had
been engaged in one or two markets or stages of the

industry outside their home countries integrated their foreign operations forward toward markets, backward toward production, or geographically. In still other instances, entries were made by companies newly organized for the purpose, or by firms previously engaged in natural gas, chemical, steel, automotive, or other industries.

Many government-owned or government-sponsored companies entered the world's oil markets, usually in competition with private companies, but sometimes with national monopoly rights or special government preferences. The entry of the giant Soviet petroleum trust was a signal event of the late 1950s and is treated separately in Chapter 8.

What caused the accelerating pace of entry into the foreign oil business? Who were the entrants and what was the nature of their activities? What effects did they have upon the structure and behavior of the industry?

THE ECONOMICS OF ENTRY

One hallmark of a competitive market is that new firms are able to—and do—enter it. They can obtain access to the necessary factors of production, such as natural resources, patents, and technology, and they can make effective contact with buyers of products. Ability to enter an industry, however, is a relative matter, rarely being perfectly free or costless (as required for "perfect" competition) or completely impossible (as required for "perfect" monopoly). The key economic consideration is the *relative difficulty of overcoming the barriers to entry,* which can be measured by the advantages of established firms in an industry over potential entrants.[3] In general, the relative difficulty of entry into any industry is determined by the amount of capital required for an efficient scale of operations, the relative ease with which the necessary raw materials, plant, and equipment can be obtained, the scarcity and costs of technical and managerial personnel, the level of technological and political risks to be borne, and the time and costs of making effective contacts with buyers in product markets. All of these costs must be weighed against any advantages the prospective entrant possesses.

We have seen that the barriers to entry into the foreign oil industry were high until after the end of World War II. The technical and governmental factors governing the supply of foreign petroleum were such as to require able and determined entrepreneurs, possessing large capital funds, with the ability to wait long periods of time for returns on their investments. Entrants were few and the structural pattern of the industry changed very slowly from the early 1920s up to the 1950s. The economic and political barriers to entry were high, the apparent risks were great, and the profit inducements were not strong enough to overcome them. The most promising areas for foreign exploration were located in undeveloped lands thousands of miles from major markets. With most of the Middle East within the British sphere of influence, diplomatic assistance was a sine qua non to entry. Producing countries preferred to grant large concessions of long duration to one or a few companies. This made it extremely difficult for new firms to get access to promising oil lands.

Moreover, most European countries rejected a competitive policy and sought to stabilize the marketing of petroleum products by establishing import and marketing quotas, thus making it hard for new firms lacking a historical import position to break in. The Great Depression of the 1930s slowed the growth of demand for petroleum throughout the world and dampened investment prospects. Indeed, many firms withdrew from foreign operations in the 1930s. Then, World War II resulted in the imposition of government controls that virtually froze the structure of the industry until controls were removed between 1945 and 1948.

As a result, there were only a handful of American companies searching for oil outside the North American continent at the end of World War II.[4] In 1945 a special committee of the United States Senate investigating foreign activities of United States oil companies between the World Wars found that some fifty United States companies had had foreign exploration concessions. By dint of ill fortune, bad judgment, or inadequate capital and enterprise, however, the great majority of these firms had sold their foreign interests or had their properties expropriated. By 1945, only six U.S. companies, other than the five largest, appeared to have any active foreign exploration interests.[5]

For several years after the war, materials and manpower were scarce. Foreign oil companies were engaged in rehabilitating facilities and organizations damaged by the war. But, by 1953, twenty-eight U.S. companies had taken preliminary steps to enter foreign operations. In 1948, Aminoil, a joint venture of ten United States companies, and, in 1949, Getty, each acquired an undivided half-interest in the onshore rights to the Neutral Zone between Kuwait and Saudi Arabia. This was the initial postwar entry into the rich Persian Gulf area. Three other American companies—Amerada, Continental, and Ohio —joined to form an active exploration venture. Atlantic, Phillips, and Sinclair had begun to develop modest but promising production in Venezuela. Powerful new forces were coming into play; the stage was set for a flood of entrants.

WHY PRIVATE FIRMS ENTERED

The factors which accounted for the rapid postwar spread of private oil enterprise throughout the world were easier conditions of entry, reduced apparent risks, and stronger profit incentives. As American influence overcame European dominance of the Middle and Far East, political barriers to entry began to give way. Many oilproducing countries began to issue smaller concessions to a larger number of companies. They also began to request the established oil companies to relinquish major

blocks of their concessions, thus increasing the accessi-
bility of potential oil-bearing lands to new firms. The
major oil-importing countries adopted progressively more
competitive economic policies and removed barriers to
trade, thus opening their markets to new firms. The advent of the European Common Market, in 1958, was a
spur to refining and marketing on a trans-European basis.

Advances were made in petroleum technology which
created opportunities for new firms not committed to
older locations and facilities. Supertankers, high-capacity
pipelines, inland and high-volume refineries situated near
centers of consumption, and the high-volume retail service stations are illustrations. Also, such technological innovations as catalytic reforming made it possible for
small-scale refineries to compete in the gasoline market.[6]
The capital and human resource requirements of entry
were also reduced by the increased availability, on a fee
or contract basis, of tankers, specialized geological and
geophysical services, and foreign contract drilling and
engineering services.

The risks of investment were reduced by the rapid
postwar growth of foreign oil consumption which provided expanding markets. Also, the striking successes of
the established international oil companies in finding
prolific reserves endowed the industry with the glamour
associated with bonanzas and lowered subjective risks in
the minds of potential entrants. The Middle East and
Latin America seemed less remote, once the trail had
been blazed and it was realized that vast deposits of low-
cost oil could be found there. Finally, rising corporate
income tax rates in the United States also shifted more
of the risks of foreign oil exploration and development to
government. They permitted the deduction from income
of intangible drilling costs, provided for percentage depletion, and allowed foreign subsidiaries to defer taxes
on their earnings until paid to the U.S. parent. Foreign
nations generally provided comparable incentives.

The relatively high rates of return earned by the largest
foreign oil companies up to 1955 constituted strong in-

ducements to new firms to enter the industry. Also, the faster growth rate of foreign oil consumption made foreign investment opportunities relatively brighter, especially in view of the rapidly rising discovery costs of American oil. Finally, the increasing governmental restriction of U.S. petroleum output under state prorationing laws led many American marketers to look abroad for crude oil sources. Later, when the U.S. government restricted entry to its domestic market by imposing import quotas, many American producers needed no further encouragement to enter foreign markets.

WHY GOVERNMENT FIRMS ENTERED

Many of the forces behind the postwar rush of private enterprises into foreign oil applied equally to government enterprises. But the entry of state-owned firms was also a response to special factors, notably national security, socialist ideology, and bargaining strength.

The massive changeover from coal to oil after World War II directed public attention to the need for reliable sources of oil. Government companies were formed, or expanded, to implement national energy policies. In some countries, national petroleum enterprises were an expression of socialist ideology or of nationalistic chauvinism which thrived after World War II. A state oil company, like an international airline, was a symbol of national sovereignty and prestige. Being under no compulsion to earn a normal return on investment, its prices could be kept at politically determined levels and could exert a "discipline" over the private oil companies with which it competed.

Some national companies were formed to explore for oil in order to reduce the drain on their foreign exchange from oil imports. Closely related to this was the formation of government companies in some oil-deficient countries to monopolize the importation of oil in the hope of getting better terms of trade. Many government companies

—prompted by the example of Italy's ENI and its relation to the Soviet Union—began to "short-circuit" the free market. They entered into trade agreements with foreign governments or government companies, often calling for the bartering of oil for other commodities.

A PROFILE OF ENTERING FIRMS

Among the 350 different firms that entered the foreign oil industry between 1953 and 1972, it is convenient to classify the *principal* ones into five groups: fifteen large U.S. oil companies, twenty medium-size U.S. oil companies, ten large U.S. natural gas, chemical, and other non-oil companies, twenty-five foreign private corporations, and fifteen foreign government oil companies.

The *fifteen large U.S. oil companies* which had by 1972 become vigorous competitors of the established firms included Amerada Hess, Aminoil, Atlantic-Richfield, Cities Service, Continental, Getty, Iricon, Occidental, Pan American, Phillips, Sinclair, Ohio Oil Company (now Marathon), Sun, Superior, and Union.[7] These were all large enterprises, well established in the United States prior to their excursions into foreign oil. By the end of 1972, each of them had found, and a dozen of them were producing, significant quantities of oil (100,000 barrels per day or more). The majority of them were operating in six to twelve countries. Most had substantial foreign refining or marketing interests. Each had the financial, technical, and managerial capability to extend and consolidate its position in world petroleum markets. The assets of eleven of the group totaled $20 billion, or an average of more than $1.9 billion each.

Twenty medium-size U.S. oil companies also went overseas on a considerable scale. These included Ambassador, Ashland, Clark, Daho-American, Delhi Taylor, Franco Wyoming, General American, General Exploration, Hunt, Kern County Land (later in Tenneco), Kerr-McGee, Mecom, Murphy, Natomas, Standard (Ohio), Pan-Coastal,

Pauley, Pure (later merged into Union), Sunray, and Texas Gulf Producing. As early as 1962, all were engaged in active exploration or production abroad, and fourteen of them had struck oil in commercial quantities. While prospects of these companies were less predictable than those of the bigger entrants, the majority appeared likely to make an enduring entry into the foreign oil industry.

Ten large U.S. natural gas, chemical, and steel companies also entered the field of foreign oil seeking profitable diversification. They included El Paso, Tennessee, Texas Eastern, United, and Western and Colorado (natural gas companies); Allied Chemical, Monsanto, W. R. Grace, and United Carbon (chemical companies); and Detroit (steel company). Up to the end of 1962, six of them had found oil. All were financially and technically capable of mounting an extensive exploratory effort.

Twenty-five foreign private firms entered the international oil industry on a major scale. The group included, from Australia, Ampol (and over sixty different Australian firms, often in joint venture with United States, British, or Canadian firms); from Belgium, Petrofina; from England, Ultramar; from France, Antar; from Israel, Paz; from Italy, Ausonia Mineraria and Montecatini; from Japan, the Arabian Oil Company (AOC), Daikyo, Idemitsu, Maruzen, Nippon Mining, and North Sumatra; from Spain, CEPSA; from Sweden, O.K. and Nynas; from Switzerland, Avia and Raffineries du Rhone; and from West Germany, Aral, DEA, Elwerath, Frisia, Gelsenberg, Preussag, and Wintershall. They were, indeed, a heterogeneous group. Some were newly formed companies, which (like AOC) had, by 1962, attained striking success. Some German companies sought to integrate established coal operations horizontally into the refining and marketing of oil, and refining operations backward to production. Some (like Ausonia Mineraria and Montecatini) were giant enterprises seeking product diversification. Their ample financial resources made them, as well as many of the others, formidable potential or actual competitors.

Fifteen foreign government companies began or significantly extended their oil operations between 1953 and 1972. Some, like the Indian Oil Company, were established to assure the government a strong position in the petroleum industry in order to implement national energy policies. The leading companies were, from Argentina, YPF; from Brazil, Petrobras; from Egypt, EGPC; from France, CFP; from India, IOC; from Indonesia, Pertamina; from Iran, NIOC; from Iraq, INOC; from Italy, ENI; from Kuwait, KNPC; from Mexico, Pemex; from Saudi Arabia, Petromin; from Spain, Campsa; from Turkey, TPAO; and from Venezuela, CVP. Every one of these enterprises was backed by the resources of a national state. Nearly all had either newly attained, or greatly extended, a position as a significant producer, refiner, or marketer of oil. The competition of government oil companies with private enterprises was often buttressed by monopoly privileges, public preferences, low-priced capital, special tax benefits, or freedom from the commercial obligation to earn a normal return on investment. These government companies, regardless of whether they had complete or partial monopolies of oil production and trade in their own countries, were part of the structure of the foreign oil industry. They could not be dismissed as "noncompetitive" with private oil enterprises.[8] During the period from 1953 to 1972, they became increasingly aggressive on both the supply and the demand sides of world oil markets, trading with other government companies as well as with private oil enterprises.

EXPLORATION AND PRODUCTION
BY THE NEWCOMERS

In 1953, twenty-eight American firms other than the five largest companies possessed foreign exploration rights. Ten had ventures in the Eastern Hemisphere and twenty in Latin America. Only four had interests in more than one foreign country. Some fifteen foreign private firms were also looking for oil abroad in 1953. In addition, some thirty-four private foreign companies were exploring for oil in their home countries or in their territories or possessions. Four government companies were exploring beyond their national borders. In total, seventy-seven private firms held exploration rights to about 520,000 square miles in some twenty-five foreign countries; and four government companies had exploration interests abroad in fifteen other nations involving 495,000 square miles.

By the end of 1972, the tempo of oil exploration had radically increased. More than 330 separate companies other than the seven largest held exploration rights to 6.8 million square miles of land, located in 122 areas of the world. Many companies were exploring simultaneously in a dozen or more countries, and in each of many nations, a dozen or more companies were participating in the search for oil. This dramatic rise of exploratory activity affected every important oil-producing region of the foreign world (see Figure 7.1 and Figure 7.2).

In the Middle East it has been seen that as late as 1953 only CFP, Aminoil's owners, and Getty, apart from the seven largest companies, had acquired concessions in the oil-producing nations. By 1962 this situation had changed significantly. Sixteen companies had exploration interests in Iran, ten in the Saudi-Kuwait Neutral Zone, two in Egypt, twelve in Israel, three in Lebanon, five in Syria, two in Yemen, two in the Hadhramaut, and one each in every other country of the region. In addition, KNPC, NIOC, INOC, and Petromin, all government-owned, held extensive acreages in Kuwait, Iran, Iraq, and Saudi Arabia respectively; and EGPC and Jazirah, newly-formed government companies, were active in Egypt and Syria. Taken together, these companies had, by 1962, discovered proven reserves of 25 billion barrels and were producing over 800,000 barrels of oil per day. The large and promising undeveloped concessions of the newcomers in this region portended further discoveries. As a result of relinquishments by the seven largest companies, vast

FIGURE 7.1
Companies Other than the "Seven Largest" with Exploration Ventures in Foreign Nations, 1953 and 1972

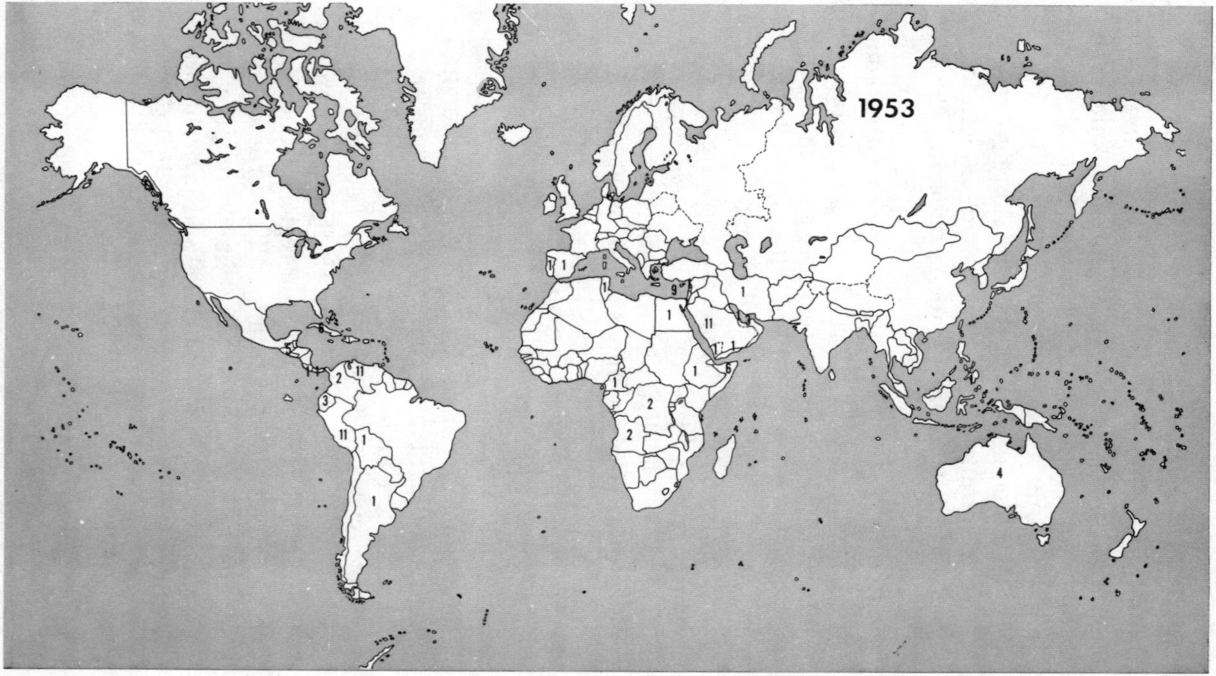

Sources: 1953 data from *Entry Data and Statistical Studies*; 1972 data from *Annual Overseas Exploration Report - 1973*, Petroconsultants, S.A.

FIGURE 7.2

Companies Other than the "Seven Largest" with Production Ventures in Foreign Nations, 1953 and 1972

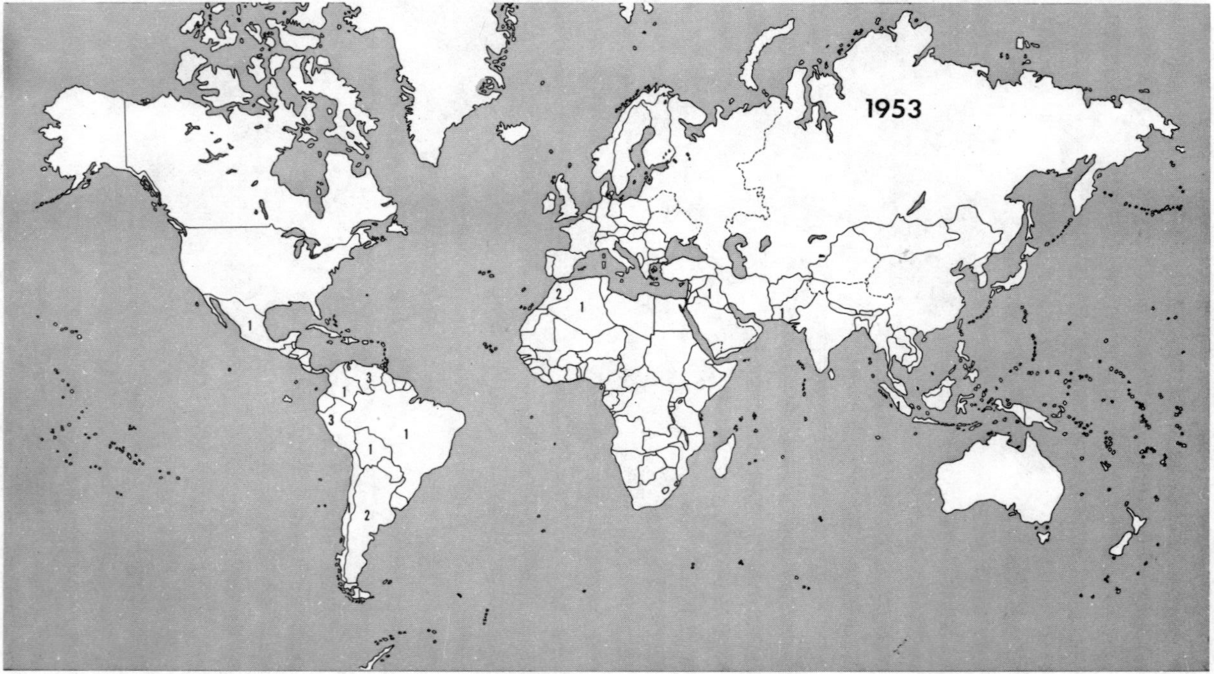

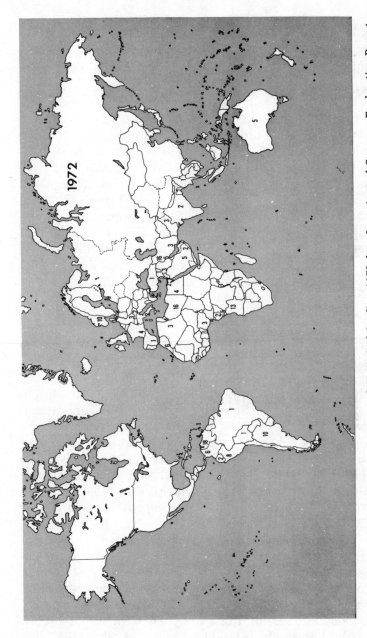

Sources: 1953 data from *Entry Data and Statistical Studies*; 1972 data from *Annual Overseas Exploration Report -
1973*, Petroconsultants, S.A.

133

Middle Eastern areas had become available. The acreage was either handed over to new national oil companies for development, or was auctioned off to the highest bonus bidder among private companies. This occurred in Iraq, Qatar, and Dubai during 1961. In 1962 Kuwait persuaded B.P. and Gulf to relinquish half of one of the world's richest concessions to KNPC, the new national oil company, and Saudi Arabia pressed ARAMCO to give up even more land. Iran's NIOC was seeking new partners to develop additional areas off its shores. Large Middle East territories, other than those relinquished in established oil-producing nations, in Egypt, Dhofar, Yemen, Sharjah, and other Trucial Coast areas, also came under active exploration. Figure 7.3 graphically depicts the spread of enterprise in this crucial oil region of the world.

In Africa, in 1953, there was virtually no oil production nor any proven reserves and less than a dozen exploration ventures were under way. By 1962 it had become the "new frontier" of the foreign oil industry; and, by 1972, the continent contained some of the world's principal oil provinces. More than one hundred companies were engaged in the search for oil in more than thirty countries of the continent as early as 1962, including twenty in Algeria, seventeen in Libya, six in Morocco, three in Nigeria, twenty in the Spanish Sahara, nine in Tunisia, and many others in central and southern Africa. Because Algeria and Libya had general petroleum laws, scores of oil companies obtained relatively small concessions under obligations to develop them quickly or relinquish them within short periods of time. As a result, the barren deserts of this region witnessed a competitive scramble for oil unmatched in recent times.

Led by CFP, an intensive exploration of Algeria and the French Sahara began in 1955. By 1962 a great bonanza had been found. From virtually none, in 1953, the French Sahara (now a part of Algeria) had, by 1972, established proven reserves of 47 billion barrels and daily production of about 1,022,000 barrels. In the deserts of nearby Libya, which produced no oil at all in 1953, exploration began in 1956 and resulted in major discoveries after 1959. At the end of 1972, proven reserves stood at 30 billion barrels, crude oil exports were over 2 million barrels per day, and the productive capacity of existing wells exceeded 3 million barrels per day—and the development of this rich area was far from complete.

By the end of 1972, North African crude oil reserves had reached 84 billion barrels and daily production more than 3.5 million barrels, despite large reductions of output by the Libyan and Algerian governments. It is significant that more than four-fifths of these reserves and more than two-thirds of the daily production were in the hands of enterprises *other than* the seven largest international companies. Atlantic-Richfield, Amerada Hess, CFP, Continental, Grace, Marathon, Newmont, Occidental, Phillips, and SONATRACH were new companies sharing in the harvest. The relatively low cost and high quality of this oil, combined with its proximity to the vast European market, gave its owners a strong competitive position. North African oil was supplying 32 percent of Europe's imports by 1972.

Angola, the Congo, Gabon, and Nigeria had also become the scene of a hectic and successful search for oil by many newcomers to the industry. Petrofina had found a commercial field in Angola, CFP in the Congo and Gabon, Phillips and Occidental in Nigeria, and it was to be expected that the exploration efforts of many others would, in time, be rewarded.

The Far East was not neglected by the new entrants in the widened search for oil. In Australia, where exploration efforts had gone unrewarded for decades, Union Oil of California, Kern County Land, and Australian Oil & Gas made the first commercial strike (in the Moonie field) in late 1961. By the end of 1972, some 132 companies were participating in a hunt extending over two-thirds of the Australian continent.

The government of Indonesia contracted with many foreign-based oil companies. One was Pan American, a four-company consortium headed by Asamera (Canada) and North Sumatra (Japan), which would develop production, in some instances on the very borders of oil fields

FIGURE 7.3

Companies Other than the "Seven Largest" Engaged in Exploration and Development in Middle East Countries, 1953

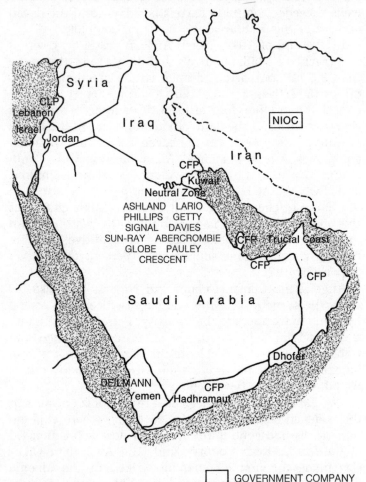

Sources: *Entry Data* and *Statistical Studies*.

Note: The location of company names does not indicate exact concession areas.

FIGURE 7.3 (Continued)
Companies Other than the "Seven Largest" Engaged in Exploration and Development in Middle East Countries, 1972

☐ GOVERNMENT COMPANY

Source: *Petroleum Press Service*, July, 1973, pp. 256–57.
Note: The location of company names does not indicate exact concession areas.
(a) 1. Occidental; (b) 1. Buttes Gas & Oil/Ashland/Skelly/Kerr-McGee, 2. Dubai Marine Areas (Conoco/CFP/Hispanoil/Sun/Wintershall); (c) 1. Vitol Exploration of Holland; (d) 1. Buttes Gas & Oil/Ashland/Skelly/Kerr-McGee/Juniper Petroleum; (e) 1. Occidental.

previously proven by Caltex and other established companies. These Indonesian government and other entering companies had, by 1972, proven 1.6 billion barrels of crude oil reserves and achieved 170,000 barrels of daily production.

In Latin America, Venezuela offered, during 1956 and 1957, new concessions in areas, some of which were adjacent to producing lands and proven acreage. Over twenty-five new firms paid large bonuses to obtain these concessions, and, by 1962, most of them had found oil and developed substantial production. American entrants had proven almost 3 billion barrels of reserves and were producing 400,000 barrels per day by 1962.

After the mid-1950s, concessions were also opened in Guatemala, Bolivia, Colombia, Ecuador, and Peru. By 1962 twenty-two companies were exploring in Peru and Guatemala, and lesser numbers in each of many other Latin American countries. During the 1960s and early 1970s, huge new reserves of crude oil were proved in the Amazon Basin regions of Peru and Ecuador by the new multinationals as well as by some of the seven largest companies. Many American oil companies entered Latin America in the hope of finding low-cost crude oil for export to the United States. After the United States imposed import quotas in 1957, these companies began marketing abroad. Between 1953 and 1972, companies other than the seven largest had expanded their proven crude oil reserves in Latin American countries from 2.7 billion barrels to 13.6 billion barrels, and had increased their daily output from about 420,000 to some 1,200,000 barrels per day.

———————

The sheer number of entrants and the worldwide scope of their activities during the years from 1953 to 1972 is deeply impressive. Even more striking, however, is the success of the new entrants in finding petroleum in commercial quantities. In 1953 no private oil company, other than the seven largest, had as much as 200 million barrels of proven foreign crude oil reserves; and among the government companies only one had reserves over this figure. By 1972 no less than thirteen "other" companies each owned more than 2 billion barrels of oil in the ground. Collectively, all the new entrants—apart from the Soviet Union—owned about 112 billion barrels of proven reserves, or not far from one-fourth of the foreign non-Communist world's oil reserves. The competitive significance of these reserves can be appreciated by recognizing that, if produced at a conservative rate of 5 percent per year, they could maintain production of 15 million barrels per day—or 58 percent of the 1972 rate of foreign non-Communist world consumption—for the next twenty years.

With regard to production, in 1953, no company—other than the seven largest—had daily foreign oil production of 200,000 barrels or more. By the end of 1972, thirteen of the new companies had passed this level. Collectively, this group of companies had attained, by the end of 1972, a daily output of about 5.2 million barrels, or more than one-sixth of the total foreign non-Communist world consumption.

REFINING BY THE NEWCOMERS

Entrance into the refining division of the foreign oil industry matched the fast pace of entry into the exploration and production phases between 1953 and 1972. To a degree, it involved the same integrated companies; but to a considerable extent, it involved a separate group of nonintegrated or partially integrated enterprises.

We have noted that most international trade in petroleum up to the end of World War II was in refined products, which moved overseas from United States, Caribbean, and Middle Eastern ports to consuming countries. The development of large numbers of medium-sized refineries in consuming countries was distinctly a postwar phenomenon. It offered opportunities to a host of new companies to enter the refining business. Governmental companies, private foreign energy distributors (such as

coal firms moving into oil), and new international producers seeking integrated outlets for their new-found oil,
took advantage of these opportunities.

During the period from 1953 to 1972, 55 percent of
new refining capacity was built by newcomers. At the
beginning of this period, no oil company other than the
three largest had daily refining capacity of 250,000 barrels per day or more. By 1972, however, seventeen "other"
companies had at least this much capacity. In 1953 companies other than the seven largest owned 27 percent of
foreign non-Communist world refining capacity; by 1972
they owned 51 percent. Their growth was rapid in every
region and important petroleum consuming country in
the foreign world.

In the Far East, refining capacity rose faster than in
any other region. In 1953 companies other than the seven
largest accounted for under one-quarter of the refining
capacity. By 1972 they had expanded their capacity to
5 million barrels per day and held 66 percent of the
regional total. In Japan, the world's fastest growing major
petroleum market, companies other than the seven
largest increased their ownership of refining capacity
from 66 percent to 78 percent over the period. Among
leading new Japanese refiners in 1972, which had had
little or no capacity in 1953 and which were not partly
owned by the seven largest firms were Idemitsu, Maruzen,
Mitsubishi, Nippon Mining, Daikyo, Kashima, Kyushu,
and Fuji. These eight companies ranked first, and fourth
through tenth, respectively, in refining in Japan.

In Western Europe as a whole, the new oil companies
had a twelvefold increase in refining capacity between
1953 and 1972. By building plants faster than their rivals,
their share of European capacity rose from 35 percent in
1953 to 45 percent in 1972. These increases were remarkable because the seven largest companies were concentrating their refining investments in Europe.

West Germany formed a booming postwar market in
which the growth of several refining enterprises—other
than those of the seven largest companies—was spectacular. They included Elwerath, Gelsenberg, Scholven,

Union-Rheinische Braunkolen, and Wintershall. Continental, ENI, Frisia, Petrofina, and Preussag were also present. In all, firms other than the seven largest comprised seven of Germany's top ten refiners in 1972, and owned 42 percent of capacity.

Italian refining capacity quadrupled during the decade. The new companies, which accounted for somewhat less than half of total capacity in 1953, owned 67 percent in 1972. Italian refiners—other than the seven largest companies—included CFP, Continental, Getty, Petrofina, Standard Oil of Indiana, and many Italian companies. Firms other than the seven largest occupied seven of the top ten positions in the industry. ENI, of course, was the largest of the "others" in its home market.

French government regulation held down the growth of refining capacity in that country between 1953 and 1972 to a moderate rate. Companies other than the seven largest, including CFP, increased their share from 53 to 56 percent over the period.

In Latin America, firms other than the seven largest owned 33 percent of refining capacity in 1953. By 1972 they had raised their share to 49 percent.

In the Middle East, the growth of refining during the years from 1953 to 1972 was relatively slow, reflecting the trend toward market-oriented locations of new refineries. Companies other than the seven largest owned only 2 percent of capacity in 1953. The new multinationals had raised their capacity to 37 percent of the regional total by 1972.

In Africa the new multinationals had two-thirds of the total refinery capacity in 1953; by 1972 they possessed 70 percent of the total.

MARKETING BY THE NEWCOMERS

Entries into foreign marketing were numerous *after* the mid-1950s, following an earlier buildup of activities by the new firms in oil production and refining. In particular, the advent of American oil import quotas in 1957 touched off a search for foreign outlets for their foreign oil production by U.S. companies.

Apart from the seven largest multinational oil companies, CFP, ENI, and Petrofina were long-established marketers which greatly expanded their activities after 1953. By 1962 CFP was retailing in more than thirty countries, Petrofina in thirteen, and ENI in twenty nations. After 1958, Aral, Avia, Continental, Getty, Phillips, Signal, Standard Oil of Indiana, and Union began multinational marketing; and there were many others. Where there were no more than two multinational marketing companies—other than the seven largest—in 1953, more than twenty companies had made substantial progress in the direction of becoming international petroleum marketing organizations by 1972, and their operations spanned the foreign non-Communist world.

In the United Kingdom, only Petrofina offered competition to the seven largest firms up to 1959. By the end of 1972, Amerada Hess (through Continental), CFP, Continental, ENI, Getty, Murphy, Occidental, Pan American, Phillips, and Standard Oil of Indiana were all selling at retail.

In Japan the focus of international competition was on the sale of crude oil to Japanese refiners and marketers not affiliated with the seven largest companies. By 1962 Idemitsu and Maruzen were the top two marketers and, together with Daikyo, Mitsubishi, Asia, Nippon Gyomo, Nippon Mining, and Toa, were eight of the fourteen largest internal marketers.

In the booming European Common Market, nine American firms entered de novo after 1957—Amerada Hess (through Continental), Aminoil, Cities Service, Continental, Getty, Marathon, Signal, Sinclair, and Standard Oil of Indiana. Aral, Avia, DEA, ENI, and Frisia expanded what were essentially one-country operations into international operations. CFP and Petrofina had expanded into all six countries. Getty, DEA, Murphy, and Petrofina had also entered Scandinavian markets, and Sweden's O.K. had entered the Common Market. Companies other than the seven largest had, through aggressive competition and hospitable governmental policies, captured a substantial part of the European Common Market for petroleum products by 1972.

The new entrants were most active and successful in the fastest growing markets of Japan and Western Europe. In Latin America, the government oil companies of most large countries were consistently important marketers between 1953 and 1972, and during 1972 it appears that government companies made over two-thirds of the product sales in most major markets. Thus it is evident that, although they began marketing operations much later than the established firms, the new multinationals had, by 1972, made significant expansions in their sales of petroleum.

TRANSPORTATION BY THE NEWCOMERS

In the transportation of petroleum by tanker, there were numerous new entrants and a strong growth of facilities owned by firms other than the seven largest oil companies between 1953 and 1972. This was true notwithstanding the fact that about 72 percent of the non-Communist world's tanker fleet was already owned by non-oil companies or by oil companies other than the seven largest in 1953. The percentages owned by non-oil companies did not change significantly; but those of oil companies other than the seven largest rose. In 1972 firms other than the seven largest owned 81 percent of the fleet (see Table 5.3).

New companies also played an important role in the rapid expansion of foreign pipeline systems after 1952. Government companies in Argentina, Brazil, France, India, Iran, and Mexico owned and operated large pipeline complexes in their respective countries. By 1962, CFP controlled a 1,200-mile system in Algeria; AOC had finished a large pipeline in the Neutral Zone; Amerada Hess,

Continental, and Marathon had completed a major pipeline to move their Libyan crude oil. Later, Union built a 200-mile line from its Moonie field to markets in Australia, and Occidental constructed a 150-mile trunk line from its Libyan fields to the Mediterranean.

Equally significant was the growth of *international* pipelines to feed crude oil to the inland refineries of Europe. The first of these was a 240-mile pipeline from Wilhelmshaven to Cologne, completed in 1959 and owned 26.5 percent by companies other than the seven largest oil companies. The next was a 175-mile line running from Rotterdam to the Ruhr, completed in 1960 and owned 20 percent by Gelsenberg and 80 percent by Caltex, Mobil, and Shell. Later, eight new oil companies joined six of the seven largest firms in building the 485-mile South European pipeline from Marseilles to the Rhine. This huge $120 million facility was completed in 1962. ENI constructed its own 650-mile Central European pipeline, running from Genoa through Switzerland into southern Germany.

These new crude oil transport facilities fostered the construction of new inland refineries, improved the competitive position of African crude oils in European markets, created opportunities for new refiners and marketers, and thus intensified competition. In addition, the immense pipeline system of the Soviet Union terminated not only at Baltic Sea and Arctic ports, but also at points within Communist countries virtually on the borders of Austria and Germany, thus giving it the capability for large deliveries into Western markets.

INVESTMENT AND CAPITAL SPENDING BY NEW FIRMS

Data assembled by the Chase Manhattan Bank show the relative increases in both the amounts and the percentages of total assets committed to foreign operations by eleven entering U.S. multinational oil companies during the period from 1953 to 1972. At the beginning of this period, the newcomers had negligible foreign investments, but by 1972 their investments amounted to $18.5 billion (see Table 7.1). Collectively, their annual foreign capital expenditures rose faster than those of the five largest U.S. oil companies, as is shown by figures for the representative years 1948, 1953, and 1972 (see Table 7.2).

AN OVERVIEW OF THE ENTRANTS
AND THEIR GROWTH

The pace of growth in the operations of the 350 "new internationals," as they have been aptly described in reports of the United Nations, was incredibly rapid in contrast to that of the seven established international oil companies. Within two decades, they collectively multiplied by many times their exploratory acreage, proven crude oil reserves, oil production, refining capacity, tanker capacity, gross investment in assets, capital expenditures, and sales of petroleum products. They captured substantial fractions of every division of the foreign non-Communist oil industry.

The evidence of massive entrance into the foreign oil industry during the period from 1953 to 1972 and of the much more rapid growth of the new enterprises as a group as compared with the established firms, clearly refutes the idea that an effective cartel of the "seven largest" companies was in operation during this period. New firms were neither excluded from petroleum markets nor were they prevented from growing at the expense of the "seven largest" firms. Of course, not all of the entrants succeeded in establishing a firm position in foreign markets. Many failed and withdrew from the industry. In an industry characterized by an explosive growth of the market and fast-paced technological changes, a substantial rate of exit of firms from the industry is evidence of vigorous competition, just as is a sustained high entry rate.

TABLE 7.1

Net Investment in Fixed Assets, Foreign and Total, of the Five Largest and of Eleven Other
U.S. International Oil Companies, at the End of 1953 and 1972

(*Amounts in Millions of Dollars*)

Company	1953			1972		
	Foreign Assets	Total Assets	Percent Foreign	Foreign Assets	Total Assets	Percent Foreign
Exxon	$1,075	$ 2,705	39.7	$ 6,334	$12,269	52.5
Gulf	155	888	17.5	1,930	5,409	35.7
Texaco	140	1,018	13.8	3,285	7,175	45.8
Mobil	74	1,064	7.0	2,479	5,145	48.2
Socal	105	1,038	10.1	2,009	5,221	38.5
Total–Five Largest Companies	$1,549	$ 6,718	23.0	$16,148	$35,219	45.9
Amerada	$ 4	$ 61	6.6	$ 376	$ 548	68.7
Atlantic	98	1,275	7.7	329	2,919	11.3
Cities Service	15	691	2.2	88	1,434	6.1
Continental	. . .	247	. . .	417	1,637	25.5
Getty	15	450	3.3	173	1,200	14.5
Marathon	3	192	1.6	180	787	22.8

Standard Oil of Indiana	8	1,325	0.6	1,027	3,799	27.0
Phillips	33	752	4.4	564	1,820	31.0
Standard (Ohio)	2	170	1.2	10	1,062	0.9
Sun	31	411	7.5	608	1,744	34.9
Union	10	574	1.7	213	1,501	14.2
Total–Eleven Other Companies	$ 219	$ 6,168	3.6	$ 3,985	$18,451	21.6
Total–Sixteen Companies	$1,768	$12,886	13.7	$20,133	$53,670	37.5

Source: Chase Manhattan Bank. Foreign assets include those in Canada.

TABLE 7.2

Foreign Capital Expenditures by the Five Largest and by
Eleven Other U.S. International Oil Companies
in 1948, 1953, and 1972

(*Millions of Dollars*)

Category of Companies	1948	1953	1972
Five Largest U.S. Oil Companies	$357.3	$372.0	$2,758.0
Eleven Other U.S. Oil Companies			
Amerada	$ 0.1	$ 2.8	$ 76.7
Atlantic	18.4	13.0	60.6
Cities Service	2.3	3.1	17.5
Continental	...	...	168.7
Getty	0.1	4.4	31.1
Marathon	...	1.8	31.4
Standard Oil of Indiana	0.2	4.1	301.9
Phillips	7.5	6.5	115.2
Standard (Ohio)	...	1.7	1.4
Sun	1.1	21.3	69.6
Union	1.0	6.7	94.6
Total–Eleven Companies	$ 30.7	$ 65.5	$ 968.7
Total–Sixteen Companies	$388.0	$437.5	$3,726.7

Source: Chase Manhattan Bank. Foreign capital expenditures include those made in Canada.

NOTES

1. "Entry" has been defined broadly to mean both the
original participation of a new firm in the petroleum industry
or a major extension of the operations of an existing firm
into a new division of the industry or into a new geographical
region. To avoid overcounting, a parent company and its

wholly or majority owned subsidiaries and affiliates were treated as one enterprise.

2. Most of the factual information presented here about entrants is drawn from and documented in the author's *Entry Data*. While the majority of postwar entrants made their debut between 1953 and 1962, some entered during the subsequent decade.

3. See J. S. Bain, *Barriers to New Competition* (Cambridge: Harvard University Press, 1956), chap. 1. The relative difficulty of entry by a new firm and the advantages of established firms can be measured by the extent to which the latter can price products persistently at a level which yields above-normal profits *without attracting new entrants*.

4. See U.S., Congress, Senate, Special Subcommittee Investigating Petroleum Resources, *American Petroleum Interests in Foreign Countries*, Hearings, 79th Cong., 1st sess., June, 1945 (Washington, D.C.: Government Printing Office, 1945), pp. 153–446.

5. They were Atlantic, the Blue Goose (Ganso Azul), Cities Service, Phillips, Richfield, and Sinclair.

6. The advent of the catalytic reforming process permitted the small refiner to produce gasolines of competitive quality without increasing the yield of gasoline per barrel of crude.

7. Since their original entry into the foreign industry, Amerada merged with Hess to become Amerada Hess, Signal sold some of its foreign oil interests to Occidental, and Atlantic merged with Richfield.

8. The staff of the Federal Trade Commission, when measuring the concentration of the world petroleum industry in 1948–1950, often excluded the state monopolies from the foreign oil industry. See, U.S., Congress, Senate, Select Committee on Small Business, Subcommittee on Monopoly, *The International Petroleum Cartel*, Staff report to, and submitted by, the Federal Trade Commission, 82d Cong., 2d sess. (Washington, D.C.: Government Printing Office, 1962), chap. 2.

8

The Reentry of the Soviet Union into Western Oil Markets

THE REENTRY of the Soviet Union into non-Communist oil markets during the 1950s was a milestone in the postwar evolution of the industry.[1] A combination of factors made this reentry significant: the rapid growth of petroleum exports to the non-Communist world—from 35,000 barrels per day, in 1953, to 1,035,000 barrels per day, in 1972; the great economic power wielded by this new competitor; its immense and still largely unproven oil resources; its complex motives as an exporter; its unorthodox trading methods and occasionally disruptive pricing practices; and the unpredictability of its behavior.

What is the historical background of the Russian oil industry? What are the measures of its postwar and probable future expansion? What have been the motives, methods, and results of the Soviet oil export drive, and its effects upon competition in the foreign oil industry?[2]

THE HISTORICAL IMPORTANCE
OF RUSSIAN OIL

It is not generally realized that the Russian oil industry began in the same era that Edwin Drake started the United States petroleum industry by drilling his first well in Titusville, Pennsylvania, in 1859. In fact, under the Czars, the growth of Russian oil production during the nineteenth century was, at first, more rapid than that of the American oil industry. Nearly all Russian oil came from the fields of Baku along the western shore of the Caspian Sea. By the turn of the twentieth century, Russia was the world's first-ranking oil producer and exporter.[3] World War I and the internal revolution which followed disorganized its oil industry, which was nationalized by the Bolshevik government in 1918. Soviet oil output in 1920 was actually no greater than it had been in 1890; and oil exports ceased.

During the 1920s and 1930s, Soviet oil production expanded at a moderate rate. However, the relatively low state of industrialization resulted in a limited domestic demand. As the need for foreign exchange was critical, about 25 percent of output was exported during the years between 1926 and 1933. The USSR provided 14 percent of the oil imported by Western European countries in the period between 1925 and 1934, and 19 percent of their imports in the period between 1930 and 1933.[4] After 1932, exports fell off as a result of a planned expansion in energy consumption by Soviet industry. By the outbreak of World War II, the Soviet Union had virtually terminated its participation in the foreign oil industry.

The German invasion of Russia again brought about partial destruction and disorganization of its petroleum industry. During the immediate postwar years, economic priorities were given to the reconstruction and expansion of heavy industry. As a result, it was not until 1951 that oil production recovered the prewar peak attained in 1944.

About 1950, according to Hodgkins, the Soviet Union

embarked upon an ambitious program of oil and gas exploration, production, transportation, and refining.[5] Consequently, it was able to begin a postwar reentry into non-Communist markets which, at times, disrupted the Western system of trade. Soviet oil production since 1890 is compared with that of the United States and the rest of the world in Table 8.1.

THE POSTWAR EMPHASIS ON OIL AND GAS DEVELOPMENT

Up to about 1950, coal formed a predominant and rising share of total Soviet energy consumption, supplying 65 percent of all energy expended. A basic postwar policy was to shift toward the increased use of oil and natural gas, and this was reflected in the allocation of funds to productive investment in energy development. The annual step-up of capital investment in the oil and gas industries was impressive, from 17.7 billion rubles in 1960 to several times that sum in 1972. Meanwhile coal investment was held down.[6]

The energy production pattern of the Soviet Union changed greatly during the 1950s and 1960s. Coal was the source of two-thirds of Soviet energy output in 1950, but it fell to 52 percent in 1960 and to 33 percent by 1971. Oil has been traveling the opposite course. From 17 percent of energy production in 1950, oil rose to 29 percent in 1960 and to 36 percent in 1971. An even more striking gain, however, was recorded by natural gas. Its share of energy output has risen from 2 percent in 1950, to 7 percent in 1960, and to 21 percent in 1971. Evidently, the USSR is moving toward an energy production pattern similar to that of the United States (see Figure 8.1 and Table 8.2).

The results of the postwar petroleum expansion program were striking. Soviet oil output, which had been 729,000 barrels per day in 1950, reached 7.9 million barrels per day in 1972. By the 1960s, the USSR had

TABLE 8.1

Crude Oil Production and Estimated Proven Reserves of the
United States, the USSR, and the Rest of the World,
1890 to 1972

Year	Production (Thousands of Barrels per Day)			Reserves (Millions of Barrels)		
	U.S.	USSR	Rest of World	U.S.	USSR	Rest of World
1972	9,441	7,880	33,493	38,823	75,000	553,060
1971	9,463	7,612	31,290	37,250	75,000	519,606
1970	9,637	7,108	28,980	37,013	77,000	497,384
1969	9,238	6,611	25,836	38,700	44,000	441,080
1968	9,096	6,170	23,270	32,500	40,000	385,546
1967	8,810	5,753	20,750	37,541	34,500	342,299
1966	8,295	5,337	19,280	38,159	32,500	318,391
1965	7,804	4,893	17,600	35,400	32,000	285,658
1964	7,614	4,490	16,062	34,492	29,250	277,531
1963	7,542	4,121	14,467	34,272	28,000	268,770
1962	7,337	3,721	13,093	35,300	28,500	249,744
1960	7,036	2,951	11,008	31,719	28,000	231,409
1955	6,805	1,397	7,211	30,012	9,500	118,629
1950	5,408	729	4,282	25,268	4,300	47,460
1945	4,696	408	2,005	19,942	5,765	37,555
1940	3,697	598	1,579	19,025	2,118	19,684
1935	2,732	499	1,304	12,400	2,408	8,796
1930	2,460	345	1,063	13,600	3,231	9,434
1925	2,093	142	693	8,500	.....	.....
1920	1,210	68	604	7,200	.....	.....
1915	770	189	225	5,500	.....	.....
1910	575	192	132	4,500	.....	.....
1905	370	151	68	3,800	.....	.....
1900	175	208	25	2,900	.....	.....
1895	195	126	14	.....	.....	.....
1890	126	79	5	.....	.....	.....

Sources: United States Bureau of Mines; *Oil & Gas Journal*; U.S., Congress, Senate, Special Subcommittee Investigating Petroleum Resources, *American Petroleum Interests in Foreign Countries*, Hearings, 79th Cong., 1st sess., June, 1945.

FIGURE 8.1

Production of Primary Energy in the USSR, by Source,
1950–1975

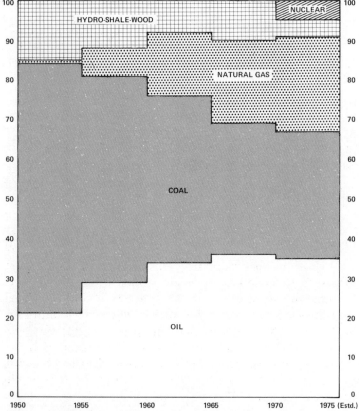

PERCENTAGES OF TOTAL ENERGY IN STANDARD FUEL EQUIVALENT

Sources: Table 8.2 and Robert W. Campbell, *The Economics of Soviet Oil and Gas* (Baltimore: Johns Hopkins University Press, 1968), pp. 1–23.

emerged once again as the foreign world's largest producing country; and it was surpassed only by Saudi Arabia in the 1970s. Its more than tenfold increase in production since 1950 represented a remarkable annual compound rate of growth of nearly 12 percent.

The Soviet government has not published estimates of its "proven crude oil reserves," taking this phrase in the

TABLE 8.2

Production of Primary Energy in the USSR, by Source,
1950, 1960, and 1971

(*Percentages of Total Energy in Standard Fuel Equivalents*)

Energy Source	1950 (Percent)	1960 (Percent)	1971 (Percent)
Oil	17.0	28.7	35.9
Coal	64.6	52.2	33.2
Natural Gas	2.3	7.4	21.0
Hydroelectric-Nuclear	2.3	3.5	3.8
Peat-Shale-Wood	13.8	8.2	6.1
Total	100.0	100.0	100.0

Sources: Robert J. Ebel, *The Petroleum Industry of the Soviet Union* (New York: American Petroleum Institute, 1961), pp. 7, 11, 12. Also, United Nations, *World Energy Supplies,* 1968–1971, 1973 eds.

American sense of reserves that are certainly and economically recoverable from oil-bearing zones within the productive limits of producing fields. Hence it is necessary to resort to conjectures based upon indirect evidence. Soviet geologists claimed, as early as 1937, that the USSR contained 55 percent of the world's oil reserves, and they have consistently maintained this position. But this estimate refers to "prospective" reserves, rather than to "proven" or even "probable" reserves.[7] After reviewing much evidence, Hodgkins concluded that in 1956 Soviet Russia certainly possessed 64 billion barrels of crude oil reserves, or about 26 percent of the world's then-known total, making it first among the oil-endowed nations of the world. *Oil & Gas Journal* credited the Soviet Union with 75 billion barrels of proven reserves in 1972.

But in the Soviet Union reserves are *not* a limiting factor on oil production or exports. The primary question is how fast should the virtually unlimited *potential* oil reserves be developed. This reasoning is substantiated by the opinions of petroleum geologists that 2.84 million square miles of Soviet territory contain promising sedimentary formations capable of yielding oil—a potential oil-producing area exceeding that of the United States by more than 34 percent. Most of this area is yet to be explored.[8] Soviet petroleum resources appear to be more than adequate to support any reasonable crude oil production program its planners choose to carry out.

The USSR significantly expanded its refining capacity during the postwar era. In 1950 it had a capacity of 944,000 barrels per day; by 1972 its capacity had risen to over 6.6 million barrels per day. The newer refineries have embodied recent and more highly developed technology which yields a higher quality of products.

Crude oil transportation facilities support Soviet export capabilities. Traditionally, rail transportation dominated all other types of carriage in the Soviet economy. In 1950 nearly two-thirds of all ton-miles of petroleum freight were carried by rail, about 30 percent by barge or ship, and only 6 percent by pipeline. Between 1950 and 1960, the mileage of available oil pipelines more than tripled; then it more than doubled to 28,000 miles by 1972. In 1972 pipelines carried the bulk of all petroleum (see Figure 8.2 and Table 8.3).

Of even greater significance is the fact that, although the USSR had built no export pipelines from the 1930s to the 1950s, the major part of the pipeline mileage in place by 1972 ran from the Urals-Volga production region to Leningrad, the Baltic ports, Poland, East Germany, Hungary, and Czechoslovakia. The Comecon ("Friendship") Pipeline ran 3,500 miles to connect with Poland, Hungary, East Germany, and Czechoslovakia. Another 5,000 miles of pipelines connect with Irkutsk. This matrix is designed to link the satellites more closely to the Soviet Union and to facilitate the movement of crude oil directly into Western Europe and other non-Communist countries.

To assess the ability of the USSR to export oil to non-Communist countries, it is necessary to examine its domestic needs. Although the Soviet government has not published statistics of USSR petroleum consumption, it can be estimated. In 1961 the USSR produced about

FIGURE 8.2
Expansion of the USSR Oil Industry, 1955, 1960, 1965, and 1972

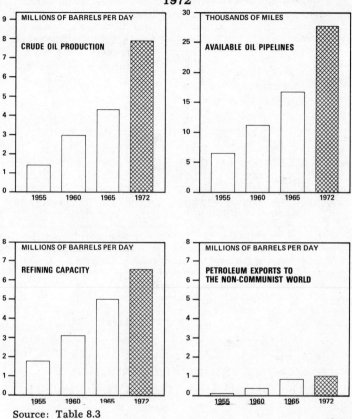

Source: Table 8.3

3,300,000 barrels per day, exported about 285,000 barrels per day to Communist bloc countries and about 540,000 barrels per day to non-Communist countries, while importing about 80,000 barrels per day, leaving some 2,555,000 million barrels per day to be accounted for by domestic consumption. By 1972 USSR production was 7,880,000 barrels per day, exports to Communist bloc countries were 940,000 barrels per day and to non-Communist countries 1,035,000 barrels per day, leaving 5,905,000 million barrels per day for domestic consumption (see Figure 8.2).

TABLE 8.3

Expansion of USSR Oil Production, Pipeline Mileage, Refining
Capacity, and Petroleum Exports, 1950, 1955, 1960,
1965, and 1972

Year	Crude Oil Production (Barrels per Day)	Available Oil Pipelines (Miles)	Crude Oil Refining Capacity (Barrels per Day)	Petroleum Exports to the Non-Communist World (Barrels per Day)
1950	758,000	3,381	944,000	. . . . . .
1955	1,412,000	6,515	1,790,000	66,000
1960	2,957,000	11,349	3,146,000	380,000
1965	4,893,000	16,875	5,036,000	900,000
1972	7,880,000	27,800	6,600,000	1,035,000

Sources: Robert J. Ebel, *The Petroleum Industry of the Soviet Union*
(New York: American Petroleum Institute, 1961); for refining capacity,
National Petroleum Council, *Impact of Oil Exports from the Soviet Bloc*
(Washington, D.C.: National Petroleum Council, 1962), vol. 2, p. 138;
United States Bureau of Mines; Robert J. Ebel, *Communist Trade in Oil
and Gas: An Evaluation of the Future Export Capability of the Soviet
Bloc* (New York: Praeger Publishers, 1970), p. 105, 115, and 329; *Petroleum Press Service*, March, 1973, p. 87, and May, 1973, p. 170.

THE GROWTH OF SOVIET
AND COMMUNIST BLOC OIL EXPORTS

The growth of Soviet petroleum exports to non-Communist markets was remarkably rapid. Even in 1955 it was exporting only 66,000 barrels per day. By 1972, however, it had multiplied exports to non-Communist countries sixteen times to around one million barrels per day. The principal countries of destination numbered nine in 1955 and twelve in 1972. Moreover, while buyers in only three nations bought 10,000 barrels per day or more from the USSR in 1955, by 1972 buyers in eight nations were purchasing over that amount.

FIGURE 8.3

Communist Bloc Petroleum Production, Consumption, and
Exports to the Non-Communist World, 1952–1972

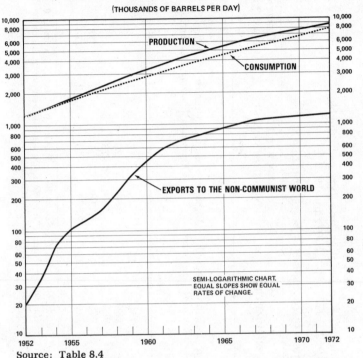

(THOUSANDS OF BARRELS PER DAY)

Source: Table 8.4

Also in 1972, the USSR was exporting about 940,000
barrels per day to its satellite nations, ten times the
94,000 barrels per day it exported to them in 1955. This,
in turn, permitted the satellites to balance their petroleum
requirements and, in the case of Rumania, to increase its
own exports to the non-Communist world. Because the
Communist bloc unified its trading under the direction of
the USSR—which produced well over 90 percent of the
bloc's petroleum output—reference will be made hereafter
to net Communist bloc exports to the non-Communist
world (see Figure 8.3 and Table 8.4).

In 1952 the Communist bloc was a negligible exporter

TABLE 8.4

Communist Bloc Petroleum Production, Consumption, and Exports to the Non-Communist World, 1952, 1957, 1962, 1967, and 1972

(Amounts in Thousands of Barrels per Day)

Year	PRODUCTION			CONSUMPTION			EXPORTS TO NON-COMMUNIST WORLD			PERCENTAGE OF NON-COMMUNIST WORLD EXPORTS TO	
	Amount	Annual Growth Amount	Percent	Amount	Annual Growth Amount	Percent	Amount	Annual Growth Amount	Percent	Bloc Production	Foreign Non-Communist World Consumption
1952	1,199	163	16	1,180	150	15	19	13	217	2	0.5
1957	2,325	291	14	2,165	262	14	160	29	22	7	2.3
1962	4,166	421	11	3,553	386	12	683	73	12	16	6.8
1967	6,334	434	7	5,328	373	8	1,118	39	4	18	6.8
1972	8,856	557	7	7,964	710	10	1,204	40	3	14	4.6

Sources: National Petroleum Council, *Impact of Oil Exports from the Soviet Bloc* (Washington, D.C.: National Petroleum Council, 1962); Robert J. Ebel, *The Petroleum Industry of the Soviet Union* (New York: American Petroleum Institute, 1961); United States Bureau of Mines; *Oil and Gas Journal; Petroleum Press Service;* and *Platt's Oilgram.*

of oil, but, by 1972, it had become an exporter of 1.2 million barrels per day to the non-Communist world. All of its exports went to Europe, mainly Scandinavia, West Germany, and Italy. The increase in exports was astonishing compared to that in Communist bloc production or consumption. Communist bloc exports rose from a negligible share of foreign non-Communist world consumption in 1952 to over 6.5 percent in 1961, but fell to 4.6 percent in 1972. Because (two-thirds of) these exports went to Europe, Communist bloc exports constituted nearly 10 percent of Western European petroleum consumption in 1972.

SOVIET EXPORT POLICIES AND PRICES

Soviet reentry into foreign oil markets during the 1950s was well organized, versatile in method, and wide in scope. The Soviet Oil Exporting Agency (Soyuzneft-export) established foreign offices. It entered into a variety of marketing arrangements, ranging from direct retailing in Finland, to establishment of foreign brokers in the United Kingdom, to direct supply contracts in Italy, to technical assistance and aid to the government petroleum company in India. By the end of 1962, the Communist bloc was doing business on four continents with at least forty-five nations; and it has since continued these widespread exports (see Table 8.5).

The Soviet Union used two key marketing strategies. One was to conclude trade agreements under which other nations committed themselves to purchase specified minimal quantities of Communist bloc petroleum in return for Communist bloc purchases of their own products. The other was to grant credits to foreign governments, payable in Communist bloc oil, engineering services, equipment, or materials in order to foster national oil industries. Even by the end of 1962, the USSR had granted over $550 million in such credits to underdeveloped nations.[9] This served the dual purposes of introducing Russian

TABLE 8.5

Petroleum Imports from the Communist Bloc by NATO Countries, 1961 and 1972

(*Amounts in Barrels per Day*)

Country	1961			1972		
	Product Equivalent of Bloc Imports	Total Product Consumption	Bloc Imports as Percentage of Product Consumption	Product Equivalent of Bloc Imports	Total Product Consumption	Bloc Imports as Percentage of Product Consumption
Belgium	6,500	170,000	3.8	16,000	612,000	2.7
Denmark	5,500	115,000	4.7	26,000	378,000	6.9
France	20,000	595,000	3.6	74,000	2,241,000	3.3
Germany	78,000	757,000	10.3	161,000	2,769,000	5.8
Greece	20,500	55,000	37.9	24,000	174,000	13.8
Iceland	6,500	7,000	93.1	8,000	11,000	72.7
Italy	121,000	528,500	22.9	152,000	2,079,000	7.3
Netherlands	400	260,000	0.1	31,000	824,000	3.8
Norway	6,000	77,000	7.6	32,000	172,000	18.6
Portugal	500	37,000	1.5	. . . . .	116,000	. . . .
Turkey	800	37,000	2.0	. . . . .	206,000	. . . .
United Kingdom	3,000	967,000	0.3	5,000	2,242,000	0.2
Total	271,000	3,608,000	7.5	529,000	11,824,000	4.5

Sources: *Soviet Economic Offensive, Special Study Mission Report; Petroleum Press Service*, May, 1973, p. 170; and United States Bureau of Mines, *International Petroleum Annual*, 1972.

technicians into foreign countries and promoting social-
ism. In addition, the Soviet Union concluded trade agreements or oil supply contracts with foreign governments,
government oil companies, and private refiners and marketers, as circumstances required.[10]

Soviet competition was often a disrupting force in
Western petroleum markets because of the unorthodox
methods of the Communist trading monopoly and its
freedom from normal commercial constraints. It was able
to barter oil with other countries having surpluses of particular commodities and even to buy up entire agricultural
crops or the output of industrial plants. It could play off
one private firm against another. It could discriminate
with impunity among purchasers or suppliers with respect
to prices. It could sell for cash to countries with "hard"
currencies, and barter with those whose currencies were
"soft." All of these advantages made it a strong competitor of private oil companies and a threat to the system of
nondiscriminatory, multilateral trade in the West.[11]

Telling evidence of the disruptive character of Soviet
competition was the blatant price discrimination practiced by its oil trust, between non-Communist buyers of
oil and the Communist buyers. Over the period from 1955
to 1960, export prices of USSR crude oil *averaged* 50 percent more, $3.31 per barrel, to Communist bloc countries
than the $2.20 per barrel it charged to non-Communist
buyers. The relative discrimination between pairs of adjacent countries was even greater. Thus, in 1960, East
Germany paid $2.60 per barrel while West Germany paid
$1.38 per barrel; Hungary paid $3.06 against Italy's price
of $1.41 per barrel; and the Peoples Republic of China
was charged $2.92 versus the $1.34 per barrel charged
Japan.[12] During 1961, prices to non-Communist countries
were substantially reduced while they held firm for the
European satellites.[13] The Soviet government evidently
preferred to promote oil exports to the non-Communist
world, even at increasingly lower prices, in order to export Soviet technicians and obtain non-Communist goods
and know-how in return. Sales of oil were based not alone

on its commercial value but also on the political value of these benefits. However, this price discrimination was reduced in the later 1960s.

Selective price discrimination was disruptive of world petroleum markets, particularly in view of the oversupply conditions prevailing after 1957. Soviet prices averaged $1.70 per barrel in Europe during 1961. Non-Communist oil would have to be priced at about $1.00 per barrel, f.o.b. the Persian Gulf—30 to 50 percent under the then-current prices and just about at cost (including taxes and royalties to Middle East nations)—to meet average Soviet prices in Southern Europe. The fact that Soviet oil had a low cost would have made the Russian export monopoly a tough competitor even if it had followed a policy of full-cost pricing. Its freedom from the requirement of covering costs made it a potentially destructive competitor.

Up through the 1960s, however, the Russians were selective in pricing. Where competition called for sharp price reductions, they made them; where they were not necessary to penetrate a market, they held to higher prices. Perhaps the only substantial constraint upon a full exercise of their competitive power in the market was a desire to avoid adverse political repercussions from the oil-producing countries. The Soviet Union could not be insensitive to charges of predatory price cutting.

SOVIET EXPORT MOTIVES

The Soviet Union had strong economic reasons for expanding its petroleum exports rooted in the comparative low cost of such exports relative to other Soviet products and foreign oil. Having abundant energy resources and a scarcity of industrial capital and technology, the USSR could reap large gains by trading petroleum for the industrial equipment and foods that its economy lacked or could produce only at a relatively high cost. Given the rapidly rising royalty and tax costs of Middle East oil, the Soviets' comparative advantage may well be greater for oil than for any other major commodity acceptable in international trade. Thus, the rapid buildup of the petroleum industry reflected a rational, strategic decision of Soviet economic planners. While it meant turning away from the policy of economic autarcky pursued under Stalin, it was a means of gaining quicker access to Western technology and equipment.[14] The major imports which the Soviet Union obtained were, in fact, such high-technology products as petrochemical plants, electronic equipment, automatic machine tools, large-diameter steel pipe and supertankers, and such products of tropical agriculture as coffee, cocoa, and sugar.

The Soviet oil export drive also had important political motives. It was a means of spreading the influence of Communism. By taking Russian personnel and Russian products into the far corners of the world, petroleum exports were a device for creating dependence of other countries upon the USSR, for fostering government-to-government trading, and for undermining the influence of private oil enterprises. The Soviet Union consistently promoted governmental intervention in the oil industry. Sixty-four percent of its crude oil and 22 percent of its product exports to the West were sold to *government-owned* companies.

What were the Soviet Union's ultimate export goals? E. B. Gurov, the head of Soyuzneftexport, said in 1960:

> We have not entered the market to upset the traditional position of other sellers; but to regain our legitimate position among the exporting nations—the position we held during the prewar period, and which we were compelled to abandon owing to the war and later on account of the need to rebuild our national industry in the immediate postwar period.[15]

Bearing in mind that the Soviet Union supplied 19 percent of European oil imports in the period from 1930 to 1933, the implication was clear that the Soviet oil export goals were still far short of fulfillment.

EFFECTS ON THE
FOREIGN OIL INDUSTRY

Soviet entry had profound effects upon both the structure and the behavior of the foreign oil industry. So long as the Russian bear stood outside the Western petroleum world, it was possible to analyze the industry solely in terms of Western enterprises. One could measure its growth, concentration, and ownership of reserves, production, transportation, and refining facilities without any reference to the historically large Russian petroleum industry. After its entry, it became clear that it possessed much larger dimensions than had been realized. The Soviet petroleum trust was one of the world's greatest oil enterprises, dwarfing many of the oil "giants" of the West. Soyuzneftexport, its foreign trading arm, was one of the world's largest exporters of petroleum during 1972, supplying a material part of Western Europe's oil needs. In calculating the market occupancy of the Western international oil companies, it has been assumed conservatively that at least the USSR's *export* sales to non-Communist countries, and the reserves, production, and refining capacity relating to those sales, should be included. This served to reduce the concentration of the Western oil industry.

Soviet entry also produced profound effects upon the behavior of the foreign oil industry. Its aggressive and ubiquitous search for markets, using the instruments of price discrimination, dumping, barter and "package deals," tended to reduce prices and to lower rates of return on private investment. These consequences became progressively more important as the Soviet export drive gained momentum in the late 1950s and the early 1960s. Because the disposition of the Soviet oil surplus was in the hands of a state monopoly, animated by political as well as by economic motives and free from the constraints of competitive private enterprises, its impact upon world oil markets was more severe than if the same quantity of exportable petroleum had been possessed by a private enterprise. In many large Western markets, the Soviet export trust was the "price leader"—downward. Western oil companies were obliged to meet its terms or lose their customers. Hence the market power of the private international oil companies was substantially diminished by the Soviet entry.

THE FUTURE OF SOVIET OIL IN WESTERN MARKETS

The widespread fear in the early 1960s that Soviet oil would inundate Western European markets had abated considerably by the early 1970s. Soviet oil production fell short of planned targets, while its own oil consumption and that of the Eastern European satellites mounted more rapidly than expected. Less was left for export to the West. After deducting Communist bloc imports from the West, *net* exports of crude oil and products amounted to under 900,000 barrels per day during 1972—less than the peak of more than one million barrels per day reached during 1968.[16] Communist bloc exports were far below the target of 19 percent of Western European oil consumption set in 1960. The former drive for rapidly rising exports to Western Europe had to be abandoned.[17]

Production from the established postwar oil fields of the Urals-Volga region appeared to be reaching a peak. The costs of the further development of these fields and of the redevelopment of the older fields of Baku were proving larger than expected. Soviet planners were staking much on the development of the Western Siberian fields from which most of the future increase in output was planned to come. However, their remoteness from tidewater would involve heavy pipeline costs, and the hostile physical environment would also raise production costs. Major investments and advanced technology would be required to wring Siberian oil and gas resources from the remote and inhospitable sub-Arctic steppes.[18] It is significant that, since the process of U.S.–Soviet détente began with the visit in Moscow of President Nixon with Secretary Brezhnev in August of 1972, a major concern of the Soviet government has been to enlist U.S. cooperation in Siberian oil and gas development. Should this cooperative effort go forward, however, many years will be required to bring large new supplies of Siberian energy to market.

Apart from the constraints of time and cost upon the expansion of Soviet oil output, domestic consumption may be expected to expand as the Russian economy motorizes. In 1970 per capita consumption of oil in the Soviet economy was less than one-third of that in the U.S. economy, being 7.5 barrels per capita.[19] In view of the rapid increase in Soviet motor vehicle production, domestic consumption of petroleum products could be expected to absorb a larger fraction of oil production than formerly. In addition, the motorization of Eastern European economies would create additional demands for Soviet oil.

Given the rising costs of Soviet oil and the greater use by the Soviet government of full costs in the pricing of oil, it does not appear likely that the future will witness either a new burst of Soviet exports to the West or a strategy of "dumping" oil in the West.[20] On the other hand, oil is likely to continue to be an advantageous export commodity for the Soviet Union and to grow rather than decline in volume over time. As a result of the quadrupled price of crude oil instituted during 1973–1974 by the OPEC members, the Soviet Union reaped great financial benefit. It supported the high prices and criticized the international oil companies for trying to bring them down. Ebel has estimated that by 1975 the Soviet Union may be able to offer non-Communist buyers as much as 1.1 million barrels per day of crude oil and petroleum products.[21] The Soviet oil trust will continue to be a significant competitor in the petroleum market of Western Europe and, some years from now, in the oil market of Japan.

NOTES

1.   Soviet entry is logically a part of the spread of public and private enterprise treated in Chapter 7. Yet the great size and the unusual nature of the Soviet oil enterprise requires that it be accorded a separate treatment.

2.   Widespread discussion of the "Soviet oil offensive" has produced a voluminous literature. In treating the postwar USSR petroleum industry, major reliance here has been placed upon two authoritative sources: Robert J. Ebel, *The Petroleum Industry of the Soviet Union* (New York: American Petroleum Institute, 1961); and National Petroleum Council, *Impact of Oil Exports from the Soviet Bloc* (Washington, D.C.: National Petroleum Council, 1962), vols. 1 and 2. These "semi-official" sources cite official USSR statistics along with estimates and adjustments by the authors.

3.   Heinrich Hassman, *Oil in the Soviet Union: History, Geography, Problems,* translated from the German by Alfred M. Leeston (Princeton: Princeton University Press, 1953), p. 112 and Figure 19.

4.   E. B. Gurov, Director of the Soviet Oil Exporting Agency (Soyuzneftexport), *Proceedings of the Second Arab Petroleum Congress,* Beirut, Lebanon, October 17–22, 1960.

5.   According to one authority, proven reserves rose from about 6 billion barrels in 1937 to around 30 billion barrels in 1950. See Jordan A. Hodgkins, *Soviet Power: Energy Resources, Production and Potential* (Englewood Cliffs: Prentice Hall, 1961), p. 105, citing Department of State, *Energy Resources of the World* (Washington, D.C.: Government Printing Office, 1949), p. 71, and J. Brian Eby, in *World Oil,* vol. 143, no. 3 (1956), p. 182. Exploration work was pressed vigorously and successfully in other parts of the vast Russian land mass.

6.   Robert J. Ebel, *The Petroleum Industry of the Soviet Union,* pp. 7–8, 21, 24.

7.   All figures on crude oil reserves are necessarily estimates, having a continuous range of credibility from near certainty to complete uncertainty. Classifications of reserves are merely checkpoints on this range. In the U.S. petroleum trade, "proven reserves" mean reserves estimated to be cer-

tainly and economically recoverable from zones within the productive limits of producing fields. "Probable reserves" are those estimated to be economically recoverable from extensions of proven zones by extrapolation of surface data and from the use of secondary recovery and other operating techniques. "Prospective reserves" are those estimated to be possibly recoverable economically from unknown or untested reservoirs.

8.   National Petroleum Council, *Impact of Oil Exports from the Soviet Bloc*, vol. 1, p. 55.

9.   Thus the USSR granted $225 million to India and granted or promised credits ranging from $2.8 to $75 million to Afghanistan, Argentina, Cambodia, Cuba, Egypt, Ethiopia, Indonesia, Iraq, Mali, Pakistan, Syria, and Yemen. *New York Times*, Jan. 21, 1962.

10.   When Ceylon expropriated property of United States and United Kingdom companies to go into petroleum marketing, the USSR was on hand to sell products at cut-rate prices until a refinery could be built.

11.   A state trading monopoly possesses competitive advantages over private enterprises in international trade. See Jacob Viner, *Trade Relations Between Free-Market and Controlled Economies* (Geneva: League of Nations, Economic and Financial Publications, II. A4, 1943).

12.   National Petroleum Council, *Impact of Oil Exports from the Soviet Bloc*, pp. 33–39.

13.   U.S., Congress, House, Committee on Foreign Affairs, *Report of Special Study Mission to Europe,* Union Calendar No. 15, House of Representatives Report 32, 87th Cong., February 7, 1963, p. 5.

14.   See, for example, U.S., Congress, Senate, Committee on the Judiciary, Subcommittee to Investigate the Administration of the Internal Security Act, *Soviet Oil in the Cold War*, a study by the Library of Congress for the Subcommittee, 87th Cong., 1st sess. (Washington, D.C.: Government Printing Office, 1961).

15.   E. B. Gurov, Address to the Second Arab Petroleum Congress, Beirut, Lebanon, October 17–22, 1960.

16.   See *Petroleum Press Service*, May, 1972, p. 162.

17.   See *Petroleum Press Service*, September, 1972, p. 323.

18.   See Robert J. Ebel, *Communist Trade in Oil and Gas: An Evaluation of the Future Export Capability of the Soviet Bloc* (New York: Praeger Publishers, 1970), p. 111.

19.   See *Petroleum in the Soviet Union: A Report to the American Petroleum Institute* (Washington, D.C.: American Petroleum Institute, January, 1973), p. 39.

20.   See Robert Campbell, *The Economics of Soviet Oil and Gas* (Baltimore: Johns Hopkins University Press, 1968), pp. 251–52.

21.   Robert J. Ebel, *Communist Trade in Oil and Gas,* p. 114.

9

Changes in the
Structure of the
Industry

THE POSTWAR BURGEONING of oil enterprises throughout the world wrought important changes in the
structure of the foreign oil industry. Competitors multiplied, concentration of the industry was reduced, and the
market positions of the "seven largest" companies shrank.
At the same time, the industry became more heterogeneous with respect to the size, nationality, goals, and
policies of its member firms.

Whether one considers exploration areas under concession, proven crude oil reserves, daily oil production,
refining capacity, tanker transportation, volume of refined
products sold, or investment, the seven largest companies,
taken together, steadily lost position relative to the rest of
the foreign non-Communist oil industry. This shrinkage
was all the more remarkable because it occurred in the
face of huge postwar investments and vigorous expansion
programs by these seven largest companies. But the annual rates of growth of the new foreign oil enterprises
materially outstripped those of the seven largest companies. Indeed, they were twice as great in virtually every

division of the industry (see Figure 9.1 and Table 9.1). Judged by accepted economic measures, during the period from 1953 to 1972, the foreign oil industry passed from a position of very *high* concentration, with less than ten important participants, to one of *moderate* concentration, with at least fifty integrated multinational oil companies, including the Soviet oil trust, plus many additional firms in particular divisions or regions.

FIGURE 9.1

Growth of the "Seven Largest" and All Other Oil Companies, by Divisions of the Industry, 1953–1972

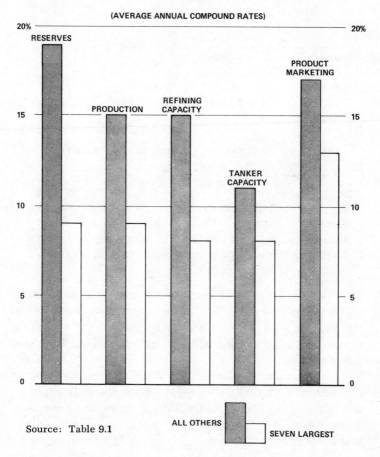

Source: Table 9.1

Table 9.1

Growth of the "Seven Largest" and of All Other Oil
Companies, between 1953 and 1972, by Division
of the Foreign Oil Industry

(*Average Annual Compound Rates*)

Division	"Seven Largest" Companies (Percent)	All Other Companies (Percent)
Proven Reserves	9	19
Average Daily Production	9	15
Refining Capacity	8	15
Tanker Capacity	8	11
Products Marketed	13	17

Sources: Other tables in this chapter.

THE MEASUREMENT OF INDUSTRIAL CONCENTRATION

In referring to the concentration of the industry around 1948, the staff of the Federal Trade Commission wrote:

> Outside of the United States, control over the petroleum industry (including reserves, production, refining, transportation and marketing) is divided, for all practical purposes, between state monopolies and seven large international petroleum companies, five of which are American and two British-Dutch.[1]

Considering the large differences among them, it is doubtful whether, even in 1948, the seven companies could meaningfully be put into one class. Yet it is certainly true that a very high degree of concentration of the industry did then exist.

The subsequent substantial declines in the market occupancy ratios of the largest firms not only diffused the structure of the industry, but, as is shown later, produced increasingly competitive behavior. Although the seven largest companies, taken together, continued in

1972 to own the major part of foreign non-Communist world crude oil reserves, production, and refining capacity, and continued to supply most of its petroleum products, they were faced in virtually every non-Communist market with vigorous competitors possessed of ample supplies of petroleum and backed by large financial resources.

In each division of the foreign oil industry, the "seven largest" companies were not the same firms in each year of the period from 1953 to 1972. There were shifts in the market shares of individual companies, and in their rankings within the industry. For example, the annual shares of the "seven largest" firms in the total crude oil produced by the industry changed unsystematically—but significantly—over the period, as did the rankings of the companies. This is evidence that no effective "market-sharing" scheme was in operation (see Figure 9.2 and Table 9.2).

Moreover, the seven companies themselves were so disparate in size, growth rates, assets, and interests that it was indefensible from a statistical point of view to group them. We have used the FTC grouping of the "seven largest" and "all other" oil companies *only* to compare recent levels of concentration with the very well-known FTC study, not because we view that grouping as meaningful.

A better method of measuring changes in concentration, also used by U.S. government agencies, groups the largest *four* and the largest *eight* firms in an industry, and observes changes through time in their combined shares of the relevant market. A refinement of this method is to observe changes in the "concentration curves" for the industry in successive periods.[2] A concentration curve is simply a line connecting a series of points which successively show the percentages of the total industry market accounted for by the largest firm, the two largest firms combined, the three largest firms combined, etc. A short, steep curve indicates high industrial concentration; a long, low-lying curve shows low concentration.

Concentration in the foreign oil industry can be meas-

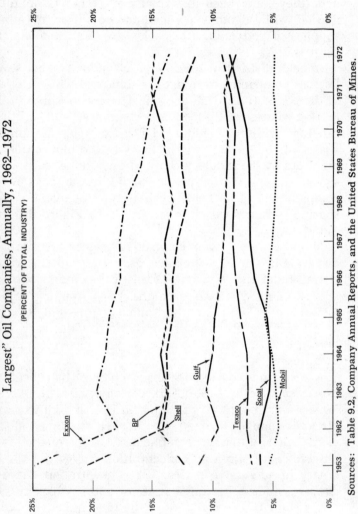

FIGURE 9.2

Shares of Crude Oil Production in the Foreign Oil Industry by Each of the "Seven Largest" Oil Companies, Annually, 1962–1972

(PERCENT OF TOTAL INDUSTRY)

Sources: Table 9.2, Company Annual Reports, and the United States Bureau of Mines.

TABLE 9.2

Shares of Crude Oil Production in the Foreign Oil Industry by Each of the "Seven Largest" Companies, 1953 and 1972

(*Percentage of Total Industry*)

Company	1953 (*Percent*)	1972 (*Percent*)
Exxon	24.9	13.7
B.P.	20.6	14.9
Shell	12.3	11.3
Gulf	11.2	8.1
Texaco	6.7	9.3
Socal	6.1	8.6
Mobil	5.3	5.0
Total—"Seven Largest"	87.1	70.9
All Others	12.9	29.1
Total	100.0	100.0

Source: Table 9.7

ured with reference to each of a number of variables, namely: exploration concessions held, crude oil proven reserves owned, crude oil production, refining capacity owned, tanker capacity, and sales of petroleum and of refined products. Whichever measure is applied, concentration diminished markedly during the period from 1953 to 1972. According to the criteria proposed by Professor J. S. Bain, the industry structure changed from one of moderately high to low concentration in exploration concessions; from high or very high to moderate concentration in the sales of petroleum, ownership of crude oil production, and proven reserves; from moderately high to moderately low concentration in the ownership of crude oil refining capacity and the volume of sales of petroleum products; and from low to very low concentration in the ownership of tanker transportation capacity.[3]

THE REDUCTION IN THE CONCENTRATION OF EXPLORATION

The area held under concession by an oil company obviously does not form an adequate basis for predicting its future proven reserves or production. Nevertheless, concessions are costly to acquire and costly to hold, and their duration is limited. Hence, concession acreages held are significant in indicating the *extensiveness of the search* being made for oil.

It appears that only sixteen U.S. companies (other than the five largest) were engaged in foreign exploration at the end of 1948 and that, excluding a concession to Sinclair to explore all of Ethiopia, their combined area was about 15,000 square miles. Fourteen companies of foreign nationality were searching for oil outside of their national boundaries or territories; and eighteen companies were exploring within their national areas. In total, forty-eight companies (other than the seven largest) were engaged in the search for oil, over a total concession area amounting to perhaps one million square miles. At that time, the seven largest companies had exploratory interests of 1.72 million square miles, or 67 percent of the total.

An examination of the concession areas held at the end of 1972 shows that the situation had completely changed. More than 330 firms other than the seven largest had foreign exploration rights located in 122 different areas on five continents. The estimated total concession area had increased from 2.9 million square miles in 1953 to 9.3 million square miles. The share under control of the seven largest firms had fallen from 64 to 28 percent and the share held by the other firms had risen from 36 to 72 percent.[4] The average annual compound rate of growth of the holdings of the seven largest companies was only 2 percent during the period; that of the others was about 10 percent (see Figure 9.3 and Table 9.3).

Clearly, the newcomers had vastly enlarged the area of their search for petroleum relative to the seven largest

FIGURE 9.3
Concentration of Foreign Non-Communist World Exploration
Concession Areas, 1953 and 1972

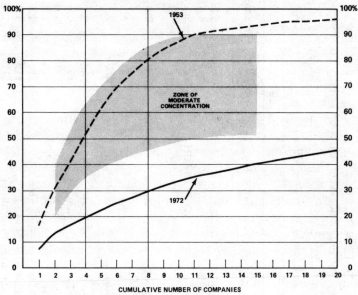

Source: Table 9.3

companies. Given the huge undiscovered petroleum deposits believed to be present in the earth's crust, and assuming average fortunes, many stood a good chance of increasing their proven reserves, and up to 1973 many did so. Concentration was very low.

THE REDUCTION IN THE CONCENTRATION OF THE OWNERSHIP OF RESERVES

Proven reserves constitute potential production of crude oil, and therefore form one significant measure of the size and importance of a company in the oil industry.

According to the FTC staff study, "outside the United States, Mexico and Russia, these seven [largest] companies in 1949 controlled about 92 percent of the estimated

TABLE 9.3

Foreign Non-Communist World Petroleum Exploration Concession Areas of Twenty Leading Companies, 1953 and 1972

(*Amounts in Thousands of Square Miles*)

	1953				1972		
Company	Amount	Percent	Cumulative Percent	Company	Amount	Percent	Cumulative Percent
1. Shell	487	16.8	16.8	1. Shell	720	7.7	7.7
2. B.P.	415	14.3	31.1	2. Texaco	526	5.6	13.3
3. Syn. pour l'Etude	300	10.3	41.4	3. SONATRACH	320	3.4	16.7
4. Socal	296	10.1	51.5	4. Continental	282	3.0	19.7
5. Texaco	290	9.9	61.4	5. Socal	262	2.8	22.5
6. Sinclair	223	7.6	69.0	6. Exxon	235	2.5	25.0
7. Exxon	192	6.6	75.6	7. Gulf	234	2.5	27.5
8. CFP	150	5.1	80.7	8. Hunt International	226	2.4	29.9
9. Mobil	118	4.0	84.7	9. ENI (AGIP)	198	2.1	32.0
10. Ampol	78	2.7	87.4	10. Aquitaine	151	1.6	33.6
11. Gulf	75	2.6	90.0	11. YPF	151	1.6	35.2
12. Deilmann	30	1.0	91.0	12. B.P.	144	1.5	36.7
13. Amerada	30	1.0	92.0	13. Santos	113	1.2	37.9
14. Continental	27	0.9	92.9	14. CFP	112	1.2	39.1
15. Marathon	27	0.9	93.8	15. Phillips	112	1.2	40.3

	1953			1972		
	Amount	Percent		Amount	Percent	
16. Cuban-Ven.	27	0.9	94.7	103	1.1	41.4
17. Jaharca	13	0.4	95.1	99	1.1	42.5
18. ENI	12	0.4	95.5	95	1.0	43.5
19. Moriqui	11	0.4	95.9	90	1.0	44.5
20. Union	8	0.3	96.2	87	0.9	45.4
All Others	110	3.8	100.0	5,084	54.4	99.8
Total	2,919	100.0	100.0	9,344	100.0	100.0

Change, "Seven Largest" and Other Companies, 1953–1972

Companies	1953		1972		Change 1953–1972		Compound Annual Rate of Growth
	Amount	Percent	Amount	Percent	Amount	Percent	Percent
"Seven Largest"	1,873	64.2	2,216	23.7	343	5.3	2
All Others	1,046	35.8	7,128	76.3	6,082	94.7	11
Total	2,919	100.0	9,344	100.0	6,425	100.0	6

Sources: *Statistical Studies; Entry Data; Annual Overseas Exploration Report-1973* (Petroconsultants S.A., Geneva, Switzerland).

crude reserves."[5] By 1972, however, the collective share of
the newcomers had risen to 31 percent of the total. Over
the period from 1953–1972, the seven largest companies,
as a group, had increased their reserves almost five times;
but other companies had increased theirs about twenty-
five times, from 6.7 to 158 billion barrels. This relative
growth of the oil stock in the hands of firms other than
the seven largest characterized all major oil-bearing regions of the world (see Table 9.4).

This measurement does not fully reflect the reduction
in concentration of ownership of proven reserves, however, by failing to take into account any of the crude oil
reserves backing up Soviet oil exports to the foreign non-
Communist world. Assuming that Soviet reserves in 1962
were allocated to the foreign non-Communist world
market in the same proportion that total 1962 Communist
bloc exports bore to 1962 USSR domestic consumption
plus its exports to Communist bloc countries, then about
5.7 billion barrels of its estimated reserves were competitive with foreign non-Communist reserves. It would increase the percentage of reserves in the hands of "other"
companies to 21 percent in 1962. A similar calculation
for 1972 would put 33 percent of reserves in the hands of
"other" companies. This represented a striking change
during the period from 1953 to 1972, considering the immense base of Middle East reserves with which the largest
firms began.[6] The proven reserves of the seven largest companies increased at a very high rate: 9 percent per year;
but those of the "others" grew at twice that rate, averag-
ing 18 percent a year.

The relative power of the seven largest oil companies
in foreign markets was, moreover, less than proportionate
to their 67 percent ownership of reserves, because a large
fraction of those reserves was *surplus* oil. Proven reserves
in 1972 would have met non-Communist world consumption at 1972 levels for nearly 35 years. When measuring
competition, the important question concerns the amount
of reserves that will come into usage within a period of,
say, twenty years. If the 171 billion barrel oil reserves of

TABLE 9.4

Foreign Non-Communist World Crude Oil Reserves Owned by the "Seven Largest" Companies and by Other Petroleum Companies, by Region, 1953 and 1972

(*Amounts in Millions of Barrels*)

Region	1953 "Seven Largest" Amount	Percent	1953 Other Companies Amount	Percent	1972 "Seven Largest" Amount	Percent	1972 Other Companies Amount	Percent
Latin America	9,166	77	2,717	23	19,565	60	13,037	40
Middle East	60,937	94	3,853	6	293,985	83	61,317	17
Far East	2,436	94	147	6	11,033	74	3,888	26
Africa	145	89	18	11	26,270	25	80,132	75
Total–Foreign Non-Communist World	72,684	92	6,735	8	350,853	69	158,374	31
Communist Countries	......	..	......	..	....	..	12,350[a]	100
Total–Foreign World	72,684	92	6,735	8	350,853	67	170,724	33

Sources: *Statistical Studies*; Company Annual Reports; and *Oil and Gas Journal*.

[a] Reserves of Communist Countries include only that proportion of their total reserves which their exports of petroleum to the Foreign Non-Communist World bore to their total crude oil production.

the "other" companies in 1972, however, were produced over a twenty-year period, it would yield over 23 million barrels per day and meet more than 50 percent of 1972 non-Communist world consumption. Hence the newcomers were in a stronger competitive position as oil suppliers than a superficial view of their share of proven reserves might suggest (see Figure 9.4 and Table 9.5).

In 1953 only nine oil companies—the seven largest plus CFP and Pemex—possessed a billion barrels or more of proven oil reserves in the foreign non-Communist world. But, by the end of 1972, the distribution of company ownership of foreign non-Communist world reserves had changed substantially. By that date, the "billion barrel club" had been enlarged to include over twenty members, and the "100 million barrel club," over one hundred companies. In consequence, the structure of the industry with respect to reserves changed from very high concentration in 1953 to moderate concentration in 1972.

The structure of ownership of proven crude oil reserves changed dramatically *after 1972*, as a result of the nationalization actions of many of the OPEC countries. The ownership of huge reserves and production facilities was transferred from private oil companies to the government oil corporations of these nations. Petromin of Saudi Arabia and KNPC of Kuwait catapulted into top position among the "seven largest" owners of reserves. Pertamina of Indonesia, NIOC of Iran, INOC of Iraq, and CVP of Venezuela were other government oil companies that displaced private companies as leading owners of the world's crude oil reserves.

THE REDUCTION IN THE
CONCENTRATION OF PRODUCTION

In 1949, according to the FTC staff report, the seven largest international oil companies produced 88 percent of the average daily output of crude oil in the world outside the United States, Mexico, and the USSR.[7] There-

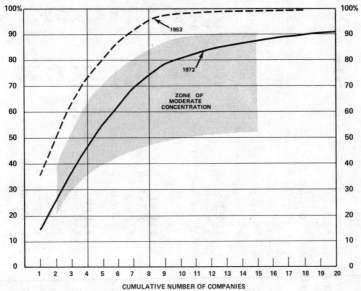

FIGURE 9.4
Concentration of Foreign Non-Communist World Proven
Crude Oil Reserves, 1953 and 1972

Source: Table 9.5

after, their collective position against other companies
deteriorated, and, by 1972, the seven largest firms had
dropped to 71 percent of the market. The seven largest
firms quintupled their output over the period, but the
new multinationals increased theirs almost fourteenfold.
The seven largest companies increased their production
by an average annual compound rate of 9 percent; but
the other companies nearly doubled this rate, reaching an
average annual compound rate of 18 percent over the
period.

The relative expansion in output of the new firms was
not confined to any single region of the world, but was
widely diffused. It rose from 19 percent to 27 percent of
total production in Latin America, from 8 percent to 17
percent in the Middle East, from 6 percent to 29 percent
in the Far East, and from 8 percent to 53 percent in Africa
(see Table 9.6).

TABLE 9.5

Estimated Foreign Non-Communist World Crude Oil Proven Reserves of Twenty Leading Companies, 1953 and 1972

(Amounts in Billions of Barrels)

	1953				1972		
Company	Amount	Percent	Cumulative Percent	Company	Amount	Percent	Cumulative Percent
1. B.P.	28.3	35.7	35.7	1. B.P.	74.6	14.3	14.3
2. Exxon	11.2	14.2	49.9	2. Exxon	61.6	11.8	26.1
3. Gulf	10.7	13.5	63.4	3. Texaco	55.7	10.7	36.8
4. Shell	8.0	10.1	73.5	4. Socal	51.4	9.9	46.7
5. Texaco	5.4	6.9	80.4	5. Gulf	44.3	8.5	55.2
6. Socal	5.2	6.5	86.9	6. SONATRACH	37.5	7.2	62.4
7. Mobil	3.9	4.9	91.8	7. Shell	37.3	7.2	69.6
8. CFP	3.2	4.0	95.8	8. Mobil	26.0	5.0	74.6
9. Pemex	1.5	1.9	97.7	9. CFP	19.5	3.7	78.3
10. YPF	0.3	0.4	98.1	10. Communist Bloc*	12.4	2.4	80.7
11. Ecopetrol	0.1	0.1	98.2	11. AOC	9.3	1.8	82.5
12. Atlantic	0.1	0.1	98.3	12. ERAP	8.1	1.6	84.1
13. Phillips	0.1	0.1	98.4	13. INOC	6.6	1.3	85.4
14. Sinclair	0.1	0.1	98.5	14. Continental	6.3	1.2	86.6
15. Trin. L. L.	0.1	0.1	98.6	15. Standard Oil of Indiana	4.0	0.8	87.4

16. Marathon	0.1	0.1	98.7	3.6	0.7	88.1
17. NIOC	0.1	0.1	98.8	3.2	0.6	88.7
18. Occidental	0.1	0.1	98.9	3.0	0.6	89.3
19. Pemex	...	...	...	2.8	0.5	89.8
20. ENI	...	...	...	2.7	0.5	90.3
All Others	0.9	1.1	100.0	51.7	9.7	100.0
Total	79.4	100.0	100.0	521.6	100.0	100.0

Change, "Seven Largest" and Other Companies, 1953–1972

Companies	1953		1972		Change 1953–1972		Compound Annual Rate of Growth
	Amount	Percent	Amount	Percent	Amount	Percent	Percent
"Seven Largest"	72.7	91.6	350.9	67.3	278.2	62.9	8.6
Others	6.7	8.4	170.7	32.7	164.0	37.1	18.6
Total	79.4	100.0	521.6	100.0	442.2	100.0	10.4

Sources: Annual reports; *Oil and Gas Journal*; *Annual Overseas Exploration Report-1973* (Petroconsultants, Geneva, Switzerland); and Communist Bloc figures from Chapter 8.

* Reserves of the Communist Bloc include only that proportion of their total reserves which their exports of petroleum to the Foreign Non-Communist World bore to their total crude oil production.

TABLE 9.6

Foreign Non-Communist World Crude Oil Production by the "Seven Largest" Companies and by Other Petroleum Companies, by Region, 1953 and 1972

(Amounts in Thousands of Barrels per Day)

Region	1953				1972			
	"Seven Largest" Companies		Other Companies		"Seven Largest" Companies		Other Companies	
	Amount	Percent	Amount	Percent	Amount	Percent	Amount	Percent
Latin America	1,829	81	420	19	3,184	73	1,196	27
Middle East	2,238	92	187	8	15,031	83	3,032	17
Far East	310	94	21	6	1,340	71	548	29
Africa	45	92	4	8	2,645	47	3,035	53
Total–Foreign Non-Communist World	4,422	87	632	13	22,200	74	7,811	26
Communist Countries	.....	..	.....	..	......	..	1,301[a]	100
Total–Foreign World	4,422	87	632	13	22,200	71	9,112	29

[a] Communist Countries include only exports to Non-Communist World.

Sources: *Statistical Studies*; Company Annual Reports; and United States Bureau of Mines.

As was true of reserves, postwar changes in the structure of foreign oil production could only be appreciated fully by pushing aside the veil of the "seven largest" versus "the others." In 1949 the foreign oil industry could fairly be described as consisting of: one giant firm (Exxon) with 30 percent of total production; two very large firms (Shell and B.P.) with 19 and 21 percent respectively; five large firms (Gulf, Texaco, Pemex, Socal, and Mobil) with between 4 and 9 percent of output each; followed by CFP and YPF, each with around one percent of total production. Eight firms accounted for 98 percent of industry output; concentration was very high.

During the years from 1953 to 1972, however, important changes took place in the shares of individual companies in world crude oil production. Some eighteen additional oil companies had become substantial producers. Concentration (the share of production held by the first eight companies) had diminished materially and by 1972 was a moderate 75 percent.

The industry in 1972 consisted of: three very large firms, each holding 11–15 percent of total production (B.P., Exxon, and Shell); six large firms (Texaco, Socal, Gulf, Mobil, the Soviet oil trust, and CFP), each holding 3–9 percent; and eleven other substantial firms (SONATRACH, Pemex, Occidental, Continental, INOC, AOC, Standard Oil of Indiana, Marathon, Atlantic-Richfield, NIOC, and ENI) each with average daily foreign production of more than 200,000 barrels per day. Over the period from 1953 to 1972, the share of the market of the eight leading firms had dropped from 91 to 75 percent. The relative market share of Exxon had fallen from 25 to 14 percent; Shell fell from 21 to 11 percent; and shares fell for four of the seven largest. In every region of the non-Communist world, there were several new major producers confronting the established companies in 1972, each seeking to supply independent refiners with their requirements for crude oil (see Figure 9.5 and Table 9.7).

The world oil revolution of 1973–74, described in Chapter 11, brought further dramatic changes in the

FIGURE 9.5

Concentration of Foreign Non-Communist World Crude Oil
Production, 1953 and 1972

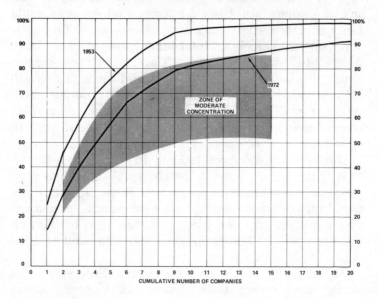

Source: Table 9.7

structure of ownership of crude oil production. As a result of the nationalization of dominant shares in the
producing subsidiaries of the private multinational oil
companies, Petromin, the national oil company of Saudi
Arabia, NIOC of Iran, and KNPC, the government-owned
oil company of Kuwait, became three of the world's "seven
largest" oil producers. Pertamina of Indonesia, INOC
of Iraq, and CVP of Venezuela also gained higher rankings among the largest producers of petroleum.

While concentration of crude oil production is moderately high in the foreign oil industry, it is relatively low in
the *domestic* industry of the United States. According to a
study by the staff of the Federal Trade Commission, in
1970 the top four companies in the foreign world accounted for 48 percent of foreign production, while the top
four companies in the United States accounted for 27 percent of domestic production. And the top eight firms in

the foreign world produced 72 percent of foreign oil, but the top eight firms in the United States produced 53 percent of domestic oil.[8] On the assumption that these measures of concentration are correct and in view of our finding that the moderate concentration of the foreign oil industry has been consistent with effective competition, it would follow that the low concentration of the domestic industry should be even more conducive to effective competition.

THE REDUCTION
IN THE CONCENTRATION
OF REFINING CAPACITY

The postwar rise of new foreign oil enterprises was even more remarkable in refining than in crude oil reserves or production. The staff of the FTC found that in 1953 the "seven largest" companies together owned more than 79 percent of the world's crude oil refining capacity outside the United States, Canada, and the Communist countries.[9] Nineteen years later, in 1972, it had shrunk to 49 percent. The proportion of crude oil processing facilities in the hands of newcomers rose from about 27 to 51 percent. Their average annual rate of growth (14 percent, compounded) was extraordinarily high, and not far from twice that of the seven largest. They added over half of the total refining capacity built between 1953 and 1972. Moreover, the active refinery construction programs of the new firms under way at the end of 1972 promised to increase their share still more in the future.[10] (See Table 9.8.)

The encroachment of the new companies on the refining market was substantial in every region between 1953 and 1962. In Latin America, the new firms' collective share rose from 33 to 49 percent; in Western Europe, from 35 to 45 percent; in the Far East, from 23 to 66 percent; in the Middle East, from 2 to 37 percent, and in Africa, from 68 to 70 percent.

TABLE 9.7

Foreign Non-Communist World Crude Oil Production of Twenty Leading Companies, 1953 and 1972

(Amounts in Thousands of Barrels per Day)

| | 1953 | | | | 1972 | | |
Company	Amount	Percent	Cumulative Percent	Company	Amount	Percent	Cumulative Percent
1. Exxon	1,261	24.9	24.9	1. B.P.	4,664	14.9	14.9
2. Shell	1,046	20.6	45.5	2. Exxon	4,299	13.7	28.6
3. B.P.	623	12.3	57.8	3. Shell	3,531	11.3	39.9
4. Gulf	571	11.2	69.0	4. Texaco	2,912	9.3	49.2
5. Texaco	339	6.7	75.7	5. Socal	2,690	8.6	57.8
6. Socal	310	6.1	81.8	6. Gulf	2,529	8.1	65.9
7. Mobil	272	5.3	87.1	7. Mobil	1,575	5.0	70.9
8. Pemex	198	3.9	91.0	8. Communist Bloc*	1,301	4.2	75.1
9. CFP	154	3.1	94.1	9. CFP	977	3.1	78.2
10. YPF	64	1.2	95.3	10. SONATRACH	925	2.9	81.1
11. Ecopetrol	34	0.7	96.0	11. Pemex	440	1.4	82.5
12. Atlantic	18	0.4	96.4	12. Occidental	424	1.3	83.8
13. Phillips	18	0.4	96.8	13. Continental	334	1.1	84.9
14. Trin. L. L.	17	0.3	97.1	14. INOC	333	1.1	86.0
15. Sinclair	16	0.3	97.4	15. AOC	331	1.1	87.1

	1953			1972		
	Amount	Percent		Amount	Percent	
16. Ultramar	12	0.2	97.6			
17. Lobitos	11	0.2	97.8			
18. Trin. Pet. D.	9	0.2	98.0			
19. Apex	8	0.2	98.2			
20. Anglo Ec.	7	0.1	98.3			
All Others	86	1.7	100.0			
Total	5,074	100.0	100.0			
16. Standard Oil of Indiana				267	0.9	88.0
17. Marathon				266	0.8	88.8
18. Atlantic-Richfield				257	0.8	89.6
19. NIOC				248	0.8	90.4
20. ENI				199	0.6	91.0
All Others				2,810	9.0	100.0
Total				31,312	100.0	100.0

Change, "Seven Largest" and Other Companies, 1953–1972

Companies	1953		1972		Change 1953–1972		Compound Annual Rate of Growth
	Amount	Percent	Amount	Percent	Amount	Percent	Percent
"Seven Largest"	4,422	87.1	22,200	70.9	17,779	67.8	9
Others	652	12.9	9,112	29.1	8,459	32.2	15
Total	5,074	100.0	31,312	100.0	26,238	100.0	10

Sources: 1953 figures from *Statistical Studies*; 1972 figures from Company Annual Reports and United States Bureau of Mines.

* Communist Bloc figures include only exports to the Non-Communist World.

TABLE 9.8

Foreign Crude Oil Refining Capacity Owned by the "Seven Largest" and by Other Petroleum Companies, by Region, 1953 and 1972

(*Amounts in Thousands of Barrels per Day*)

Region	1953				1972			
	"Seven Largest" Companies		Other Companies		"Seven Largest" Companies		Other Companies	
	Amount	Percent	Amount	Percent	Amount	Percent	Amount	Percent
Latin America	1,131	67	566	33	3,316	51	3,228	49
Western Europe	1,200	65	644	35	9,542	55	7,668	45
Middle East	989	98	21	2	1,562	63	922	37
Far East	344	77	105	23	2,693	34	5,223	66
Africa	25	32	54	68	303	30	691	70
Total–Foreign Non-Communist World	3,690	73	1,389	27	17,416	50	17,732	50
Communist Bloc	.....	..	.....	..	......	..	674[a]	100
Total–Foreign	3,690	73	1,389	27	17,416	49	18,406	51

Sources: *Statistical Studies*; and *Oil and Gas Journal*.

[a] Communist Bloc includes only that required to refine products exported to the Foreign Non-Communist World.

An examination of the structure of the ownership of foreign non-Communist refining capacity by individual companies reveals further striking changes. In 1949 the industry consisted of three giant firms (Exxon, Shell, and B.P.) with 66 percent of capacity, followed by four large firms (Texaco, Socal, Mobil, and Gulf) with another 14 percent, and followed by a considerable number of medium-sized and smaller firms with the balance of 20 percent. The level of concentration was high.

By the end of 1972, however, the degree of concentration had become much more diffuse. Concentration had become moderately low. Dozens of firms each had a capacity of 100,000 barrels per day or more. Exxon and Shell, with 13 and 12 percent respectively, and B.P. with 8 percent, were still far ahead of the field; but their combined total had fallen from 59 to 33 percent of capacity. Texaco, Mobil, Socal, and Gulf each had capacities of 2.8 to 5 percent of the total. In addition, thirteen other firms had capacities of between 260,000 and 800,000 barrels per day (see Figure 9.6 and Table 9.9).

By 1972, in most of the major petroleum importing countries, refineries of the large integrated oil companies competed with unaffiliated domestic refiners. Many national companies owned capacities in their countries greater than those owned by any of the seven largest firms except Exxon, Shell, and B.P. Thus, in Japan, four of the seven biggest refining companies were not affiliated with any of the "seven largest" multinational oil companies.

In Germany, affiliates of Exxon, Shell, and B.P. ranked first, second, and third in refining capacity, but the next seven were primarily German companies. In Italy, the three largest refiners were Italian firms. In France, CFP's capacity far outstripped that of any other refiner. The concept of the "seven largest" firms had as little relevance to the refining markets of many important countries as it had to refining in the foreign non-Communist world area as a whole.

FIGURE 9.6
Concentration of Foreign Non-Communist World Crude Oil
Refining Capacity, 1953 and 1972

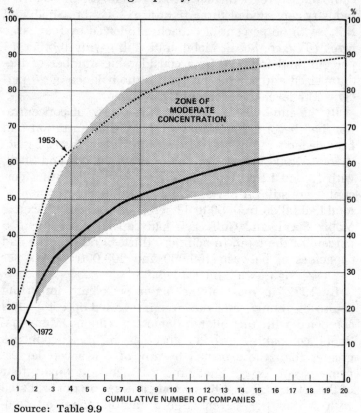

Source: Table 9.9

THE REDUCTION
IN THE CONCENTRATION
OF TANKER CAPACITY

The staff of the FTC estimated that, in 1948, the "seven largest" international oil companies owned or controlled under long-term charter about 50 percent of the non-Communist world's total tanker tonnage. Including only *owned* capacity, the seven largest firms possessed about 35 percent of the fleet. During the postwar years, there was a steady erosion of their position as a result of the much faster growth of tanker tonnage owned by other oil companies, by private shipping companies, and by governments. By 1953 the seven largest oil companies owned or managed 29 percent, and by 1972 the figure was 19 percent. Their compound annual rate of growth during the period from 1953 to 1972 was about 8 percent compared to the 11 percent growth rate achieved by other companies. The largest—and most rapidly growing—fraction of the tanker fleet was owned and managed by non-oil companies and by oil companies other than the seven largest. Facing immense requirements for capital in other divisions of the industry, oil companies were content to let other firms supply more of their shipping requirements (see Figure 9.7 and Table 9.10).

Between 1953 and 1972, total deadweight tanker tonnage of the non-Communist world sextupled, although the number of ships in the fleet rose very little. The reason for this was that most of the newly constructed vessels were of large size, capable of moving oil at higher speeds and at lower per-barrel costs than the older smaller tankers. In 1953 the seven largest oil companies collectively owned 47 percent of total "supertanker" tonnage; by 1972, their ownership of these carriers represented only 19 percent of non-Communist tonnage of this type. In 1974 a commonly quoted size for a "supertanker" was at least 100,000 deadweight tons. Tankers over 200,000 deadweight tons were called "Very Large Crude Carriers" (VLCCs), and those over 500,000 deadweight tons, "Ultra Large Crude Carriers" (ULCCs).

THE REDUCTION IN THE CONCENTRATION OF PRODUCT MARKETING

Because the ultimate aim of business is to sell products profitably to consumers, concentration in the occupancy of petroleum product markets is a matter of prime importance.

Table 9.9
Foreign Non-Communist World Refining Capacity of Twenty Leading Companies, 1953 and 1972
(Amounts in Thousands of Barrels per Day)

	1953				1972		
Company	Amount	Percent	Cumulative Percent	Company	Amount	Percent	Cumulative Percent
1. Shell	1,132.6	22.3	22.3	1. Exxon	4,697	13.1	13.1
2. Exxon	960.6	18.9	41.2	2. Shell	4,295	12.0	25.1
3. B.P.	909.4	17.9	59.1	3. B.P.	2,910	8.1	33.2
4. Texaco	225.1	4.4	63.5	4. Texaco	1,810	5.1	38.3
5. Pemex	209.5	4.1	67.6	5. Mobil	1,352	3.8	42.1
6. Mobil	205.8	4.1	71.7	6. Socal	1,346	3.8	45.9
7. Socal	195.2	3.8	75.5	7. Gulf	1,006	2.8	48.7
8. CFP	154.0	3.0	78.5	8. CFP	739	2.1	50.8
9. YPF	141.7	2.8	81.3	9. Communist Bloc*	674	1.9	52.7
10. Trin. L. L.	80.0	1.6	82.9	10. Petrobras	660	1.8	54.5
11. Gulf	61.1	1.2	84.1	11. Pemex	625	1.7	56.2
12. Petrofina	36.0	0.7	84.8	12. Idemitsu	532	1.5	57.7
13. Antar	34.9	0.6	85.5	13. Mediterranean	480	1.3	59.0
14. Ecopetrol	32.5	0.6	86.1	14. Pertamina	420	1.2	60.2
15. CEPSA	28.2	0.6	86.7	15. YPF	359	1.0	61.2

	1953 Amount	Percent	Cum.		1972 Amount	Percent	Cum.
16. Un. Rhein.	28.0	0.6	87.3	16. Sincat	314	0.9	62.1
17. Gelsenberg	28.0	0.6	87.9	17. ELF	307	0.9	63.0
18. ANCAP	25.2	0.5	88.4	18. Maruzen	283	0.8	63.8
19. ENI	25.1	0.5	88.9	19. Yugoslav Gov.	274	0.8	64.6
20. Nippon Oil	24.0	0.5	89.4	20. CEPSA	262	0.7	65.3
All Others	542.2	10.6	100.0	All Others	12,477	34.7	100.0
Total	5,079.1	100.0	100.0	Total	35,822	100.0	100.0

Change, "Seven Largest" and Other Companies, 1953–1972

Companies	1953 Amount	Percent	1972 Amount	Percent	Change 1953–1972 Amount	Percent	Compound Annual Rate of Growth Percent
"Seven Largest"	3,689.7	72.6	17,416	48.6	13,726	45.0	8.5
Others	1,389.4	27.4	18,406	51.4	17,017	55.0	14.6
Total	5,079.1	100.0	35,822	100.0	30,743	100.0	10.8

Sources: *Statistical Studies*; figures for Communist Bloc from Chapter 8; and *Oil and Gas Journal*.
* Communist Bloc capacity includes only that required to refine products exported to the Foreign Non-Communist World.

FIGURE 9.7
Concentration of Owned Non-Communist World Tanker
Capacity, 1953 and 1972

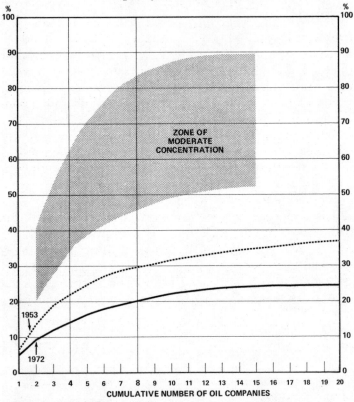

Source: Table 9.10

In discussing this matter for the years 1949 and 1950, the staff of the FTC wrote:

> . . . it does not appear necessary to develop any elaborate statistical argument to support the conclusion that the seven international oil companies have a highly concentrated control over marketing. Such control would seem to be inevitable for the simple reason that there are no other companies operating in international markets capable of supplying petroleum products in substantial quantities.[11]

Accepting the logic of this argument, and noting that scores of substantial public and private enterprises (including the Soviet Union) had entered the industry between 1953 and 1972, that collectively these firms had increased their ownership of crude oil reserves from one-twelfth to one-third of the total, that they had raised their percentage of annual production from 13 to 29 percent of the total, and that they had moved from ownership of 27 percent of refining capacity to 51 percent of the total, it would follow that there was *not* by the 1970s a high concentration in foreign petroleum product marketing.

While simple logic leads to this conclusion, there is also direct evidence to support it. In 1953 only a handful of firms other than the seven largest were marketing petroleum products outside their own countries, and few were important factors even in their national markets. By 1972, as has been seen, dozens of Americans and foreign firms had moved into the European, African, Asian, and Latin American markets. Most of the new firms began international marketing in the late 1950s and early 1960s.

Estimates were made by the author of sales in principal Eastern Hemisphere (Europe, Africa, and Asia) markets during 1953 and 1972. The estimates show that the seven largest companies increased their sales elevenfold while the new companies (including the Communist bloc) increased theirs twenty times.

The newcomers accounted for almost half of the additional estimated sales of petroleum products between 1953 and 1972. Their average annual compound rate of growth was 17 percent—far higher than the 13 percent rate registered by the seven largest companies. As a result, the newcomers' share of the market rose from 28 percent to 46 percent, while that of the seven largest firms dropped from 72 to 54 percent. The relative gain of the newcomers was most pronounced in the fast-growing markets of Japan and the EEC.

Analysis of the aggregates for the "seven largest" and "the other" marketing firms discloses significant changes in the structure of Eastern Hemisphere petroleum prod-

TABLE 9.10

Non-Communist World Tanker Capacity Owned or Managed by Twenty Leading Companies, 1953 and 1972

(Amounts in Thousands of Deadweight Tons)

	1953				1972		
Company	Amount	Percent	Cumulative Percent	Company	Amount	Percent	Cumulative Percent
1. Shell	2,518	7.3	7.3	1. Exxon	10,922	5.0	5.0
2. Exxon	2,168	6.3	13.6	2. Shell	9,755	4.5	9.5
3. B.P.	1,851	5.4	19.0	3. Socal	5,540	2.5	12.0
4. Texaco	1,033	3.0	22.0	4. B.P.	5,327	2.4	14.4
5. Gulf	882	2.6	24.6	5. Texaco	5,119	2.3	16.7
6. Socal	827	2.4	27.0	6. Moller, A. P.	3,296	1.5	18.2
7. Mobil	562	1.6	28.6	7. Mobil	2,798	1.3	19.5
8. Atlantic	349	1.0	29.6	8. CFP	2,153	1.0	20.5
9. Sun Oil	344	1.0	30.6	9. Gulf	2,086	1.0	21.5
10. YPF	333	1.0	31.6	10. Idemitsu	1,336	0.6	22.1
11. Cities Service	233	0.7	32.3	11. Getty	1,238	0.6	22.7
12. Petrobras	230	0.7	33.0	12. Petrobras	836	0.4	23.1
13. Standard Oil of Indiana	226	0.7	33.7	13. Atlantic-Richfield	754	0.3	23.4
14. Hunting	215	0.6	34.3	14. ENI	741	0.3	23.7
15. Sinclair	208	0.6	34.9	15. Mediterranea Raff. Siciliana	709	0.3	24.0

Rank & Company	1953 Amount	1953 Percent	1953 Cumulative Percent	1972 Amount	1972 Percent	1972 Cumulative Percent
16. Cities Service	183	0.5	35.4	659	0.3	24.3
17. Petrofina	176	0.5	35.9	609	0.3	24.6
18. Standard Oil of Indiana	173	0.5	36.4	566	0.3	24.9
19. Chinese	79	0.2	36.6	526	0.2	25.1
20. Phillips	50	0.1	36.7	480	0.2	25.3
All Others*	21,882	63.3	100.0	163,440	74.7	100.0
Total	34,523	100.0	100.0	218,890	100.0	100.0

Change, "Seven Largest" and Other Companies, 1953–1972

Companies	1953		1972		Change 1953–1972		Compound Annual Rate of Growth
	Amount	Percent	Amount	Percent	Amount	Percent	Percent
"Seven Largest"	9,841	28.6	41,547	19.0	31,705	17.2	7.9
Others	24,682	71.4	177,343	81.0	152,661	82.8	10.9
Total	34,523	100.0	218,890	100.0	184,367	100.0	10.2

Sources: *Statistical Studies; Clarkson's Tanker Register;* and *Skinner's Oil and Gas International Yearbook, 1973.*
* "All Others" includes several large private shipping companies which are not otherwise engaged in the oil industry.

uct markets. In 1953 the level of concentration was moderately high. Shell, Exxon, and B.P. were the giants, with 55 percent of the market. They were followed by Mobil, Socal, and Texaco with a collective share of 15 percent. CFP, Nippon Oil, Campsa, NIOC, Gulf, Petrofina, and ENI had a total of 13 percent. Many local firms shared the remaining 17 percent.

By 1972 the market position of the "big three" combined had fallen (by quite unequal amounts) from 55 to 36 percent. Texaco, Mobil, and Socal followed with a combined share of 16 percent. CFP, Nippon Oil, Aral, Idemitsu, the Communist bloc, Kyodo, and ENI had enlarged their collective market occupancy to 16 percent. The balance of 32 percent was shared by a multitude of marketers, many of them local firms. The level of concentration for the eight leading sellers was moderately low, in contrast to the high concentration in 1953 (see Figure 9.8 and Table 9.11).

THE INSTABILITY OF
THE MARKET SHARES
OF LEADING COMPANIES

Changes in three structural characteristics of an industry are commonly held to be of value in judging the effectiveness of competition. They are the relative concentration of business among the largest firms, the rate of entry of new firms, and the relative stability of the market shares of leading companies. Consistent high concentration, lack of entrants, and stable market shares do not per se constitute proof of monopoly. But if an industry exhibited these characteristics over a long period, especially in combination, it would be logical to suspect collusion among its dominant members, or at least a mutual recognition of interdependence resulting in a coordination of pricing and production policies. Conversely, the presence of diminishing concentration, numerous entrants, and much instability of market shares of the leading companies in

FIGURE 9.8

Concentration of Sales of Petroleum Products in the Non-Communist Eastern Hemisphere, 1953 and 1972

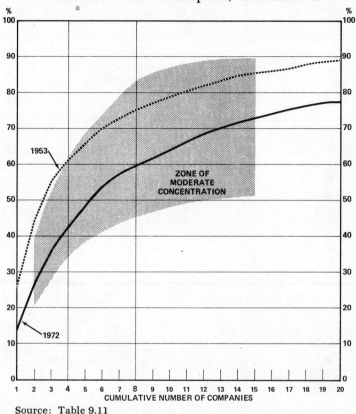

Source: Table 9.11

an industry constitutes presumptive evidence of effective competition.[12]

As we have seen, the foreign oil industry was marked by rapidly diminishing concentration and a spate of new entrants during the postwar era. But there was also much instability in the annual market shares of the leading international oil companies between 1953 and 1972. Whether attention is focused upon the exploration, reserve, production, refining, transportation, or marketing division of the industry, the market shares of the individ-

TABLE 9.11

Estimated Sales of Petroleum Products in the Non-Communist Eastern Hemisphere Markets by Twenty Leading Companies, 1953 and 1972

(Amounts in Thousands of Barrels per Day)

	1953				1972		
Company	Amount	Percent	Cumulative Percent	Company	Amount	Percent	Cumulative Percent
1. Shell	457	26.2	26.2	1. Shell	3,235	14.0	14.0
2. Exxon	315	18.0	44.2	2. Exxon	2,950	12.8	26.8
3. B.P.	196	11.3	55.5	3. B.P.	2,180	9.4	36.2
4. Mobil	105	6.0	61.5	4. Texaco	1,536	6.7	42.9
5. Socal	76	4.3	65.8	5. Mobil	1,255	5.4	48.3
6. Texaco	76	4.3	70.1	6. CFP	979	4.2	52.5
7. CFP	47	2.7	72.8	7. Socal	956	4.1	56.6
8. Nippon	38	2.2	75.0	8. Nippon	644	2.8	59.4
9. Campsa	38	2.2	77.2	9. Idemitsu	556	2.4	61.8
10. NIOC	29	1.6	78.8	10. Communist Bloc	540	2.3	64.1
11. Gulf	27	1.5	80.3	11. Kyodo	481	2.1	66.2
12. Petrofina	27	1.5	81.8	12. ENI	444	1.9	68.1
13. ENI	26	1.5	83.3	13. Gulf	401	1.7	69.8
14. Aral	25	1.4	84.7	14. Petrofina	340	1.5	71.3
15. Idemitsu	15	0.9	85.6	15. Mitsubishi	336	1.5	72.8

	Amount	Percent			Amount	Percent	
16. Mitsubishi	14	0.8	86.4	16. Maruzen	325	1.4	74.2
17. Antar	13	0.8	87.2	17. Daikyo	188	0.8	75.0
18. Maruzen	12	0.7	87.9	18. Showa	178	0.8	75.8
19. OK	10	0.6	88.5	19. Aral	176	0.8	76.6
20. Nynas	8	0.4	88.9	20. NIOC	104	0.5	77.1
All Others	192	11.1	100.0	All Others	5,296	22.9	100.0
Total	1,746	100.0	100.0	Total	23,100	100.0	100.0

Change, "Seven Largest" and Other Companies, 1953–1972

Companies	1953		1972		Change 1953–1972		Compound Annual Rate of Growth
	Amount	Percent	Amount	Percent	Amount	Percent	Percent
"Seven Largest"	1,252	71.7	12,513	54.2	11,261	899	12.9
All Others	494	28.3	10,587	45.8	10,093	2,043	17.5
Total	1,746	100.0	23,100	100.0	21,354	1,223	14.6

Sources: *Statistical Studies*; Communist Bloc figures from Chapter 8; *Entry Data* and Company Annual Reports; *Japan Petroleum Weekly*.

ual companies fluctuated materially from year to year. These changes were sporadic and unsystematic. They reveal no pattern.

The amount of variation over time in the market shares of the leading firms under effective competition will, of course, vary among industries. In general, such variation will be proportional to changes in the products and costs of firms, to the rate of the growth of demand, to the pace of technological change, and to the degree of uncertainty about the future. The postwar foreign oil industry was characterized by changing differences in the costs of oil (primarily because of new discoveries of oil reservoirs), by an explosive growth of demand, by rapid technological changes, and by considerable uncertainty. It would be expected that the fortunes of individual companies and their market shares would vary from year to year, as their management pursued different operating strategies in their efforts to gain sales and profits, and were later proved right or wrong in the marketplace. In such an industry, instability of market shares is an expected consequence of competition, viewed as a multivectored dynamic process. Certainly, the sporadic and unsystematic annual changes in the market shares of the largest firms were inconsistent with the existence of any effective cartel agreement or tacit understanding to share markets.

THE INCREASED HETEROGENEITY OF THE INDUSTRY

The increasing diversity of member firms was another structural change in the foreign oil industry during the postwar era. New entrants not only enlarged the number of competitors, but also introduced heterogeneity. They included companies with interests in production or marketing in a single region as well as those with far-flung interests; refiners and marketers who reached backward for crude oil production, as well as producers who integrated forward for markets; government oil monopolies;

government-interest companies as well as private enterprises; and a miscellany of powerful automotive, chemical, transportation, and other non-oil firms seeking investment diversification.

There was also a growing divergence in the economic interests of the established multinational oil companies. As time passed, new oil discoveries (e.g., North Africa and the North Sea), the rise of new markets to prominence (e.g., Japan), and heavier taxation changed the balance of interests of these companies. The management of each firm had a more complex task of achieving its goal of maximizing its net returns after taxes on integrated operations. This led to more diverse policies.

The rising heterogeneity of the industry eliminated any real possibility of an effective concert of action among its members. Concerted control of an industry presupposes not only a small number of firms but also a strong community of interests. By the 1960s, the foreign oil industry was composed of many types of firms in its various divisions, each with a different motivation, strategy, and economic interest. The market action of none of them could be predicted confidently by competitors. It would be fanciful to suppose that this heterogeneous group of enterprises could be brought together voluntarily to agree on a single petroleum pricing and production policy. Nor could a smaller subgroup limit production or raise prices without provoking a large number of differently motivated firms to invade its markets. The absence of these possibilities is, however, a salient characteristic of an effectively competitive market.

A SUMMARY OF
THE STRUCTURAL CHANGES
IN THE INDUSTRY

The foregoing analysis has produced the following major conclusions regarding the postwar structural changes in the foreign oil industry:

First, there was a large increase in the *number* of substantial enterprises competing with the "seven largest" firms in each functional division of the industry. To a considerable extent, these new competitors differed from division to division.

Second, in every functional division, the "seven largest" companies, taken together, suffered marked declines in market positions as a result of the relatively more rapid expansion of other petroleum enterprises.

Third, the widely disparate sizes of the "seven largest" firms, combined with the rapid growth of many of the "others," made it invalid to describe the structure of any division of the industry in terms of this dichotomy.

Fourth, substantial and erratic shifts took place in the market occupancy ratios of individual companies within the "seven largest." These were inconsistent with any tacit or overt market-sharing among them.

Fifth, the decline in concentration of the industry is conventionally measured by the percentages of the market occupied by the largest four and by the largest eight companies in each division. These measures reveal that, relative to U.S. manufacturing industries in general, the foreign oil industry passed from a position of very high concentration in ownership of crude oil reserves and daily crude oil production, in 1953, to a status of moderate concentration in 1972. It moved from moderately high concentration with respect to refining capacity and product sales to moderately low concentration. It moved from high concentration to low concentration in regard to ownership of exploration concessions. And the low concentration in the ownership of ocean shipping capacity became even lower.

Sixth, many new types of entering companies, as well as discoveries of new oil pools and differential rates of market growth, produced a significant rise in the heterogeneity of participants in the industry. Their widening diversity of interests eliminated any real possibility of an effective concert of action in regard to production or pricing policies.

A summary of changes in the market shares of the "seven largest" and of "all other" companies, in each division of the foreign oil industry, over the period from 1953 to 1972, is shown in Table 9.12.

TABLE 9.12

Summary of Changes in Concentration of the Foreign Oil Industry, by Division, 1953 and 1972

Division of the Industry	1953		1972	
	"Seven Largest" Companies Combined (Percent)	*All Other Companies Combined (Percent)*	*"Seven Largest" Companies Combined (Percent)*	*All Other Companies Combined (Percent)*
Concession Areas	64	36	24	76
Proven Reserves	92	8	67	33
Production	87	13	71	29
Refining Capacity	73	27	49	51
Tanker Capacity	29	71	19	81
Product Marketing	72	28	54	46

Source: Other tables in Chapter 9.

NOTES

1. U.S., Congress, Senate, Select Committee on Small Business, Subcommittee on Monopoly, *The International Petroleum Cartel*, Staff report to, and submitted by, the Federal Trade Commission, 82d Cong., 2d sess. (Washington D.C.: Government Printing Office, 1962), p. 21.

2. For a discussion of methodology in measuring concentration, see, for example, J. S. Bain, *Industrial Organization* (New York: John Wiley and Sons, 1959), pp. 124–33. Also, Gideon S. Rosenbluth, "Measures of Concentration," in *Business Concentration and Price Policy* (Princeton: Princeton University Press, 1959), pp. 57–99.

3. Bain suggests approximately the following standards for manufacturing industries; these are adopted here:

Percent of Market Occupied by the First 4 Firms	Percent of Market Occupied by the First 8 Firms	Degree of Concentration
75% or more	90% or more	Very High
65%–75%	85%–90%	High
50%–65%	70%–85%	Moderately High
35%–50%	45%–70%	Moderately Low
Under 35%	Under 45%	Low

4.   The study *excluded* enormous areas in countries in which government oil enterprises held petroleum exploration rights *within* their national borders.

5.   U.S., Congress, Senate, Select Committee on Small Business, Subcommittee on Monopoly, *The International Petroleum Cartel*, p. 230.

6.   United States and Canadian reserves were excluded from consideration because they were distinctly marginal to the foreign non-Communist world market. To include them would reduce concentration ratios significantly in all years.

7.   U.S., Congress, Senate, Select Committee on Small Business, Subcommittee on Monopoly, *The International Petroleum Cartel*, p. 24.

8.   Joseph P. Mulholland and Douglas W. Webbink, *Economic Report: Concentration Levels and Trends in the Energy Sector of the U.S. Economy*, A Staff Report to the Federal Trade Commission by the Bureau of Economics, Department of Commerce, March, 1974, pp. 62, 63, and 90.

9.   U.S., Congress, Senate, Select Committee on Small Business, Subcommittee on Monopoly, *The International Petroleum Cartel*, p. 25. The report gave a figure of 77 percent for the foreign non-Communist world *including* Canada. We have relied upon the data used by the FTC staff to adjust its figures to exclude Canada.

10.   The weakening of the position of the seven largest firms was even greater than the figures suggest because almost 40 percent of their refinery investments were in locations of declining advantage.

11.   U.S., Congress, Senate, Select Committee on Small Business, Subcommittee on Monopoly, *International Petroleum Cartel*, p. 29.

12.   See Neil H. Jacoby, "The Relative Stability of Market Shares: A Theory and Evidence from Several Industries," *Journal of Industrial Economics* (March 1964), pp. 83–107.

10

Changes in the Behavior of the Industry

HAVING SHOWN how postwar forces affected the structure of the foreign oil industry, it remains to examine their influence upon its behavior. Did the behavior of the industry change significantly in response to the dynamic forces bearing upon it? What happened to competition in crude oil and petroleum product markets, to price movements and pricing methods, to innovation and technological improvements, and to the level of profits and returns on investment?

MARKET MODELS
AND TESTS OF COMPETITION

In analyzing industrial markets, economists have found it helpful to utilize certain abstract models. Among these are the models of perfect competition, perfect monopoly, and oligopoly. The model of perfect competition envisages a market with a very large number of sellers and buyers, none of which is important enough to influence price by its own actions. Participants trade in a standardized commodity, possess complete information, and act under no uncertainty. Entry into and exit from the market are costless. Under these conditions, market price always equals marginal cost and, in the long run, just covers the average costs of production per unit, including a normal profit.

No market in the real world conforms to the model of perfect competition. In reality, information is incomplete and uncertainty is present. Entry into an industry involves varying degrees of cost or difficulty. To realize the economies of large scale and of vertical and horizontal integration, there cannot be an almost infinite number of firms in an industry.[1] Markets are not large enough to absorb supplies from an unlimited number of firms, each of optimum size and efficiency. Moreover, there would be no product variation, innovation, or development of new products in a perfectly competitive market.

The model of perfect monopoly involves a market in which one seller controls the entire supply of a commodity and into which it is impossible for other sellers to enter. A perfect monopolist is in a position to extort abnormally high profits from buyers by holding up his price and restricting his sales volume. And just as the real world lacks perfect competition, it likewise lacks perfect monopoly. Buyers are able to find substitutes for monopolized products, and new firms can usually enter into competition, even though with great difficulty.

Neither perfect competition nor monopoly form desirable goals of public policy. Our society properly rejects private monopoly as incompatible with the public interest. But perfect competition would also be incompatible with the public interest, because consumers would have to pay higher prices to cover the higher costs of small-scale production, and they would have to forego the new and improved products from technological innovation.

Between the theoretical poles of perfect competition and perfect monopoly lies a broad range of market structures. One of these is oligopoly, a market in which sellers are comparatively few and trade with numerous buyers.[2]

In such a market, each seller's contribution to supply is so important that he is in a position to influence price. Each seller is aware that, if he reduces price in an effort to take business away from his few rivals, they may well respond in kind. Unless demand for the product is highly elastic, in the end, all sellers would end up selling little more than before, but at lower prices and profits. From such mutual awareness, there may arise a spontaneous coordination of pricing and output policies without any collusion among sellers. However, tacit coordination of business policies (as well as overt collusion) is limited by uncertainty regarding future changes in the relative costs and bargaining strength of the different sellers.[3] Its probability diminishes as the number of firms increases and as they become more heterogeneous in their interests and policies. Collusion by oligopolists—often called "shared monopoly"—is uncommon because tacit agreements are very difficult to maintain.

Because perfect competition is neither an attainable nor a desirable standard of behavior, we propose the standard of *effective competition,* by which the degree of competition in an industry is judged by the actual *effects* on consumers as measured by the price and quality of products and services.[4] As has been observed previously, the essence of effective competition is *rivalry between independently managed enterprises* in the offering of a mixture of products, services, terms of sale, and prices to the public—a mixture which itself changes through time. The competitive process consists of a continual series of moves and countermoves by individual firms, each seeking to protect or improve its position in the market against its rivals and thereby to enhance its earnings.

What makes the real world of business different from the abstract world of the economic theorist is mainly its *dynamism.* In the contemporary world, the whole matrix of conditions surrounding the firm is constantly changing.[5] In such an environment, the management of every firm is under constant pressure to adapt its capital structure, organization, personnel, strategy, products, services, and processes to shifts in the external forces that impinge upon it. Even more, the management must try to foresee future changes in the environment and make timely adjustments. Change inevitably enlivens competition in an industry because it requires actions and reactions by its member firms. A highly dynamic industry, therefore, will tend to behave competitively, whatever its structure.[6] But a competitive structure—meaning essentially an adequate number of independent firms and the ability of new firms to enter—naturally increases the probability of effectively competitive behavior.

An industry in which competition is effective will exhibit a number of behavioral characteristics. Each member firm will act and react independently. The productive efficiency of each will approach the maximum obtainable. The prices of products will sensitively reflect changes in costs and demand. The rate of return on investment will tend toward a normal level which suffices to retain investment and to finance innovations. Opportunities to make innovations, to reduce costs, to improve products, and to develop new products will be quickly seized. And there will be active rivalry among sellers for the patronage of buyers.[7]

We will apply these criteria of effective competition to four critical aspects of the performance of the foreign oil industry during the postwar period. They are: the behavior of crude oil prices, the behavior of prices for refined petroleum products, the pace of technological change and innovation in the industry, and the returns on investment and the annual volume of new investment in the industry.

COMPETITION AND PRICING PROCESSES IN PETROLEUM MARKETS

Most foreign crude oil is marketed through the refining and marketing affiliates of the integrated oil companies. But a growing fraction is sold, on long-term contracts or in the "spot" market, by the integrated companies and by nonintegrated producers to unaffiliated refiners. Refiners sell petroleum products to wholesale distributors and to large commercial consumers. Wholesalers sell products to retail service station operators. And retailers sell to ultimate consumers. Thus competition in the sale of crude oil and its products takes place at several levels of distribution.

Because of horizontal integration in the industry, a given supplier often sells petroleum in many national markets, each with its own pattern of demand and mode of public regulation. Sellers, therefore, are obliged to differentiate their competitive strategies among countries and among marketing levels in the same country.

The nature of competition in the foreign oil industry is strongly influenced by the heterogeneity of the products and by the importance of transportation costs in delivered prices. Crude oils vary widely in specific gravity, impurities, yield of the various refined products, and, therefore, in value. At any given time and location, there is a whole family of crude oil prices—not *a* single price.[8] Moreover, crude oils are relatively low-valued in relation to their weight and bulk, and are generally produced far from major centers of consumption. Hence, transportation charges form a substantial element of delivered prices and international tanker rates fluctuate widely.[9]

Competition is also influenced by the characteristics of buyers at each of the three levels of distribution. In general, buyers are numerous and sophisticated. In each major national market, several refining companies purchase crude oil. Because its cost is a dominant factor in the profitability of a refining company, its purchase is normally a function of a major full-time executive. Having expert knowledge of conditions in world crude oil markets, these buyers are hard bargainers who cannot be taken advantage of, and they constrain the market power of the crude oil vendor, whether it is a major integrated company or a nonintegrated producer. Likewise, bulk buyers of refined products are numerous and well-informed. They comprise the purchasing agents of manufacturing and commercial companies, building corporations, and railroad and air transportation companies, as well as operators of chains of retail service stations. These buyers often ask vendors to submit sealed bids to supply their requirements of petroleum products. Being aware of alternatives, they cannot be victimized. At the third level of distribution are the millions of buyers of gasoline for automobile operation and fuel oil for home heating. They are indubitably numerous, although perhaps not as sophisticated as buyers at other levels. In summary, the structure of the buying sides of petroleum markets are conducive to effective competition.

A "posted price" in the foreign oil industry traditionally has been a *public offering price by the seller, f.o.b. port of origin,* based on his assessment of the value of petroleum to him, in terms of replacement and opportunity costs, and its value to buyers around the world.[10] While the posted price is by its very nature the most visible to the public, the competitively significant price, is the *actual transaction price of oil delivered to refiners* in the consuming countries. It is an individually negotiated price. An unaffiliated refining company in, say, West Germany, is interested only in the net delivered price per barrel because this is the price which determines his competitive ability to sell refined products in his market area. Typically, various oil-producing firms will offer him a variety of deals designed to satisfy his requirements. Each proposal will involve a somewhat different package of attributes including for instance: a specified *type* of crude oil, an *f.o.b. price* per barrel at the port of origin, a *transportation charge* per barrel from that port of origin to a refinery, a *schedule of deliveries,* and specified *terms* of *payment.* In addition, a seller may suggest a variety of other features to make his proposal more attractive. These may include agreements to provide technical assistance, to make loans or extend special credits, to buy back surplus products from the refiner, or to provide a variety of quid pro quo's. Indeed, the number of different factors that may be involved in sellers' negotiations with the buyer is limited only by the ingenuity of the human mind.

In the end, the refiner will choose that deal which offers him the best combination of factors. A crude oil sale will be completed at a certain price per barrel. Yet it is evident that the specified delivered price is only one of many dimensions of competition.[11] Lack of comprehensive information about other factors in the competitive process makes it necessary, however, to focus upon the behavior of prices.

Because most port-of-origin prices were publicly posted and did not change very frequently up to 1973, whereas delivered prices were not readily available in detail, studies of the foreign oil industry have traditionally concentrated attention upon the movements of posted prices. They have in particular noted the increasingly prevalent practice, after 1958, of "discounting" f.o.b. posted prices to buyers by amounts reportedly ranging from 10 to 25 percent.[12] The downward movement of posted prices after 1957 and the increasing size and prevalence of discounts from posted prices formed evidence of the vigor of competition between sellers. However, competition in petroleum markets also involved rivalry in the quotation of transportation rates, credit terms, and other factors that enter into delivered prices. It would be an oversimplification to regard discounts simply as reductions in f.o.b. prices, without also taking into account the other factors in sales transactions.

If competition were effective in foreign petroleum markets, one would expect delivered prices to behave in certain ways:

First, prices for each major type and quality of crude oil would *sensitively reflect changes in the demand-supply conditions of the products manufactured from it,* rising when demand increased proportionately more than supply, and declining when supply increased proportionately more than demand.

Second, a substantial number of sellers would offer a variety of crude oils to buyers at *prices which varied with their relative refining values in each national market.*

Third, competition among sellers would produce *unsys-*

tematic price discrimination—that is, a random scattering of individual transaction prices around their average —as a result of the imperfect knowledge of buyers and sellers of the actual transaction prices in markets where prices are individually negotiated.[13]

The behavior of foreign crude oil prices during the later 1950s and the 1960s reveals that, measured by these criteria, price competition was effective.

COMPETITION AND THE BEHAVIOR OF CRUDE OIL PRICES

POSTWAR CHANGES IN THE PRICE FORMATION PROCESS

Before World War II, the United States Gulf and the Caribbean were the foreign world's primary sources of crude oil. Eastern Hemisphere consumption was relatively small and yet its crude oil production supplied less than half of its petroleum needs. Hence, crude oil produced in the Eastern Hemisphere was priced to meet U.S. crude oils delivered into foreign markets. At any given point in the Eastern Hemisphere, the price of oil approximated the price at the United States Gulf *plus* tanker rates from there to the point of delivery, irrespective of the actual origin of the oil.

This pricing structure, known as "Gulf-Plus," passed into history as Middle East crude oil came into large-scale production during the later 1940s and displaced Western Hemisphere oils in Eastern Hemisphere markets. During 1948 and 1949, crude oil prices, f.o.b. Middle Eastern ports of origin, were cut from about $2.20 per barrel to $1.70 per barrel. This enabled Middle East crude oils, at prevailing freight rates, to undercut Western Hemisphere oil throughout Europe, and even to compete with American oil in the United States (see Table 10.1).

For nearly a decade after 1949, foreign crude oil prices rose moderately because of the very strong growth of con-

TABLE 10.1
Changes during 1948–1949 in Prices of Leading Crude Oils at Ports of Origin
(Dollars per Barrel)

Quarterly Posted Prices	Saudi Arabia (Ras Tanura) — Exxon	Saudi Arabia (Ras Tanura) — Caltex	Kuwait (M. al Ahmadi)	U.S. Gulf (Houston) 34°	Venezuelan (Puerto La Cruz)
1948					
January	$2.18	$2.18	$2.11	$2.65	$2.61
May	2.18	1.99	2.11	2.65	2.61
July	2.03	1.99	1.98	2.65	2.61
October	1.99	1.99	1.93	2.65	2.61
1949					
January	1.99	1.99	1.93	2.65	2.61
April	1.84	1.84	1.78	2.65	2.61
July	1.84	1.84	1.71	2.65	2.61
September	1.71	1.71	1.71	2.65	2.61

Source: Based on transaction prices reported to E.C.A., adjusted for gravity.

Notes: These prices apply to 34° gravity Arab Mix, Kuwait oil, West Texas sour, and Oficina, at their regular loading ports. Gravity differentials of two cents per barrel were used to reflect adjustments in port-of-origin prices in order to standardize gravities of crude oil. During 1948 and 1949, the Persian Gulf prices were commonly quoted in terms of 36° gravity crude oil, and the Western Hemisphere crude oils in terms of 35°.

Approximate prevailing freight charges per barrel fell radically from 1948 to 1949 as follows:

	1948	1949
Persian Gulf to Northwest Europe	$1.45	$1.00
Persian Gulf to East Coast United States	1.70	1.15
United States Gulf to Northwest Europe	1.00	0.70
United States Gulf to United States East Coast	0.40	0.25
Puerto la Cruz to Northwest Europe	0.86	0.60
Puerto la Cruz to United States East Coast	0.40	0.25

sumption which outran new production capacity. Beginning in 1950, prices were posted in the Persian Gulf, and they were raised twice—in 1953 and again in 1957.[14] Although the oil-producing capacity of the foreign non-Communist world rose rapidly, the Korean conflict (1950–1953), the Iranian oil nationalization (1951–1954), and the Suez Canal crisis (1956–1957) curtailed civilian supplies, and there was a sellers' market throughout most of the period.

The reopening of the Suez Canal in 1957 marked a radical shift from a sellers' market to a buyers' market in the foreign oil industry. Many new crude oil producers entered the market and aggressively sought outlets for their oil. Sharply dropping tanker rates after the Suez Canal reopened brought remote markets "closer," in terms of delivered prices, and thereby permitted more crude oils to compete in each of many national markets. Exports of crude oil and petroleum products by the Communist bloc began to assume major proportions. The rising competition thus engendered was magnified by the action of the United States government in imposing "voluntary" oil import quotas in 1957 and mandatory quotas in 1959, thus limiting access to the huge U.S. market as an outlet for the swelling flood of foreign oil. The rising competition in crude oil markets was further compounded in the 1960s as North and West African oil was added to the supplies available to the foreign non-Communist world.

These basic enlargements of the foreign crude oil supply led to reductions in the prices charged to *nonaffiliated* refining companies. The share of these companies in foreign non-Communist refining capacity was 40 percent by 1962; and their refineries were located in the largest and fastest-growing national markets. Most of the new oil-producing companies lacked refining and marketing outlets of their own. They led the competitive battle by offering lower prices to unaffiliated refiners. The latter frequently used their lower crude oil acquisition costs to reduce their product prices to distributors and, hence, to expand their markets. Competing refiners were forced to meet these prices. Reductions in the level of product prices necessarily reduced the "refining value" of crude oil: the price at which a refiner could profitably sell the products of a barrel of crude oil, after recouping his processing costs. With a growing number of firms eager to sell oil, the whole level of crude oil prices declined (see Figure 10.1 and Table 10.2).

The refining and marketing affiliates of the integrated companies had to compete in national product markets with the nonaffiliated refiners. They, too, had to cut their product prices in order to retain their customers. However, integrated companies usually did not cut the prices at which crude oil was transferred to their affiliates. Thus, with lower gross revenues from sales, some refining and marketing affiliates had lower profits—or even losses—in their operations.[15] The reductions in crude oil

FIGURE 10.1
Quoted Prices of Leading Crude Oils at Ports of Origin,
1948–1972

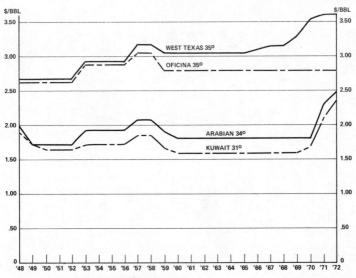

Sources: Table 10.1 and Table 10.2
Note: Year-end data each year.

TABLE 10.2

Posted Port-of-Origin Prices of Leading Crude Oils, Year-end, 1950, 1953, 1957, 1959, 1960, and 1962–1972

(Dollars per Barrel)

Year	Arabian 34° (Ras Tanura)	Kuwait 31° (M. al Ahmadi)	U.S. Gulf 35° (Houston)	Venezuelan 35° (Puerto La Cruz)	Libyan 39° (Brega)	Algerian 40° (Bougie)
1950	$1.71	$1.65	$2.67	$2.63	....	....
1953	1.93	1.72	2.92	2.88	....	....
1957	2.08	1.85	3.17	3.05	....	....
1959	1.90	1.67	3.05	2.80	....	$2.77
1960	1.80	1.59	3.05	2.80	$2.21	2.65[a]
1962	1.80	1.59	3.05	2.80	2.21	....
1963	1.80	1.59	3.05	2.80	2.21	....
1964	1.80	1.59	3.05	2.80	2.21	2.35
1965	1.80	1.59	3.05	2.80	2.21	2.35
1966	1.80	1.59	3.10	2.80	2.21	2.35
1967	1.80	1.59	3.15	2.80	2.21	2.35
1968	1.80	1.59	3.15	2.80	2.21	2.35
1969	1.80	1.59	3.29	2.80	2.21	2.65
1970	1.80	1.68	3.54	2.80	2.51	2.65
1971	2.29	2.19	3.60	2.80	3.38	2.65
1972	2.48	2.37	3.60	2.80	3.61	2.65

Primary Source: *Platt's Oil Price Handbook.*
[a] Posting withdrawn.

prices extended to all levels of operation and to all participants.

Under the impact of rising supplies and growing competitive pressures, posted f.o.b. prices of leading foreign crude oils were reduced repeatedly during 1959 and again in 1960. By August of 1960, they stood about 15 percent below their 1957 level, and even below the level prevailing in 1953. But the percentage decline during the years from 1957 to 1961 in *delivered* prices of crude oils into the major consuming countries was considerably larger: 29 to 38 percent depending upon the crude oil involved. A 1961 report by the OEEC, an organization of the principal foreign oil-importing countries, stated:

> During the greater part of 1959 and 1960, however, posted prices of crude oil have not accurately reflected current market conditions. . . . [T]he pressures caused by: a) the excess capacity in both production and transport, b) the competition coming from companies who were not previously operating on an international scale and for many of whom quick return on their investment is essential, c) the effects of United States import controls and similar governmental restrictions elsewhere, and d) the influx of greater quantities of Soviet oil, much of it at substantial discounts, all led to widespread discounts and other allowances being offered on posted prices.[16]

By 1962 prices of crude oils were being determined from day to day by their refining value in major national markets. The refining values, in turn, depended upon the retail sales prices of refined products in those markets. The costs of crude oil to refiners were not determined by the prices posted by leading oil companies at major ports of origin plus the standard ocean freight rates to the country of destination. Instead, *crude oil price formation had changed from primarily a seller-announced basis to essentially a market-determined basis*. The sensitive reaction of crude oil prices to changes in product prices showed that no company possessed the power to "control" crude oil prices, even in the short run.

The fierce competition that developed in foreign crude oil markets during the late 1950s can be appreciated best by examining the markets of individual countries. The markets of Japan and of the European Economic Community are of special interest because of their large size and rapid growth.

THE JAPANESE CRUDE OIL MARKET

Japan had become the foreign non-Communist world's largest importer and refiner by 1962. Its government released figures on the delivered prices of *individual* crude oil import transactions between 1957 and 1962, which permit a detailed analysis.[17] This analysis revealed a random variation of individual transaction prices around their mean, rather than a single rigid price, a behavior that is characteristic of imperfectly—but effectively—competitive markets in which prices are privately negotiated.

Concurrent with the explosive postwar expansion of the Japanese economy, annual crude oil imports multiplied many times. So did the number of crude oil suppliers and primary marketing firms. By the early 1960s, sixteen companies were importing and/or refining crude oil. Unaffiliated Japanese firms owned the preponderance of the refining capacity. Each refiner characteristically purchased crude oil from two to six different suppliers, who vied with each other to supply his requirements. The crude oils emanated from nearly every oil-producing area of the Eastern Hemisphere and were supplied at a bewildering variety of prices.

The average delivered price of all crude oils sold to Japan during 1957 reached a peak of $3.48 per barrel following the Suez Canal closure. After the canal's reopening, the decline in prices was startling. The price fell steadily over the thirteen-year period from 1957 to 1970 by 48 percent—from $3.48 per barrel to $1.80 per barrel—in the face of a rapidly growing Japanese demand. Prices of different crude oils all fell, but by amounts which were quite unequal from year to year, and without any systematic pattern (see Figure 10.2 and Table 10.3).

This dramatic decline in the *average* prices of crude oil from 1957 to 1970 tells only part of the story. Each Persian Gulf crude oil was supplied by different sellers at

FIGURE 10.2

Prices of Leading Crude Oils Delivered in Japan, 1958–1972

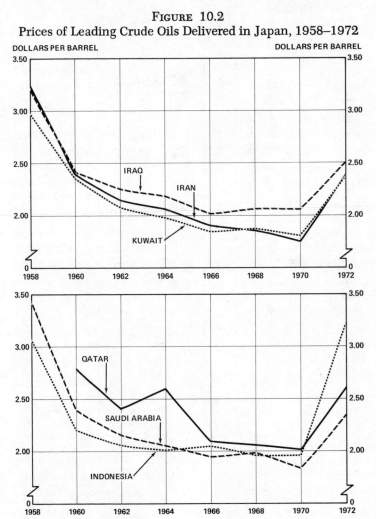

Source: Table 10.3

TABLE 10.3

Crude Oil Prices Delivered in Japan: Weighted Average Prices of Leading Crude Oils

(Dollars per Barrel)

Source of Crude Oil	1958	1960	1962	1964	1966	1968	1970	1972
Iran	$3.26	$2.38	$2.16	$2.07	$1.90	$1.86	$1.76	$2.38
Iraq	3.23	2.40	2.26	2.19	2.02	2.06	....	2.50
Kuwait	2.97	2.35	2.07	1.98	1.85	1.87	1.80	2.37
Qatar	....	2.81	2.41	2.61	2.09	2.07	2.02	2.61
Saudi Arabia	3.42	2.40	2.16	2.07	1.96	1.99	1.84	2.34
Indonesia	3.07	2.20	2.06	2.01	2.05	1.97	1.97	3.20

Source: United Nations, Commodity Trade Statistics, 1958–1972.

prices varying widely around the average. The *range* of individual transaction prices for each type of crude oil was remarkably wide, and the relative spread between the highs and lows in each range differed considerably, both from crude oil to crude oil and from year to year.

The same random variation was apparent in the prices charged by *individual sellers* of crude oil to Japanese importer-refiners. The prices of all vendors fell substantially between 1957 and 1970, but at varying rates and by varying amounts, so that the "price profile" of each vendor reflected his unique response to the particular marketing situation that confronted him, as well as the different "product mixes" offered to customers. Evidently, these differences reflected variations in the relative bargaining powers and skills of buyers, and in the value of delivery, credit, and other nonprice factors in the transactions. They show an absence of control of crude oil prices by any seller or group of sellers.

The competitive character of the Japanese crude oil market is only incompletely revealed by this record of the behavior of prices. Many sales were made upon unusually generous credit terms. Some suppliers agreed to buy back surplus refined products from their customers. Others sold crude oils especially "enriched" with refined products to enhance their refinery yields—a form of quality competition. Large loans were made to refiners at low interest rates by crude oil sellers, and no doubt many other competitive techniques were employed.

Thus there can be no doubt that during the late 1950s and the 1960s competition was effective in the crude oil market of Japan. To be sure, this was not the perfect competition described in economic textbooks, yet it was rigorous and dynamic, as a relatively large number of independent buyers and sellers sought to increase their respective shares of a rapidly growing market.

EUROPEAN CRUDE OIL MARKETS

The prices of crude oils delivered to Western Europe rose by an average of 22 percent between 1953 and 1957, from $3.08 to $3.75 per barrel. With the emergence of a buyers' market after the reopening of the Suez Canal, however, the average price dropped between 1957 and 1965 by nearly 40 percent, from $3.75 to $2.27 per barrel. The net result was that 1965 crude oil prices were about 16 percent lower than they had been twelve years earlier. These lower prices were maintained through the 1960s, despite a gathering general price inflation after 1965, until they were increased in the early 1970s. Even so, the average price of $2.95 per barrel in 1972 was lower than it had been two decades earlier in 1953 (see Figure 10.3 and Table 10.4).

There were wide disparities in the prices paid in the various markets into which crude oils moved. What stands out are the considerable inter-country differences between the average levels of prices, and the unequal upward movements of prices before the Suez Canal crisis and the disparate downward movements thereafter. Differences in transportation costs per barrel and in the mixtures of crude oil types and qualities imported into each country clearly accounted for some of these disparities. Yet significant variances between *adjacent* European countries in the average prices paid even for the *same* type of crude oil remained. These discrepancies could only be explained by differences in national product prices based on the refining values of imported crude oils, in the relative bargaining powers of buyers, and in the importance of nonprice factors in individual transactions.

Price data for *individual* crude oil purchase transactions are not available for Western European markets. The strong swings of *average* prices in response to changes in crude oil supply-demand conditions suggest, however, that such data would show the same random scatter of individual transaction prices around the averages as were observed in the Japanese market. This presumption is borne

FIGURE 10.3
Average Prices of Crude Oil Delivered in Six European
Markets, 1953, 1957, 1961, 1965, and 1972

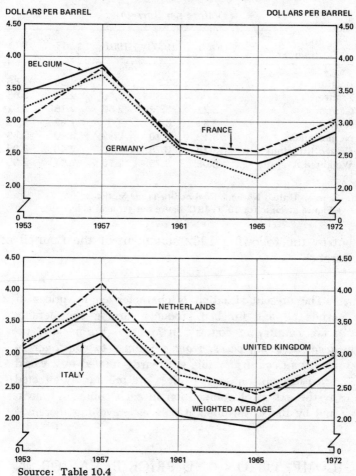

Source: Table 10.4

TABLE 10.4

Average Prices of Crude Oils Delivered in Six European
Markets, 1953, 1957, 1961, 1965, and 1972

(*Dollars per Barrel*)

Country of Destination	1953	1957	1961	1965	1972
Belgium	$3.45	$3.86	$2.60	$2.36	$2.86
France	3.00	3.83	2.66	2.54	3.05
Germany	3.21	3.72	2.56	2.13	3.01[a]
Italy	2.81	3.34	2.07	1.89	2.81
Netherlands	3.12	4.10	2.82	2.40	2.88
United Kingdom	3.19	3.78	2.70	2.46	3.02
Weighted Average	3.08	3.75	2.56	2.27	2.95

Source: United Nations, *Commodity Trade Statistics*.
[a] Figure given is for 1971; 1972 figure not yet available.

out by the following 1962 statement of the Council of
Europe:

> The present situation is characterized by prices of
> crude oil and finished products varying considerably
> from country to country in Western Europe *and in-*
> *deed, in many cases, from consumer to consumer in*
> *the same country*. While still partly related to a world
> price mechanism, actual prices are profoundly affected
> by the extent of competition in each country or area,
> and by the Governmental policies prevailing therein.[18]

COMPETITION AND PRICE BEHAVIOR IN
THE PETROLEUM PRODUCT MARKETS

The postwar behavior of foreign national markets for
petroleum products was too diverse to permit a general
description. Each market differed from others because
each was strongly influenced by a particular pattern of
national government regulation. Attention is first directed
to the international product market, involving petroleum

products moving from the large "export" refineries in the Persian Gulf and the Caribbean, and then to the national product markets of Italy and Japan.[19]

THE INTERNATIONAL PRODUCT MARKET

Prior to 1950, large refineries were built by the multinational oil companies in the Persian Gulf and the Caribbean, near major sources of crude oil. Most of the prewar international trade in petroleum involved products from these refineries and from refineries situated on the Gulf Coast of the United States. During the postwar period, however, products became distinctly subordinate in volume of trade. As petroleum consumption boomed, local refineries mushroomed under the protection of national energy policies. Although products continued to move from the great export refineries, they had become a marginal source of supply in most large consuming countries. The primary source was domestic refineries processing imported crude oil. Prices of imported products thus had to meet those of local refiners, most of whom steadily reduced their prices as the cost of crude oil declined after 1957.

Competition and price behavior in the international product market underwent a postwar evolution similar to that in the crude oil market, although it came somewhat later in time. Before the mid–1950s, "Gulf-Plus" was the pricing rule. Buyers in nearly every importing country paid prices for most products which approximately equaled the f.o.b. prices posted in the Caribbean or the United States Gulf plus freight to destination.[20] Between 1953 and 1957, the posted price of gas oil and residual fuel oil rose—as did the price of crude oil— although the price of gasoline fell. After the reopening of the Suez Canal in 1957, the prices of all three petroleum products dropped heavily and maintained a low level until the 1970s. In 1972 they rose in response to higher taxes by the oil-producing countries and dollar devaluation (see Figure 10.4 and Table 10.5).

Movements in the *delivered* prices of petroleum prod-

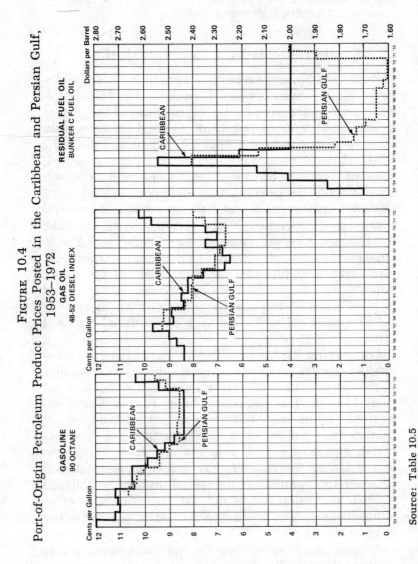

FIGURE 10.4

Port-of-Origin Petroleum Product Prices Posted in the Caribbean and Persian Gulf, 1953–1972

Source: Table 10.5

234

ucts are far more meaningful than movements in posted prices at ports of origin, however, because they take into account discounts from the posted prices, changing transportation charges, and many other nonprice factors. Just as sellers of crude oils to unaffiliated refiners had to meet competition on the basis of delivered prices, so did exporters of products have to lay down their commodities in consuming countries at prices which would meet those offered to distributors by the growing number of local refiners. The average prices of petroleum products imported into the major Western European countries during the period from 1957 to 1972 fell between 22 percent and 46 percent. These declines were of the same order of magnitude as those in the delivered prices of crude oils, as would be expected in markets that are effectively competitive and functionally interrelated. And, as was the case with crude oil prices, movements of the annual averages were diverse among countries and over time (see Table 10.6 and Figure 10.5).

THE ITALIAN PRODUCT MARKET

The national petroleum product market of Italy illustrates vividly what happens when the government favors competition in a market characterized by strong growth.

Over the period from 1950 to 1961, the Italian real Gross National Product rose by 6 percent a year. But annual consumption of petroleum quintupled, rising almost 16 percent per year. Much of this striking gain was achieved at the expense of coal. Lacking significant indigenous energy, virtually all of Italy's crude oil requirements were imported from various countries of the Middle East and from the Soviet Union.

Italy embarked upon a liberal economic policy after World War II. One primary objective was to create an oil industry capable of meeting domestic requirements through local refining. Most wartime economic controls were removed by 1951, after which petroleum refining and marketing were open to free competition. These liberal government policies, superimposed upon a booming

TABLE 10.5

Prices of Petroleum Products at Leading Ports of Origin in the Caribbean and Persian Gulf, Annually, 1952–1972

CARIBBEAN

Year	Gasoline (90 Octane)		Gas Oil (48–52 D.I.)		Residual Fuel Oil	
	Per Barrel	Per Gallon	Per Barrel	Per Gallon	Per Barrel	Per Gallon
1953	$5.04	12.0¢	$3.53	8.4¢	$1.70	4.0¢
1954	4.70	11.2	3.53	8.4	1.85	4.4
1955	4.62	11.0	3.65	8.7	2.01	4.8
1956	4.66	11.1	3.78	9.0	2.14	5.1
1957	4.70	11.2	4.07	9.7	2.55	6.1
1958	4.37	10.4	3.70	8.8	2.21	5.3
1959	4.41	10.5	3.74	8.9	2.00	4.8
1960	4.41	10.5	3.53	8.4	2.00	4.8
1961	4.16	9.9	3.57	8.5	2.00	4.8
1962	3.99	9.5	3.44	8.2	2.00	4.8
1963	3.86	9.2	3.44	8.2	2.00	4.8
1964	3.70	8.8	3.19	7.6	2.00	4.8
1965	3.53	8.4	2.81	6.7	2.00	4.8
1966	3.53	8.4	2.73	6.5	2.00	4.8
1967	3.53	8.4	2.86	6.8	2.00	4.8
1968	3.53	8.4	3.15	7.5	2.00	4.8
1969	3.53	8.4	2.94	7.0	2.00	4.8
1970	3.53	8.4	3.15	7.5	2.00	4.8
1971	3.95	9.4	4.07	9.7	2.00	4.8
1972	4.37	10.4	4.28	10.2	2.00	4.8

PERSIAN GULF

Year	Gasoline (90 Octane)		Gas Oil (48–52 D.I.)		Residual Fuel Oil	
	Per Barrel	Per Gallon	Per Barrel	Per Gallon	Per Barrel	Per Gallon
1953	not posted	not posted	not posted	not posted	not posted	not posted
1954	"	"	"	"	"	"
1955	"	"	"	"	"	"
1956	"	"	"	"	"	"
1957	4.49	10.7	3.91	9.3	2.40	5.7
1958	4.41	10.5	3.86	9.2	2.13	5.1
1959	4.33	10.3	3.86	9.2	1.82	4.3
1960	4.20	10.0	3.53	8.4	1.74	4.1
1961	3.95	9.4	3.40	8.1	1.73	4.1
1962	3.95	9.4	3.40	8.1	1.69	4.0
1963	3.78	9.0	3.36	8.0	1.65	3.9
1964	3.61	8.6	3.19	7.6	1.65	3.9
1965	3.65	8.7	2.98	7.1	1.65	3.9
1966	3.65	8.7	2.98	7.1	1.65	3.9
1967	3.61	8.6	2.90	6.9	1.62	3.9
1968	3.61	8.6	2.81	6.7	1.60	3.8
1969	3.61	8.6	2.81	6.7	1.60	3.8
1970	3.61	8.6	2.81	6.7	1.60	3.8
1971	3.86	9.2	3.15	7.5	1.89	4.5
1972	4.03	9.6	3.36	8.0	2.01	4.8

Source: *Platt's Oil Price Handbooks*, 1953–1972. Prices are annual averages.

FIGURE 10.5
Prices of Petroleum Products Imported into Leading Markets,
1957–1972

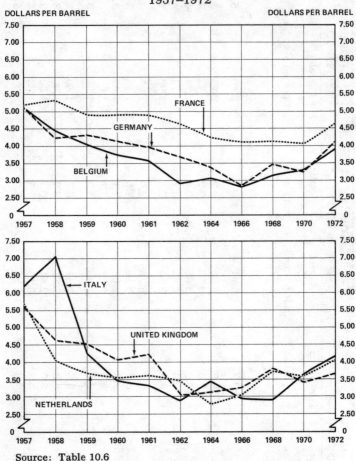

Source: Table 10.6

market, were eminently successful. In 1953 refining capacity was just over 300,000 barrels per day. By 1972 no less than thirty-four refineries, having a total rated capacity of 3.6 million barrels per day, were in operation. Except for some fuel oil and specialty products, all of Italy's petroleum needs were met by the early 1960s by domestically refined products.

TABLE 10.6

Average Annual Prices of Petroleum Products Imported into Leading Markets, 1957–1972

(Dollars per Barrel)

Importing Country	1957	1958	1959	1960	1961	1962	1964	1966	1968	1970	1972
Belgium	$5.11	$4.45	$4.06	$3.75	$3.57	$2.91	$3.07	$2.81	$3.16	$3.27	$3.92
France	5.21	5.35	4.91	4.92	4.90	4.64	4.22	4.10	4.12	4.05	4.64
Germany	5.11	4.22	4.33	4.13	3.99	3.67	3.37	2.82	3.49	3.24	4.07
Italy	6.22	7.05	4.25	3.45	3.33	2.87	3.48	2.93	2.93	3.65	4.14
Netherlands	5.66	4.05	3.69	3.53	3.61	3.49	3.29	3.02	3.72	3.54	4.02
United Kingdom	5.55	4.65	4.54	4.05	4.22	3.05	3.61	3.26	3.80	3.39	3.66

Sources: United Nations, *Commodity Trade Statistics;* also United Kingdom Ministry of Power, *Statistical Digest.*

Italy's refining industry, always comparatively diffuse, became more so. Many of the multinational oil companies owned refineries, plus some twenty-eight nonaffiliated Italian companies. Refineries were supplied by crude oil purchased directly from the multinational oil companies, from seventeen other primary importers, and from the Soviet oil trust. Thus there were many crude oil suppliers and many refiners operating outside of the seven largest firms.

The fast growth of Italian petroleum consumption naturally elicited a rapid expansion of internal marketing facilities. By 1962 there were already forty-six primary marketers doing business. As in the case of refining capacity, there was a decline in the market shares of the seven largest firms. Most of the largest oil companies suffered a marked erosion of position. ENI, the government-owned marketing company, reportedly gained 25 percent of the market and first rank in 1962 as a result of heavy price cutting in gasoline. Petrofina and "other" firms also gained ground. Such unsystematic shifts were, of course, symptomatic of the intense competition that prevailed. By 1962 Italian gasoline prices were the lowest in all Europe, and most integrated refiners and marketers were operating at a loss.[21]

One may summarize the salient developments in the Italian petroleum product market in the 1960s in this way: prices to consumers declined, margins to retail dealers were maintained, returns to independent owners of outlets rose, and returns to integrated primary suppliers declined. Italian consumers were undoubtedly enjoying the fruits of effective competition. The vigor of price competition is shown by the fact that up to 1972 actual market prices were *below* official maximum market prices set by the government by 5–10 percent.[22]

THE JAPANESE PRODUCT MARKET

The spectacular postwar growth of the Japanese economy was accompanied by a rocketing increase in its annual petroleum consumption, to 4.4 million barrels per day in 1972.[23] Governmental policy aimed to minimize the costs of imported oil and to support domestic refining by imposing low tariffs on crude oil and high tariffs on refined products, as well as by utilizing exchange controls for these purposes. Crude oils of the Japanese-owned Arabian Oil Company, which had found large reserves in its offshore Neutral Zone concession, were favored by the government, which put pressure on all refiners in Japan to process it.

Under the stimulus of exploding demand and a protected market, refining capacity increased almost 110–fold between 1953 and 1972, to 4.5 million barrels per day. Among non-Communist foreign nations, Japan rose from thirteenth in refinery capacity, in 1953, to first, in 1972. All of this expansion was financed privately, much of it by joint equity ventures of foreign and Japanese companies or by loans from foreign oil companies, in accordance with governmental policies requiring major Japanese participation. In addition to five of the seven largest oil companies, CFP, Union, and Getty participated heavily in this expansion. Where there had been eight refineries in Japan prior to World War II, by 1972 some forty-six refineries were being operated by thirty different companies, all importing crude oil and distributing products. Japanese marketing became diffuse and pluralistic in structure.

Japanese petroleum product prices sensitively reflected the rising abundance of supplies and the internal competition that developed after the Suez crisis of 1957. Prices of imported crude oil, wholesale prices to dealers, and retail prices to consumers all declined steeply after mid-1957. The average price of imported crude oil fell 48 percent from the peak of the Suez crisis in April of 1957, to June of 1969. This decline in crude oil prices was reflected in the wholesale price of gasoline, which fell proportionately from 1957 to 1969 as did retail prices.

A rising number of competitors and more vigorous rivalry in the sale of petroleum products was characteristic of most foreign non-Communist countries during the postwar era. Developments in the markets of West Germany and of the United Kingdom, for example, paralleled many of those described in Italy and Japan. Throughout the 1960s, consumers of petroleum products were benefiting from active rivalry among many competitors seeking to supply them with their requirements.

INNOVATION AND TECHNOLOGICAL PROGRESS OF THE INDUSTRY

Another test of the presence of effective competition in an industry is whether market pressures are strong enough to force the managements of firms to foster technological development and to make innovations in products and in production processes. Innovation and competition are mutually interacting processes. Successful innovation by one firm compels its rivals to make innovations of their own, thus enlivening competition. The basic question is whether multinational oil companies exerted strong efforts during the postwar period to accelerate technological progress, in order to offer the public better petroleum products at minimum cost.

Petroleum has long been regarded as a progressive industry by students of technology.[24] The discovery, production, refining, transportation, and distribution processes of the oil industry involve the application of a wide range of sciences, notably, geology, physics, chemistry, engineering, economics, and management. In their assessment of the technological performance of the industry up to the end of World War II, Mikesell and Chenery concluded:

> The technology of the industry is as varied and highly developed as that of any industry. Technological progress has proceeded at a very rapid rate. Most developments have been made in the United States, where the

industry is quite competitive, and transferred to the international sphere quite promptly, since the companies involved are the same.[25]

The great size of the technological effort of the oil industry can be realized by the amount of company funds that were expended on research and development. Although figures are lacking for foreign oil companies as a group, those of American oil companies, which, according to the Chase Manhattan Bank, owned 36 percent of foreign oil assets in 1972, may be considered representative. American petroleum firms spent $462 million of company funds on research and development during 1972, continuing a level of outlays for these purposes that they have maintained for many years. Although outranked by the chemical, machinery, electrical equipment, transportation equipment, aircraft, and instruments industries in the *amount* of such outlays, the petroleum industry ranked first in the *proportion* of total research and development expenditures financed by company funds.[26] Evidently, the petroleum industry put forth a respectable technological effort, relative to the opportunities afforded by its scientific base.

Research and experimentation has produced a myriad of practical innovations in all divisions of the industry during the postwar era. The average payoffs of investment in new knowledge were high.[27] In addition to important breakthrough innovations, there was a large accumulation of less spectacular, evolutionary changes so important to overall technological progress that they have been described as a "quiet revolution."[28]

In exploration, research resulted in advances in aerial surveys (photographic, magnetic, and gravimetric), marine seismic surveys, paleontological studies, and computerized seismic analysis. The last technique has recently resulted, through highly sophisticated data processing, in the so-called "bright spot" technique, which in a large percentage of cases seems to indicate accumulations of gas directly.

In the development and production of oil much has been accomplished. Phenomenal advances have been made in offshore and underwater operations which, with minor exceptions, have been postwar developments. The capability of deep drilling has progressed to the point that wells have been drilled to depths of more than 30,000 feet. Innovations have been made in the recovery of oil in place. They include improved completion techniques, such as acidizing formations to enlarge the drainage channels, or hydraulic fracturing, which converts reservoirs that would otherwise be marginal into economic producers. Research in extending the life of producing wells and fields has resulted in the development of such secondary and tertiary recovery methods as water floods, miscible floods, and firefloods (in situ combustion).

The costs of transporting crude oil and its products were virtually halved by the development of supertankers and large diameter pipelines. Supertankers with capacities of one million barrels or more plied the oceans. Pipelines of 48–inch diameter, capable of moving 1.5 million barrels per day, became commonplace.

Striking improvements were made in refining, notably in the development of continuous processing, the diversification and upgrading of products, and in the automation of processes. All this called for heavy investments in modern equipment, making the value added per employee in petroleum refining many times that in manufacturing as a whole.[29] The quality of gasolines increased steadily, as the "octane race" spread to foreign markets. Companies vied with each other to improve quality by the use of a diverse array of additives. The development of catalytic reforming enabled smaller refineries to manufacture top quality gasolines. Exxon pioneered the development of a "vest pocket" or miniaturized refinery (2,500–5,000 barrels per day) which could be used in the smaller markets of developing nations and which could be operated at costs and with product yields and unit prices that compared favorably with plants ten or twenty times its size.[30]

In marketing, B.P. installed a worldwide data processing system to allow it to cut costs and increase profits on complex integrated operations. B.P. also introduced the multi-grade gasoline blending pump to Europe; but it was Murphy of the United States who introduced it to England.

Finally, it must be noted that a vast amount of technological effort went into the burgeoning field of petrochemicals, which, although outside the scope of this study, increased the need for new oil refining plants and opened wide new markets for petroleum producers.[31]

The evidence thus points to vigorous postwar technological development of the foreign oil industry. Competitive pressures made managers act to defend their firms' market positions by imitating the innovations of competitors and making new innovations of their own.

BEHAVIOR OF PROFITS
AND RETURNS ON INVESTMENT

The ultimate test of effective competition is whether market pressures tend, over time, to equalize the attractiveness of investments in different industries. Competition affects profits and the rate of return on investments, and hence the flow of capital into alternative uses. If competition is effective, a high rate of earnings in an industry, resulting from a rise in demand for its products or a fall in its costs, will increase the rate of investment in that industry. The resulting expansion of supply, by established firms and by new entrants, will subsequently lower prices and reduce the earnings rate to a normal level for investments carrying the same degree of risk. This fall in the rate of return will then bring about a decline in the rate of new investment in the industry. Thus effective competition, through its influence on the profit rate, reallocates economic resources in socially desired ways. *The foreign oil industry forms a classic case of competitive adjustment to changed supply-demand relationships in the years after 1950.*

The explosive postwar growth of foreign non-Communist demand resulted in rising prices for crude oil and its products. High levels of profitability followed for established oil companies. Up to 1958, the rate of profit earned on foreign investments in petroleum was conspicuously higher than the rates earned on foreign investments in manufacturing, mining, and other industries.[32] In fact, the rate for oil averaged more than twice the rate earned on investment in mining, an industry which also carried relatively high risks. These high returns of 20–30 percent generated huge investments by the established companies and by many new entrants.

The ensuing rapid expansion of oil supply began to reduce the high profit rates after 1952; but the crises of Iran, the Korean War, and the Suez Canal closure postponed the glut of oil and kept the profit rate above 20 percent until 1958. With the reopening of the canal during 1957, severe competition to sell the new supplies of petroleum forced down prices and profits drastically. By the early 1960s, foreign investment in oil was yielding 11 to 13 percent—the same return as in manufacturing industries and a lower return than in mining and smelting. This continued to be true through the 1960s and during 1970 and 1971, after which the "world oil revolution" changed the parameters of the industry. Competitive forces had brought the rate of earnings on foreign oil investment down to—and, considering the risks, probably somewhat below—the normal level for foreign investment as a whole.[33] (See Figure 10.6 and Table 10.7.)

The steep drop in profitability after 1957 served to reduce the growth of capital expenditures of the foreign oil industry in accordance with theoretical expectations. The growth ended in 1957 in the case of the seven largest companies combined and in 1959 in the case of all other companies combined. The faster reaction of the largest firms to the lower investment return was probably due to their earlier buildup of assets, which enabled them to complete expansion programs more quickly than the newcomers. The flattening of capital expenditures lasted until

FIGURE 10.6

Rate of Earnings on U.S. Direct Investment in Foreign Industries, 1955–1972

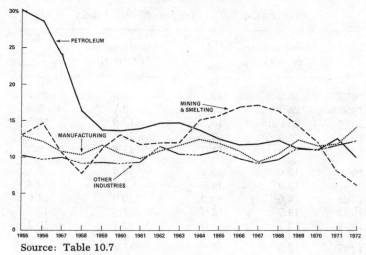

Source: Table 10.7

the late 1960s, when accelerating price inflation boosted them again. Seldom does one find so clear a statistical demonstration of an effective competitive process.[34] (See Figure 10.7 and Table 10.8.)

A CONSPECTUS OF POSTWAR BEHAVIOR

This chapter began with two basic questions: Did important changes take place during the postwar era in the behavior of the foreign oil industry? Did the industry become effectively competitive? This study leads to affirmative answers to both questions. Progressive changes did occur in the industry's structure and behavior, reflecting the dynamic forces acting upon it. Competition did, indubitably, become effective.

Up to the mid–1950s, petroleum consumption expanded more rapidly than supplies, and prices and profits rose. These high profit rates soon induced the investment of billions of dollars in the expansion of oil-producing,

TABLE 10.7
Rates of Earnings on U.S. Direct Investment in Foreign
Industries, Annually, 1955–1972

(*Percentage of Net Income to Net Assets*)

Year	Petroleum (Percent)	Mining and Smelting (Percent)	Manufacturing (Percent)	Other Industries (Percent)
1955	30.2	13.1	13.0	10.2
1956	28.8	14.6	12.1	9.7
1957	23.8	10.7	10.8	10.0
1958	16.2	7.7	10.3	9.2
1959	13.8	11.0	11.6	9.3
1960	13.6	13.1	10.5	9.1
1961	13.9	11.7	9.9	9.4
1962	14.6	12.0	10.9	11.6
1963	14.7	12.0	11.6	10.4
1964	13.7	15.0	12.4	10.3
1965	12.5	15.6	11.9	10.9
1966	11.7	16.8	10.9	9.8
1967	11.8	17.1	9.3	9.2
1968	12.3	16.3	10.4	9.7
1969	11.1	14.4	12.4	11.3
1970	11.0	11.9	11.6	11.1
1971	12.5	8.1	11.9	11.7
1972	9.9	6.2	14.1	12.2

Sources: Petroleum data from the Chase Manhattan Bank; United States Department of Commerce, *Survey of Current Business,* various issues, for Mining and Smelting, Manufacturing and Other Industries. Figures include investments in Canada.

refining, and marketing capacity. Scores of new firms entered the industry. Output caught up with demand, and later substantial excess productive capacity appeared. The prices of crude oil and its products reflected this shift in supply-demand relationships with increasing sensitivity. Prices fell deeply and unsystematically. Rates of return on foreign oil investment turned sharply downward, to the level of other foreign investment. This stopped the growth of capital expenditures through the mid–1960s,

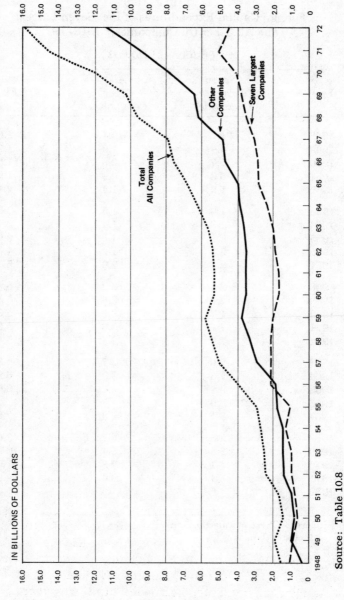

FIGURE 10.7

Foreign Capital Expenditures of the "Seven Largest" and All Other Oil Companies,* 1948–1972

IN BILLIONS OF DOLLARS

Source: Table 10.8
* Includes Canada.

249

TABLE 10.8
Foreign Capital Expenditures of the "Seven Largest"
and All Other Oil Companies,* 1948–1972

(*Billions of Dollars*)

Year	"Seven Largest" Companies	All Other Companies	Total All Companies
1948	$1.2	$ 0.4	$ 1.6
1949	0.9	1.0	1.9
1950	0.7	0.8	1.5
1951	0.8	0.9	1.7
1952	1.0	1.4	2.4
1953	1.0	1.5	2.5
1954	1.3	1.4	2.7
1955	1.1	1.8	2.9
1956	2.1	1.9	4.0
1957	2.1	2.9	5.0
1958	2.1	3.3	5.4
1959	2.0	3.8	5.8
1960	1.7	3.6	5.3
1961	1.7	3.6	5.3
1962	1.9	3.5	5.4
1963	2.0	3.7	5.7
1964	2.3	3.9	6.2
1965	2.8	4.0	6.8
1966	2.9	4.7	7.6
1967	3.1	4.8	7.9
1968	3.5	6.1	9.6
1969	3.8	6.4	10.2
1970	4.1	7.8	11.9
1971	5.1	9.4	14.5
1972	4.6	11.3	15.9

Source: Chase Manhattan Bank.
* Includes Canada.

after which dollar investment began an accelerating rise as a result of worldwide price inflation. The movements of prices and investment returns in the foreign oil industry over the period from 1948 to 1972 are a classical example of the adjustment processes of effective competition.

Scholarly critics of the oil industry have commonly viewed it as an oligopoly dominated by a few huge companies that "administer" the prices of crude oil and its products. Integration, concentration, and a good deal of tacit cooperation among the leading firms have led, in their view, to too little competition. And undoubtedly there is truth in the contention that competition in the industry falls short of perfect competition. But the basic issue is whether the industry is *effectively* competitive, in the sense that there are strong forces that make for an efficient use of resources and for petroleum prices that reflect average costs including a normal return on investment. The evidence shows that competitive forces are sufficiently strong—and growing stronger—to guard the public interest effectively. New entrants progressively encroached upon the markets of established companies. Prices tended to cover costs and to provide a normal return on investment, showing an absence of monopoly profits.

Indeed, it has been argued that during the 1960s the rising pluralism and heterogeneity of the industry led to *excessive* competition of a destabilizing kind. Petroleum prices kept falling throughout the 1960s in the face of accelerating price inflation. Rates of return on investment were, in this view, on the average subnormal, considering the relatively large risks. The industry became composed of so many firms having such diverse interests as to be incapable of offering an adequate counterpoise to the rising power of the oil-producing nations.

As will be seen, powerful new political and economic forces were beginning to mold the future of the foreign oil industry as the world entered the decade of the 1970s. They came to a head during 1973 and 1974—years that inaugurated a new era in the history of the world oil industry. The parameters of the industry were radically changed; and the new parameters could only dimly be discerned.

NOTES

1. Some branches of agriculture may be an exception to this rule.

2. Other market models include those of monopsony (one buyer), oligopsony (few buyers), monopoly-monopsony or bilateral monopoly (one seller–one buyer), and oligopoly-oligopsony (few sellers–few buyers).

3. W. H. Fellner, "Collusion and Its Limits Under Oligopoly," *American Economic Review*, 40 (May, 1950): 54–62.

4. A critical commentary of the economic literature on effective competition is given by Stephen H. Sosnick in "A Critique of Concepts of Workable Competition," *Quarterly Journal of Economics* 72 (August 1958): 380–423. See also the author's *Corporate Power and Social Responsibility: A Blueprint for the Future*, p. 138–40.

5. Changing factors include the number, location, wants, preferences, and per capita incomes of consumers in markets; the attitudes of people toward work, leisure, saving, and consumption; the stock of resources, scientific knowledge, technology, and know-how; and the forms of governmental regulation and social attitudes toward enterprise.

6. This vital point is made by J. M. Clark in his *Competition as a Dynamic Process* (Washington, D.C.: The Brookings Institution, 1961), p. 490: "The imperfectly competitive mixed economy we have is better than the impossible abstraction of 'perfect competition' largely because of its dynamic quality; and because, while competitive *processes* continue to change their forms, competitive *pressures* continue to be forceful, including what is probably an increasing role for various forms and degrees of potential competition."

7. Approximately this formulation was suggested by J. S. Bain in "Workable Competition in Oligopoly: Some

Theoretical Considerations and Some Empirical Evidence,"
American Economic Review, 40 (May, 1950): 35–47.

8.   Crude oil prices at a given location vary widely according to current supply-demand conditions for oils of particular qualities. High-gravity or "light" crude oils yield more
gasoline than low-gravity or "heavy" crude oils, and normally
command higher prices. Other things being equal, each added
degree of gravity normally adds to the market value of a
barrel of oil. Also, no refinery can economically process all
types of crude oil, so that the demand curve of each refiner
for crude oils will vary from those of other refiners.

9.   At any given time, moreover, ships currently in service will be operated under charters made at different dates
and calling for very different short-, medium-, and long-term
charter rates. Also, about 35 percent of tanker capacity is
owned by firms which also trade in crude oil, while about 65
percent is owned by firms which do not. These facts compli-
cate the computation of the average freight rate and comparisons of delivered prices.

10.   In the United States, the *buyer* (usually a refiner)
posts the price at which he is willing to buy; abroad, the
seller posts the price at which he is willing to sell.

11.   Crude oil is often sold under two separate contracts:
one a contract for the sale of oil f.o.b. a loading port, and the
other a contract of affreightment to the buyer's port of entry.
The two agreements are commonly negotiated and signed
simultaneously. By the early 1960s, many buyers owned, or
hired, their own tankers; but most crude oil moved in tankers
owned or supplied by crude-oil-producing firms. The latter
often emphasized price reductions via low ocean transport
rates instead of lower crude oil prices f.o.b. ports of origin.
(Compare the practice of automobile dealers in giving large
"trade-in allowances" to their customers instead of cutting the
prices of new cars.)

12.   See, for example, J. E. Hartshorn, *Politics and World
Oil Economics* (New York: Frederick E. Praeger, 1962). Also
Wayne E. Leeman, *The Price of Middle East Oil* (Ithaca:
Cornell University Press, 1962), *passim.*

13.   *Unsystematic* or random price discrimination will
occur in imperfect markets under effective competition.
(Compare the retail automobile market in the United States.)

Systematic price discrimination by the seller, on the other hand, is characteristic of a monopolized market. In a theoretically perfect market, price discrimination is not possible because buyers and sellers are presumed to have complete knowledge of all relevant facts.

14. In general, it appears that up to 1957 most sellers were able to realize posted f.o.b. prices on most or all of their sales of crude oil.

15. Affiliates began to show losses in 1958. See Edward Symonds, *Oil Advances in the Eastern Hemisphere* (New York: First National City Bank of New York, December, 1962), p. 5.

16. Organization for European Economic Cooperation, *Oil—Recent Developments in the OEEC Area* (Paris: OEEC, 1961), pp. 27–28.

17. These data were compiled by Japan's Ministry of International Trade and Industry (MITI). They run from the beginning of the second quarter of 1957 through May of 1962.

18. Council of Europe, *European Energy Problems,* Document No. 1463, p. 70 (emphasis added).

19. In markets for refined products—as in crude oil markets—the competitive process was a multi-vectored phenomenon. Competition involved pricing, changes in product quality, provision to buyers of equipment, credit, financial assistance, delivery services, locational conveniences, sales promotion, and product differentiation through branding and advertising. Ralph Cassady, Jr., provided detailed descriptions of the competitive process in U.S. petroleum markets in his *Price Making and Price Behavior in the Petroleum Industry* (New Haven: Yale University Press, 1954).

20. Product prices were not posted in the Persian Gulf until 1957, when they were posted at levels somewhat under Caribbean postings.

21. *Petroleum Intelligence Weekly,* July 30, 1962.

22. During the period from 1950 to 1962, maximum prices of liquid and solid fuels were fixed by the Comitato Interministeriale del Prezzi with the aim of protecting consumers. However, vendors were free to sell at lower prices.

23.   Oil accounted for only 6 percent of Japanese energy in 1950, but 40 percent in 1962. By 1972 it had risen to 77 percent.

24.   As an example, the development of high-performance aviation fuels by the oil industry paced the development of the aviation industry. Robert Shlaifer and S. D. Heron, *Development of Aircraft Engines and Fuels* (Boston: Division of Research, Graduate School of Business Administration, Harvard University, 1950).

25.   See R. F. Mikesell and H. B. Chenery, *Arabian Oil* (Chapel Hill: University of North Carolina Press, 1949), pp. 173–74.

26.   See *National Science Foundation Databook* (Washington, D.C.: January, 1974), p. 44.

27.   In his paper "Invention and Innovation in the Petroleum Refining Industry," in *The Rate and Direction of Inventive Activity: Economic and Social Factors* (Princeton: Princeton University Press, 1962), pp. 311–13, John L. Enos estimated that the returns to oil companies that had innovated major advances in oil-refining processes were very high. See also, John L. Enos, *Petroleum Progress and Profits: A History of Progress Innovation* (Cambridge: The M.I.T. Press, 1962), p. ix.

28.   The phrase is Miller B. Spangler's, whose *New Technology and the Supply of Petroleum* (Chicago: Miller B. Spangler, 1956) shows the relation of technological progress to the recovery of crude oil and the adequacy of crude oil reserves.

29.   See U.S., Department of Labor, *Studies of Automatic Technology: A Case Study of a Modernized Petroleum Refinery* (Washington, D.C.: Government Printing Office, 1957), p. 4.

30.   See *Chemical Week,* November 17, 1962, pp. 66–8; *Oil and Gas Journal,* February 11, 1963, p. 62.

31.   Also of great significance, but beyond the scope of this study, were major innovations in the intercontinental transportation of *natural gases* by pipeline and in the overseas transportation of liquefied natural gases in cryogenic tankers.

32.   Because profit rates for the *entire* foreign oil industry are not available, the rates for *U.S.* direct investment in the

industry, which forms 36 percent of total investment, have been taken as representative for the whole industry. Because of defects in the Department of Commerce figures on foreign oil profits, the data of the Chase Manhattan Bank on rates of return on the book value of foreign petroleum assets have been used. It is unnecessary for present purposes to present profit rates for each division of the industry, because all divisions are interdependent and the whole investment of an integrated company is necessary to give value to crude oil in the ground.

33. Petroleum investment in the United States—carrying less risk than foreign investment—has yielded after-tax net income of total net assets of around 10 percent per annum under normal conditions, for integrated companies.

34. The author presented a model of effective competition among large firms in *Corporate Power and Social Responsibility: A Blueprint for the Future* (New York: Macmillan and Co., 1973), chap. 6.

11

The World Oil Revolution of the 1970s and the Future

URING THE EARLY 1970s, the foreign oil industry underwent revolutionary political and economic changes. Crude oil pricing and production decisions, traditionally initiated by the international oil companies, were taken over by the oil exporting nations, whose basic policies were coordinated through the OPEC and the OAPEC. Most of these countries progressively nationalized private petroleum properties and acquired majority —and, in some countries, total—ownership of oil reserves and producing facilities. Most important, they *quadrupled* the price of crude oil during 1973 and 1974, and—in the case of the Arab countries—cut back production and placed an embargo on shipments to the United States for political reasons.

These actions produced an earthquake in the political, economic, and financial structure of the non-Communist world, whose reverberations and aftershocks will be felt for many years.[1] They set in motion radical changes in national energy policies, in patterns of energy production and consumption, in international balances of payments, and in the role of multinational oil companies and their relationships with governments. Just as World War II formed a watershed in the history of the world oil industry, so will historians look back on the early 1970s as another watershed, separating a vanished age of cheap energy and private oil enterprise from a new age of expensive energy and governmental domination of oil pricing and production decisions. For good or evil, political considerations have become dominant in both exporting and importing countries.

Why did the OPEC evolve into the world's most effective international export cartel, and why did it act so aggressively? What are the prospects for the future supply and price of crude oil? What institutional machinery is needed to determine oil prices and production levels? And what will be the future role of private oil enterprises and their relationships with governments?

PRICE INFLATION AND THE OPEC TAKEOVER OF OIL PRICING

Among the motivating forces behind the world oil revolution of the early 1970s three factors stand out: global price inflation, rising nationalism, and the Arab-Israeli conflict. The latter half of the 1960s and the early 1970s were marked by an accelerating inflation of the price level in most of the industrialized world. In the United States, the Consumer Price Index rose 23 percent during the five-year period from 1965 to the middle of 1970. In the following two and one-half years up to the end of 1972, the Index rose another 20 percent; and thereafter the rise accelerated still further. Comparable or greater increases were recorded in most European nations and in Japan. What made this inflation so ominous was its pervasive and accelerating character.

Worldwide price inflation initially affected manufactured products and services. It did not touch petroleum, the price of which remained virtually constant through the 1960s. But beginning in 1970 several events put upward pressures on oil prices. Petroleum consumption in North America as well as in Europe spurted upward unexpectedly. In May of 1970, the Trans-Arabian Pipeline, which carried 500,000 barrels of crude oil per day from Saudi Arabia to the Mediterranean, was shut down because of an accident and remained closed the rest of the year. This increased the importance of Libyan oil in European markets. The revolutionary government of Libya under Colonel Qadaffi, which had overthrown the regime of King Idris the preceding year, used its increased bargaining power to demand a higher price for oil. That demand was met by Occidental Petroleum Corporation in September of 1970, after Libya had cut back crude oil production; and later, in the face of a threatened stoppage of all production, the demand was met by the other companies operating in Libya. This action put in motion pressures for increases in posted prices by other OPEC countries.

In December of 1970, the OPEC called for immediate negotiation with the oil companies over the following demands: the establishment of a 55 percent income tax rate, a general increase in all posted prices of crude oil, the elimination of disparities in prices among the OPEC members, and the elimination of special discounts on sales of crude oil. These demands were substantially met in the historic Teheran Agreement of February, 1971, which was supposed to run for five years. Also, in December of 1970, the OPEC had adopted a resolution that oil prices should be adjusted to reflect changes in the exchange rates of currencies. This led to the Geneva Agreement in January of 1972, raising the price of oil by twenty cents per barrel to offset the devaluation of the U.S. dollar during August of 1971, and to a second agreement in June of 1973 to raise the price another fifteen cents per barrel to offset the dollar devaluation of February, 1973.

All this, however, was a mere overture to the opera that was to follow. The OPEC countries viewed themselves as trading their low-priced oil for increasingly expensive industrial products. The terms of international trade were moving against them, as price inflation accelerated. This they saw as an inequitable exchange of their national patrimonies of an exhaustible resource. The crude oil price increases made at Teheran as a result of the U.S. dollar devaluations totaled about 35 percént and did not offset the more than 50 percent inflation of the general price level up to that time. In September of 1973, they called for a renegotiation of the Teheran Agreement, noting that the current rate of inflation far exceeded the 2.5 percent rate contemplated in that Agreement. During the following month, the oil companies proposed an escalator clause that would have caused crude oil prices to rise pari passu with general inflation—but the negotiations were never completed. In that same month, October, the OPEC members in the Persian Gulf *unilaterally* increased the posted price of crude oil by an unprecedented amount. For the first time, the oil-exporting nations took the pricing function completely into their own hands. This increase was followed by a staggering increase in January of 1974. Within two years the price of crude oil had quadrupled. The Saudi Arabian government raised its posted price from $2.59 per barrel in early 1973 to $11.65 per barrel in January of 1974. The price of Arabian oil delivered to the Atlantic Coast of the United States shot up from about $3.65 per barrel to $12.25 per barrel in early 1974. Comparable increases were made at Japanese and European ports. And so the age of inexpensive oil passed into history.

In one perspective, this oil price revolution can be seen as a natural reaction—or overreaction—by the oil-exporting nations to an inflationary world economy they had no part in creating and as an expression of resentment by the Arab members of U.S. aid to Israel. The industrialized nations in the Organization for Economic Cooperation and Development (OECD) were merely suffering the inescapable consequences of their inflationary economic policies. To those who argued that the OPEC overreacted, the OPEC members could reply that their fourfold increase in the price of oil merely matched the fourfold increase in the free market price of gold from the $42.50 per ounce value set by the U.S. Treasury. From another perspective, the OPEC can be viewed as a dangerous export cartel, exploiting its monopolistic power to extract tribute from energy-short nations! While there is some truth in both contentions, the pertinent task now before the world is to establish an institution for determining price levels and production schedules for crude oil that will meet the needs of the oil-exporting countries and also maintain viable economies in the oil-importing countries.

RISING NATIONALISM AND THE TAKEOVER OF OIL PRODUCTION FACILITIES

The other motive behind the oil revolution of the early 1970s was the rising nationalism in the OPEC countries, which stimulated their progressive takeover of production facilities. Most of these nations were formed after the breakup of colonial empires or were formerly within imperial spheres of influence. Their sense of national awareness and identity had sharpened during the 1960s. It became more strident and activist as they strove to develop their economies and began to wield economic power over the industrialized countries that had become heavily dependent upon them for energy. The closure of the Suez Canal during the six-day Arab-Israeli War of 1967 had shown them the vulnerability of Europe to a reduction of oil supplies. The OPEC countries began to question the policy of unlimited oil production by foreign-owned corporations. Some already had larger reserves of foreign exchange and more oil revenue than they could invest productively at home.

As early as June of 1968, the OPEC began to exert pressures for the participation of host governments in the ownership of concessions. It resolved that where an existing contract did not provide for participation, the host government might acquire it on the grounds of "changing circumstances." At the same time, it advanced the thesis that the oil resources of its members were being "exploited" detrimentally to their economic development. It instructed its Economic Commission in June of 1970 to study ways of integrating the petroleum industries into the economies of member countries. The following year the OPEC called upon member countries to take immediate steps to implement the principle of national participation. Each country went its own way in carrying out this policy.

Again the revolutionary government of Libya led the way. In December of 1971, it nationalized British Petroleum's 50 percent interest in the Sarir field in retaliation for the British government's purported role in allowing Iran to occupy three Arab islands in the Persian Gulf. Then, in June of 1973, it nationalized Bunker Hunt's 50 percent interest in the same field in retaliation for U.S. support of Israel. And, in the following month, it demanded a 51 percent interest in the production properties of all remaining oil companies. Occidental agreed to sell such an interest to the government; and later some other companies followed suit.

Iraq also steadily increased its control of the oil industry. Following a lengthy dispute, the government nationalized IPC during 1972. In the following year, it nationalized American and Dutch interests in the Basrah Petroleum Company as a penalty for their home countries' support of Israel.

Some of the Persian Gulf states, including Saudi Arabia, signed a General Participation Agreement with the oil companies in December of 1972 to acquire a 25 percent interest in oil operations immediately and additional shares each year thereafter, leading to 51 percent by 1982. However, Kuwait insisted on a larger share and obtained 60 percent effective in January of 1974. ARAMCO and Saudi Arabia subsequently revised their earlier agreement to transfer to the Saudi Arabian government a 60 percent share as of the same date. Although compensation to ARAMCO had not been determined up to mid-1974, when the Saudi government had acquired a 25 percent interest, it had agreed to pay the companies "updated book value" and to give them long-term access to government oil at favorable prices.

The fluidity of conditions and the fragility of agreements were demonstrated once again in June of 1974 when it was reported that the government of Saudi Arabia was negotiating for the complete ownership of ARAMCO.[2] The OPEC countries appeared to be aiming for complete ownership of the oil production resources within their boundaries.

THE EFFECTS OF A
QUADRUPLED OIL PRICE
ON THE WORLD ECONOMY

The drastic actions of the OPEC and its members during 1973 and 1974 dealt the international economy its heaviest shock since the outbreak of World War II. The quadrupling of the price of crude oil immediately increased the demand for other sources of energy (coal, natural gas, uranium), leading to large increases in their prices. This action also reduced the level of energy consumption and will probably slow its growth. It fundamentally changed the international balances of payments of virtually every non-Communist country and brought about a revision of national economic plans. The OPEC members changed the roles of multinational oil companies and their relationships to producer governments. Suddenly, the parameters of economic and social planning were altered—favorably for the members of the OPEC and unfavorably for other countries. The heavy dependence of Western Europe and Japan, and the rising reliance of the United States, on foreign oil were thrust into sharp relief.

Oil-importing countries reacted with oil conservation

measures to minimize the adverse shifts in their balances of payments and to lessen their dependency on foreign energy. Throughout the foreign non-Communist world, governments restricted the use of gasoline and other petroleum products. Scheduled flights of aircraft were reduced. Ships were detained in port. Manufacturers of automobiles, aircraft, petrochemicals, textiles, and other oil-dependent operations laid off workers and curtailed activities. A ban on the use of private automobiles on Sundays and holidays was instituted in some European countries. Some governments made plans to ration gasoline.

In the United States, where long lines of motorists formed in front of service stations during the Arab embargo on crude oil shipments, many of these same measures were taken. In addition, President Nixon proposed "Project Independence," a new energy policy for the United States designed to enhance national security by making the nation essentially self-sufficient in energy by 1980. The Common Market countries and Japan—for whom energy independence was practically impossible—also scrambled to develop new energy policies. Among the measures already taken, or which are likely to be taken, are oil storage programs, the establishment of governmental bodies to centralize oil purchasing, bilateral agreements with oil-exporting countries in the hope of gaining an assured supply, and intergovernmental agencies (such as the OECD) to bargain with producers and to cooperate in the development of alternative energy sources.[3] These countries also speeded up their nuclear energy development. According to the Chairman of the U.S. Atomic Energy Commission, they purchased many American-designed nuclear power plants and so much enriched uranium that by the fall of 1973 the Atomic Energy Commission held firm contracts for the sale of $20 billion worth of enriched uranium to foreign countries.[4]

The most critical problem, however, was that of financing the immense international movements of oil, now worth $12 instead of $3 per barrel. Vast new faults had opened up in the world's balance of payments structure.

Even after allowing for the immediate reduction in petroleum consumption, the *net increase* in payments due to the OPEC countries from oil-importing nations was estimated at $63 billion for 1974. And this huge annual transfer would rise in future years if oil consumption increased or if the OPEC members pushed oil prices up further.

The Secretary-General of the OECD estimated that, instead of earning a current account surplus of $10 billion during 1974, the OECD countries as a group would go into deficit about $30 billion. If an individual country sought to escape from this swing, it would only put the current account balances of other OECD countries into deeper deficits. Huge deficits in the overall balances of international payments of the OECD countries could be avoided only if each country attracted a return flow of capital from the OPEC members sufficient to offset its deficit on current account.[5]

While the oil-importing nations had to find the money to pay for high-priced oil, the OPEC countries faced the more agreeable problem of deciding how to invest the proceeds. To a large industrialized country like the United States, whose oil imports were not a large factor in total energy consumption, the $17 billion in additional annual payments could be met, in the main, by an expansion of U.S. exports. Those advanced countries that were heavily dependent upon foreign oil, such as Japan, France, and Italy, would be compelled to borrow funds in the international money markets or from the International Monetary Fund. The most severe problems were faced by the thirty or more oil-deficient, less-developed countries, such as India, that lacked ready access to world money markets. They would require assistance from some source, perhaps the proposed special energy fund of the IMF. Financing $60 billion of additional payments for oil during 1974 would create severe strains and hardships. Yet the problem appeared to be manageable.[6]

The OPEC members, beneficiaries of the new world oil order, fall into two groups. One, including Algeria, Indonesia, Iran, Iraq, Nigeria, and Venezuela, is able to absorb the new oil revenues in productive domestic investment. The other, whose members' new revenues are so large in relation to the size of their various economies that they have huge surpluses available, includes Abu Dhabi, Kuwait, Libya, Qatar, and Saudi Arabia. The "petro-money" surpluses of these nations will have to be cycled back to the rest of the world. The major options included development loans to the less-developed countries, loans to the IMF energy fund, purchase of the assets or securities of the international oil companies, or investment in non-oil assets such as foreign real estate or securities. In mid-1974 it appeared likely that all of these media of investment would be utilized. The World Bank estimated the aggregate oil revenues of the producing countries would amount to $86.6 billion during 1974, or nearly four times the $23.2 billion they realized in 1973. The largest 1974 revenues would accrue to Saudi Arabia ($19.4 billion), Iran ($14.9 billion), Venezuela ($10 billion), and Libya ($8 billion).[7]

The immediate effects of the quadrupled price of oil upon the economies of the oil-importing countries was similar to that of a very heavy excise tax from which foreign governments benefited. Public expenditures on petroleum and its products were greatly increased. Had incomes and spending propensities remained constant, outlays on other commodities would have been reduced proportionately. On this assumption, the net effect would have been deflationary, or, in view of the worldwide inflation then raging, anti-inflationary. However, in an inflationary era, incomes usually rise and spending propensities increase, so that spending on other products was probably maintained at customary levels, while spending on petroleum products rose sharply. The probable net effect was thus to pour more fuel on the fires of inflation.

Although the international financing problems created by the oil revolution appeared to be manageable during 1974, *the long-term consequences of a $12-per-barrel price for oil would be profound, and they could be cata-*

strophic. The cumulative effects, even over a decade, of vast monetary transfers to the members of the OPEC from other countries would be to change the world's economy substantially. Abundant capital would accelerate the economic development of the OPEC members and transform them into creditor nations of the first rank. The Persian Gulf countries, in particular, would become heavy investors in the OECD countries. Higher costs of energy in the oil-importing countries would elevate production costs and would slow their economic growth. Higher energy costs would visit severe hardships on the less-developed nations, for which ameliorative measures would be needed. *To reduce the threats of financial breakdown and further price inflation, a reduction of the 1974 price of oil to a moderate level should be a primary objective of world economic policy.*

Of course, all problems of world economic adjustment would be aggravated if the members of OPEC decided to raise oil prices and to restrict output even further. At some point, this policy could precipitate a breakdown of the international financial system. However, the OPEC members, as potentially important creditor and investor nations, have a strong self-interest in the viability of the international financial system. Presumably, this will be a constraint upon their actions.

THE DAMPENED GROWTH OF FOREIGN OIL CONSUMPTION

The quadrupling of oil prices during late 1973 and early 1974 ended the long boom in oil consumption. It quickly led to heavy price increases for coal, natural gas, and nuclear fuels, the primary competing sources of energy. Despite the relative inelasticity of demand for energy in general, the rate of consumption dropped significantly. Official estimates of future energy consumption were revised downward. The anticipated role of oil in the future pattern of energy use was reduced, while that of coal, natural gas, and nuclear fuels was increased. The Common Market Commission of the EEC approved, in June of 1974, a new energy strategy which anticipates a 10 percent cut in the total energy use which was previously estimated for 1985. It forecast, by 1985, a reduction in the role of oil from 65 percent to 42 percent of energy consumption, and a rise in nuclear energy from 9 to 15 percent and of natural gas from 17 to 24 percent.[8]

During the next decade, the growth of foreign non-Communist petroleum consumption will be much less rapid. *How much* less depends upon many factors. Assuming that the new era of expensive fuels endures, higher-priced petroleum products will lead consumers progressively to conserve their usage. As time passes, additional conservation measures, such as conversion to other energy sources, insulation of buildings, and fuller utilization of mass transportation facilities, will become effective. Despite the past relative inelasticity of demand, the consumption of oil is likely to contract considerably in response to a very large change in price. In addition, governments have restricted oil consumption for national security reasons and to reduce balance of payments problems.[9] The process of developing energy-intensive societies, already well advanced in Western Europe and Japan, would, in any event, have proceeded less rapidly in the future as they approached the American level of per capita consumption. But it will continue to be strong in foreign countries still catching up with the leading consumer societies.

The substitution of oil for coal will assuredly diminish, and, indeed, this process may be reversed, while reliance upon nuclear fuels and natural gas (in Europe) will rise. Despite a sharp increase in coal prices, the quadrupled price of oil has given coal a decisive advantage over oil in cost per BTU. The main handicap of coal is its generation of pollution; but if a technology for the inexpensive removal of sulphur from coal is developed this would induce a massive substitution of coal for oil in the generation of electricity. An economical process for converting coal into liquid petroleum—also a distinct possibility—would have the same effect.

The future growth of energy consumption in the non-Communist world is thus likely to be depressed by government conservation measures as well as by higher prices. Walter Levy, a respected specialist on energy, believes that higher prices per se will bring only a modest reduction in the growth rates of energy and of oil consumption, between 1974 and 1980, in the non-Communist world, from those that prevailed during the period from 1968 to 1972. Energy use, he estimates, will expand by 4.6 percent a year instead of 5.6 percent, and oil by 5.1 percent instead of 7.5 percent. He advocates governmental policies of "genuine austerity," which would cut the growth of energy consumption to 3.3 percent a year and of oil to 2.7 percent a year. Only austerity, in his view, will enable the industrialized nations to hold their balance of payments deficits within manageable limits.[10]

The major uncertainty in gauging the future consumption of oil concerns the pricing and production policies of the OPEC members. Our conclusion here is that the national interests of the oil-exporting countries will be best served by a moderate price for oil under current (mid–1974) conditions. Such a price would approximate the $7 to $8 per barrel, delivered to the United States, predicted by U.S. Secretary of the Treasury William E. Simon in July of 1974.[11] If such a price comes into effect, the curtailment of oil consumption would be less drastic, and the development of substitutes for liquid petroleum (from shale, tar sands, coal conversion, liquified natural gas, etc.) would be less rapid than it would be under a restrictive OPEC policy. Under a moderate pricing policy, it is likely that the growth rate of oil consumption in the *foreign* non-Communist world during the balance of the 1970s will decline from 11 percent to between 4 and 8 percent a year. Under a severely restrictive pricing policy, annual growth could fall to 4 percent, or even much less. Considering the 10 billion barrel yearly consumption base in 1972, this would still entail a healthy increase in the size of the foreign oil industry.

THE OPEC'S CONTROL OF THE FUTURE SUPPLY AND PRICE OF OIL

We have noted that the margin of spare oil producing capacity present in the United States, Canada, and Venezuela vanished during 1971 and 1972, leaving most of the world's quickly expansible oil production concentrated in the Middle East, and particularly in the Persian Gulf. The nations of that region, and especially Saudi Arabia (holding about one-quarter of the non-Communist world's proven reserves) were elevated to a position of vast economic power. By turning down the valves on ARAMCO's massive oil flow of 8.5 million barrels per day, the Saudi Arabian government could quickly bring the industrialized world close to a state of darkness and immobility. Saudi Arabia has become the "swing" producer; and it will continue to play that role because it will probably account for a large fraction of the increment in the proven reserves of the non-Communist world during the next decade.

With OPEC oil at around $8 per barrel, it would be profitable for the oil companies to develop the oil resources of the deep jungles, the arctic wastes, and the ocean beds of the continental shelves. And there is still much oil to be found. In a report prepared for the United Nations in 1973, Weeks estimated that the potential oil and gas ultimately recoverable from the offshore areas of the world alone were 2,272 billion barrels, about 60 percent of which was believed to be present in the continental shelves.[12] Beyond these liquid petroleum resources are the hydrocarbons locked in the oil shales, tar sands, and coal beds of the world—estimated at many times the amount of liquid petroleum. The oil supply problem is not, in essence, a lack of hydrocarbons in the earth's crust; the problem is one of maintaining adequate incentives to look for and produce available energy resources.[13] If governments do not foolishly tax away petroleum profits or foreclose investment opportunities, the foreign oil industry will assuredly maintain a high rate of investment in oil exploration and development.

Naturally, companies will be motivated to search for oil in nations that offer relatively attractive returns on investment. History teaches that a determined effort, if spurred by strong profit incentives, has a good chance of success. Just as the hectic search for oil during the 1950s uncovered huge deposits in the Middle East, Venezuela, Indonesia, North Africa, and the USSR, and searches in the 1960s revealed equally important reserves in West Africa, Alaska, and the North Sea, so we may expect the future to witness important increments to the world's reserves. Indeed, the vast unexplored central desert of Saudi Arabia may prove to be as prolific as presently productive areas.[14] Another glut of oil is distinctly possible.

But it appears improbable that, during the next decade, such large oil reserves will be found outside of the OPEC's jurisdiction as to destroy its ability to control the price and supply of oil. The key issue is whether the OPEC will be able to restrict crude oil production in order to support high prices and thus avoid the creation of surpluses. To succeed, the OPEC must become another Texas Railroad Commission, prorating "allowable" outputs among its members to levels the market will absorb at the price it has established. The OPEC has formulated oil production control plans from time to time since its establishment in 1960. In June, 1970, the organization resolved to adopt a production plan limiting output to a level that would meet estimated world "demand," a la the Texas Railroad Commission. It decided a year later, however, to hold the program in abeyance. With increasing evidence of oil surpluses during 1974, it appeared that the ability of OPEC to control crude oil production would inevitably be put to a test.

Skeptics of the OPEC's ability to restrain oil production

and to hold up prices in the long run point to the negative history of international commodity cartels. Generally, they have been beset by defections of their members, by rising external competition, by technological displacement, and by ultimate failure.[15] These skeptics believe that the same growing pluralism and diversity of interests that eroded the ability of the oil companies to bargain effectively with the OPEC member governments during the 1960s will probably erode the OPEC's economic power during the 1970s. For example, the government oil companies of Iran, Saudi Arabia, Kuwait, and other nations may well compete with each other. The OPEC's power could also be curbed by the discovery of major new oil reserves in the Arctic, the continental shelves, the North Sea, the USSR, and elsewhere, and by the emergence of alternative fuels.

Nevertheless, it is conservative to assume that the OPEC *will* maintain sufficient cohesion to dominate strategic oil pricing and production decisions, at least during the balance of the 1970s. After all, its members have savored the sweet taste of financial success from their collaboration so far. This experience may make their international oil cartel an exception to the rule. As Adelman has astutely observed: "The cartel can endure as long as potential competition [for OPEC crude oil] is not translated into actual."[16] Because several years at least will elapse before substantial competing sources of petroleum or other fuels can be developed outside of the OPEC control, and even more time may be needed to forge a common petroleum policy for the oil-importing countries, the prospect is that the OPEC cartel will remain effective for some time. Let us make this assumption and inquire what oil pricing and production policies will best serve the interests of its members.

The factors that would lead the OPEC to a relatively *liberal* (low price, large output) policy are the potential competition of new crude oil supplies outside its control, the development of alternative energy sources, and its financial interest in a stable world monetary order.

Huge reservoirs of oil, rivaling the multi-billion-barrel

fields of the Middle East, could be found in regions outside of the OPEC's control. Even today there are indications that the North Sea may ultimately yield 100 billion barrels or more. Eastern and Western Siberia, the North Slope of Alaska, the continental shelves of the United States and of West Africa are all candidates for giant new oil pools. The managers of the OPEC cannot fail to assess these probabilities, knowing that a restrictive policy will accelerate worldwide exploration and hasten the day when OPEC oil will have to compete with vast new supplies.

The OPEC must also be cognizant of the possibility that advances in technology will soon make alternative sources of energy available at falling costs. With crude oil at around $8 or more per barrel, the extraction of oil from shale, tar sands, and coal becomes economic; so does the conversion of coal into gas, the transportation of liquified natural gas, and the development of geothermal and solar energy. In his imaginative model of energy use in the long run, Nordhaus envisages a world economy moving in stages from today's heavy reliance upon oil and natural gas to deep-mined and strip-mined coal, gasified and liquified coal, shale oil, and light-water nuclear reactors during the twentieth century until in the late twenty-first century, breeder reactors supply almost all energy needs. His analysis (published before the 1973–1974 OPEC price increase) indicates that the world is not running out of energy sources, and that although the cost of fuel will gradually rise, the increase will not be alarmingly rapid.[17] Should oil be pushed up to, say, $15.00 per barrel, however, efforts to develop alternative energy sources, including the expansion of fission and the development of fusion energy, would be pressed forward on crash schedules. A fortunate scientific breakthrough could even solve the world's energy problem, leaving the OPEC members with oil in the ground useful only for fertilizers and petrochemicals. Thus the OPEC decision makers may find it advisable to price their oil at levels which do not too quickly make it an unattractive source of energy.

Finally, as noted previously, the OPEC will no doubt consider the interests of its members in the stability of the international financial system. As huge potential investors in foreign nations and as holders of vast deposits in the world's banks the OPEC countries will have a most compelling interest in the viability of the international financial system. Even military intervention in the Persian Gulf by the industrialized nations could become a possibility—although remote—that the OPEC members could not ignore should the world be confronted with imminent financial disaster as a result of highly restrictive petroleum policies. It is thus in the interest of the OPEC to price and to produce oil at levels which enable importing countries to maintain productive economies and to balance their international accounts.

The principal factors making for a *restrictive* (high price and low output) oil policy by the OPEC cartel would be the continuation of world price inflation, limited opportunities for its members to invest their surplus oil revenues abroad, and the insensitivity of oil exports to the price charged.

It will be recalled that one of the major causes of the assumption of oil pricing decisions by the OPEC members in 1973 and 1974 was the failure of the price of oil to rise proportionately to the accelerating world price inflation. Further declines in the purchasing power of money would, no doubt, strongly motivate the OPEC toward a restrictive policy. Its members would prefer to keep their oil in the ground rather than to accept paper money of diminishing real value. The oil-importing nations, therefore, have a powerful reason for taking strong measures to arrest the galloping inflation that has enveloped the world and to stabilize the value of money. The restoration of monetary order in the world is necessary to avert future energy "crises."

A restrictive OPEC policy might also arise from the inability of some of its members to invest their surplus oil revenues abroad. Saudi Arabia, Kuwait, and Libya do have an interest in restricting their oil production and revenue flows. Sheik Yamani, Saudi Arabia's Minister of Petroleum, has stated repeatedly that the Saudi Arabian government serves the interests of consuming nations, rather than its own, in programing large increases in ARAMCO's output. This being so, it behooves the OECD countries to enlarge the opportunities for foreign investment which they offer to the governments of the oil-rich countries. By making such opportunities available, they would mitigate the pressure on several OPEC members to curtail production.

The oil-importing nations would help to induce the OPEC cartel to fix a moderate price for crude oil by making the volume of their oil imports highly elastic with respect to price. For example, they could vary the rates of their import taxes sharply and directly with the price of petroleum, thus restraining imports when prices were high and expanding imports when prices were low. Finally, as George W. Ball has observed, "the Arab states would feel a greater obligation to meet the soaring requirements of the Western world for oil that comes out of their soil . . . if the Western world, and particularly the United States, were to change its attitude toward Israel."[18]

The OPEC's future oil price and output policy will be determined by its evaluation of these factors. Our judgment is that the balance of considerations probably will lead the OPEC to pursue a moderate policy.

THE FUTURE ROLE OF GOVERNMENTS —THE OPEC AND THE OECD

The future political economy of the world petroleum industry is necessarily obscure. Many paths are open for its evolution; and one would be rash indeed to attempt to predict the specific course it will take. Yet one conclusion can be expressed with some confidence: *strategic* oil pricing and production decisions are unlikely to be returned to the multinational oil companies. The system under which multinational oil companies took the initiative in changing the posted prices of crude oil in response to shifts in supply-demand relationships and adjusted their liftings of oil to their estimated future sales passed into history with the oil revolution of the early 1970s. Although that system on the whole served petroleum consumers well, as we have seen, it is unlikely to be revived. The OPEC members possess the crude oil the world needs. They have profited richly by seizing control of pricing and production and by coordinating their actions through the OPEC and the OAPEC. They will retain these powers to the maximum extent possible. Strategic oil decisions have become political decisions, made by the governments of the oil-exporting countries.

But the question remains: what kind of institution and process for the formulation of strategic oil pricing and production decisions will best serve the world in the future? Few would contend that these decisions, concerning so vital a commodity as petroleum, should be left to the unilateral determination of a cartel of oil-exporting nations, containing a very small fraction of the world's population and gross production. The present process is unstable because it expresses only producer interests and accords little weight to consumer interests. The OPEC members have not only brought to bear the power of sovereign governments, but they have magnified that power by forming a multinational government monopoly. It would be unrealistic to expect that the governments of the oil-importing nations will for very long passively accept a radically inferior bargaining position. They will assuredly act to redress the balance. What options are open to them?

Some have urged that, since the oil-exporting countries have formed a monopoly of sellers, the oil-importing countries should organize a buyers' monopsony to bargain with the OPEC with a single voice and thus countervail its power. Such a development would create the classical case of monopoly-monopsony, or bilateral monopoly, described in economic textbooks. Economic theory teaches that the price and output decisions reached in such a market are unpredictable over wide ranges and are dominated by the relative bargaining strengths of the contending parties. It also teaches that such bargaining can result in an impasse, with a breakdown of supply. There is no doubt that pitting the OPEC and the OECD members against each other would tend to generate frictions and to exacerbate national differences.

It has also been suggested that the governments of the major oil-importing countries should assist the multinational oil companies to organize a consortium to bargain with the OPEC cartel. Those who espouse this idea believe that the governments of the oil-deficient nations should now support their home-based corporations in the formation of a bargaining bloc which would be a counterpoise to the OPEC bloc. This "chosen instrument" approach appears to possess both drawbacks and advantages in comparison with alternative solutions. It is open to the same objection as that made against a monopoly-monopsony of governments: it pits the buyers and sellers of oil against each other in an adversary relationship. And, because governments are able to offer inducements not available to corporations, such as technical assistance and economic and military aid, it can be argued that they have more bargaining leverage than would their corporations. On the other hand, the multinational oil companies have superior expertise to bring to the bargaining table. And oil pricing and production decisions that are made in the commercial arena are less likely to provoke international tensions than are decisions made in the diplomatic arena.

AN INTERNATIONAL
COMMODITY AGREEMENT
ON PETROLEUM

A third approach, which appears superior to the others in many ways, is to create an International Petroleum Policy Organization, consisting of representatives of the principal oil-exporting and oil-importing nations as well as the multinational oil companies whose expertise is essential, which would negotiate an international commodity agreement on petroleum. Conceivably, such an agreement would fix for several years in advance the amounts of royalties and taxes to be imposed by the OPEC members, the price-range of their sales of oil, and the range of production levels they would agree to maintain. Provision would be made for adjustments of oil prices by an index of world price movements. In return for commitments by the OPEC members to thus stabilize the supply and price of oil within specified ranges, the oil-importing countries might pledge technical aid in economic development and opportunities for the investment of surplus oil revenues.

Such a commodity agreement could be reviewed periodically and adjusted in the light of changing circumstances. Its purpose would be to provide a stable framework within which world petroleum markets could function. *The organization would not supplant markets*. It would specify only the agreed ranges of prices and outputs. Competition among oil enterprises in open markets would continue to play their important role of allocating petroleum supplies and of determining actual transaction prices. The broad concept of an international commodity agreement on petroleum was advanced as long ago as 1963 by Sheik Abdullah Tariki of Saudi Arabia at the Fourth Arab Oil Congress. Perhaps it is an idea whose time has come.

As has been noted, the potential support for an international commodity agreement on petroleum is strong, because many of the oil-importing nations—as well as the oil-exporting nations—favor an ample price for crude oil.[19] Such importing nations require a substantial price for imported oil in order to protect their domestic supplies and also to maintain an incentive to develop alternative energy sources.[20] Thus there is a large enough core of common interests in petroleum pricing and production policies to make a meeting of minds feasible.

A step toward multinational action was taken by President Nixon in March, 1974, when he convened the Washington Energy Conference of the OECD countries. The stated aim was to avoid a vicious cycle of unilateral action and national autarky which could threaten the world economic order. Secretary of State Kissinger proposed a seven-point program of international cooperation, involving the oil-exporting as well as the oil-importing countries. The program embraced oil conservation, expansion of alternative energy sources, research and development of new sources, emergency sharing of available oil supplies, aid to less-developed countries, and a consultative organization of producer and consumer nations to establish "just" petroleum policies reflecting the interests of all. Unfortunately, the French attitude was recalcitrant. France made clear her intention of "going it alone" in establishing relations with the Arab countries. Common Market and OECD internal relationships were put under severe strain.[21]

Following this unsuccessful effort to forge a multinational approach to energy problems, President Nixon signed on June 5, 1974, an agreement between the United States and Saudi Arabia for mutual cooperation in economic development and national security. Hopefully, this bilateral agreement between the most important oil exporter and the most powerful oil importer will be the precursor of a wider multinational consultative body to be formed in the future.

Nevertheless, an effort to organize an effective world petroleum policy organization and to negotiate a multinational agreement confronts formidable obstacles, as the Washington Energy Conference illustrated. Within both groups of oil-importing and oil-exporting countries, national interests, goals, and policies diverge. Reconciliation of differences could be a time-consuming process. For this reason, the best interim approach may be to build toward a multinational organization on a foundation of bilateral agreements between major oil-importing and oil-exporting nations. The agreement of June, 1974, between the government of the United States, the world's largest consumer of oil, and Saudi Arabia, the largest oil-producing country, could be a prototype. It could treat oil policy within the broad context of economic development and technical assistance. In carrying out that agreement, ARAMCO, which is jointly owned by the Saudi Arabian government and the four American multinational companies that market most of Saudi Arabia's oil, should play an important role. A three-way organization for collaboration, including the governments of the producing and the consuming nations and the multinational oil companies that serve both, could emerge from this.

THE FUTURE ROLE OF MULTINATIONAL OIL COMPANIES

Whether strategic oil pricing and output decisions continue to be made by the members of the OPEC or become the subject of an international commodity agreement, the role of multinational oil enterprises has changed. In most of the members of the OPEC, oil companies have become minority shareowners of crude oil reserves and production facilities, or contractors, exploring and producing oil for governments. They function mainly as buyers of crude oil from government oil companies, and as refiners and marketers of petroleum products. They have also become, as the Chairman of British Petroleum has wryly said, the "OPEC's tax collecting agency."

Should all oil-exporting nations ultimately take over 100 percent ownership of the producing operations within their borders, then, as Jamshid Amouzegar, a former president of the OPEC, has said, "We will have done with posted prices, taxes, and royalties."[22] The OPEC governments will simply sell oil to multinational companies at specified prices per barrel, and the companies will resell it, or refine and sell the products, on the best terms they can get in the market.

So far, most OPEC governments have chosen to market their oil through the companies whose producing facilities they have nationalized. They have given an option or a preferential purchase arrangement to those companies which have been affected. Companies then market such oil

—known in the trade as "buy-back oil"—to their customers through ordinary channels, along with their own oil, known in the trade as "equity oil." As time passes, the OPEC governments may invite sealed bids for their oil, or else auction it off to the highest bidder, thus creating highly competitive markets for crude oil. International oil companies would then compete for their raw material, just as they now compete in selling crude oil to independent refiners, or in selling refined products to independent jobbers and retailers. While this change would create a new area of competition, it does not pose a threat to the viability of private oil enterprises.

Multinational oil companies will not be without assets under the new world petroleum order. Even if all of their foreign crude oil reserves and production assets were taken over by governments, this would involve only $32 billion of a total of $134 billion, or less than 24 percent, of the total gross investment of the industry in fixed assets in foreign countries.[23] More than three-quarters of the industry's investment is in pipelines, tankers, refineries, chemical plants, and marketing facilities lying outside the control of OPEC members. Of course, much of it would be worthless without the OPEC's oil. But OPEC members need markets for their oil as urgently as the oil companies need to market their oil. Given the innumerable varieties of crude oil, the multiplicity of its uses, the multitude of buyers, and the many locations where it is needed, the business of marketing oil is highly technical. The government oil companies of the OPEC will need the expertise of the multinational oil companies in finding oil along with their refining, petrochemical, transportation, and marketing facilities. The members of OPEC may well acquire substantial equity investments in multinational oil companies. The oil industry is a natural repository of their surplus funds because it is the industry in which they have the deepest economic interest and about which they possess the most knowledge.

A foreign oil industry consisting mainly of private international companies competing in open markets has unique values to the Western World. Profit-motivated enterprises are better adapted to accept the long risks and to allocate multinational investment economically than are governments. They are under stronger pressures to seize emerging opportunities quickly and to avoid impending obstacles. They make it possible to transfer from the political to the commercial arena many international problems that would otherwise generate frictions among governments. As experts in world oil logistics, they balance production with consumption, adjust supplies from diverse sources in accordance with changes in relative costs, and compare prospective returns from many regions in allocating investments.

Private management, disciplined by competition, brings a greater flexibility of operations and adaptability to changing circumstances than would civil-servant management of socialized oil firms. Being prepared to invest in any country, the multinational oil company seeks the most profitable—which is normally the most efficient—way to meet petroleum demands. It takes a world view rather than a national view of consumers' requirements. Thus it promotes freedom of international trade and payments, and moderates the forces of extreme nationalism which tend to compartmentalize markets.

An old stereotype still shapes much contemporary thought about the foreign oil industry. This is the notion that an oligopoly or cartel of seven big companies holds up oil prices and exacts exorbitant profits. Although there may have been some substance to this view prior to World War II, our analysis has shown it to be inapplicable in the postwar era. The record shows that *effective* competition prevails. The proof lies in the fact that the rate of return on investment in the industry has been at or below normal levels for many years. Perhaps this truth about the performance of the industry will become more widely appreciated now that consumers of petroleum products have seen what happened to the supply and prices of oil when a real cartel, the Organization of Petroleum Exporting Countries, took command!

NOTES

1. See James E. Akins, "The Oil Crisis: This Time the Wolf is Here," *Petroleum Intelligence Weekly*, March 26, 1973, pp. 12–15.

2. See *Wall Street Journal*, June 6, 1974, and *Los Angeles Times*, May 24, 1974.

3. See James W. McKie, "The Political Economy of World Petroleum," *American Economic Review*, vol. 64, no. 2 (May, 1974), p. 51.

4. Statement of Dr. Dixy Lee Ray, Chairman, United States Atomic Energy Commission. See *The Energy Crisis*, an AEI Round Table (Washington, D.C.: American Enterprise Institute for Public Policy Research, Inc., 1974), p. 63.

5. See address of Emile van Lennep, Secretary-General of the OECD, to the Consultative Assembly of the Council of Europe on January 23, 1974, published as "Consequences of the Oil Price Rise," in *The OECD Observer* 68 (February, 1974): 3.

6. This conclusion was expressed by the Bank for International Settlements. See its *Annual Report 1973* (Basel, Switzerland: May 1974).

7. See the *Petroleum Economist*, vol. 41, no. 5 (May, 1974).

8. *Platt's Oilgram*, vol. 52, no. 106C (June 3, 1974).

9. The degree to which governments should augment the consumption-reducing effects of higher market prices for energy is a central issue of public policy. Most observers agree that governments should curb oil demand. See McKie, "The Political Economy of World Petroleum." Also, *Exploring Energy Choices: A Preliminary Report of the Energy Policy Project of the Ford Foundation* (Ford Foundation: Washington, D.C.: 1974).

10. Walter J. Levy, "World Oil Coöperation or International Chaos," *Foreign Affairs*, vol. 52, no. 4 (July, 1974), pp. 707–8.

11. U.S. Secretary of the Treasury William E. Simon was reported to have predicted that the price of crude oil, landed in the United States, would fall to $7 to $8 per barrel by mid–1975. See *New York Times*, July 25, 1974.

12. Lewis G. Weeks, "Subsea Petroleum Resources," in *Economic Significance of Sea-bed Mineral Resources of the Various Limits Proposed for National Jurisdiction* (New York: United Nations, April, 1973).

13. To provide a firm basis for planning shale extraction, coal conversion, and other such projects, the U.S. government's energy policy should include the establishment of an official "floor" for synthetic crude oil prices.

14. Exploratory drilling by ARAMCO in the Rub-al-Khali ("the empty quarter") has already found oil of very high quality. See the *Arizona Republic*, July 12, 1974.

15. See George S. Stocking and Myron W. Watkins, *Cartels in Action* (New York: Twentieth Century Fund, 1946), and George S. Stocking and Myron W. Watkins, *Cartels or Competition* (New York: Twentieth Century Fund, 1948), and the author's review article, "Perspectives on Monopoly," *Journal of Political Economy*, vol. 59, no. 6 (December, 1951), pp. 514–27.

16. See M. A. Adelman, "The Energy Problem," *Business Problems of the Seventies*, ed. Jules Backman (New York: New York University Press, 1973), p. 133.

17. See William D. Nordhaus, "The Allocation of Energy Resources," *Brookings Papers on Economic Activity*, 3 (1973) (Washington, D.C.: The Brookings Institution, 1973), p. 529.

18. See *The Energy Crisis*, An AEI Roundtable (Washington, D.C.: The American Enterprise Institute for Public Policy Research, June, 1974).

19. M. A. Adelman, *The World Petroleum Industry* (Baltimore: The Johns Hopkins University Press, 1972), pp. 248–49.

20. The latter point is made by McKie, "The Political Economy of World Petroleum." Walter Levy has also emphasized this point: "Completely free market prices for traded oil are not a practical alternative: in a free market the existence of large reserves and the very low costs of developing and producing oil would mean a market price that would be very low indeed. Such a price would not be acceptable to the producing countries. Nor would it in fact serve the interests of importing countries as a whole since it would lead to wasteful consumption of oil on the one hand and on the other would provide no inducement to the major countries to push

forward in good time with research on new and more costly sources." See Walter J. Levy, "World Oil Coöperation or International Chaos."

21.   See "The Washington Energy Conference," *The Atlantic Community Quarterly*, vol. 12, no. 1 (Spring, 1974), pp. 22–64.

22.   *Wall Street Journal*, July 8, 1974.

23.   See Chase Manhattan Bank, *Capital Investments of the World Petroleum Industry 1972*, (New York: Chase Manhattan Bank, 1973), p. 21. Canadian investment is considered "foreign" in this calculation.

12

The Competitive Dynamics of the Foreign Oil Industry: A Review

WHEN ECONOMISTS set about their "dismal" profession, the bricks with which they work are numbers, expressed in quantities, percentages, statistics, tables, and graphs, mortared together with theories, models, and, extrapolations. Numbers and computations are absolutely basic to adequate economic analysis, but the great quantity of them required, as well as their abstractness, frequently render their meaning impenetrable to the layman and, indeed, may cause an economist's colleagues to scratch their heads in wonder.

If an economist wants his work to escape from the stacks of the university libraries, the bookshelves of his colleagues, and the remainders tables of booksellers, he is obliged to try to say in ordinary language what he has so laboriously said in the specialized language of his profession. Indeed, in attempting to render his arcane investigations into the language of those who are interested without being deeply learned, the scholar imposes a valuable discipline upon himself. If his theoretical conclusions cannot be expressed in propositions that permit the layman to make an informed decision about the economic realities under examination, then he may have produced an elegant study, but it will do nothing for the world but satisfy the aesthetic cravings of his fellow economists.

Wanting our study to make a difference in the way the foreign oil industry is viewed, we now attempt to draw together our principal findings and conclusions, through brief reviews of each chapter. After these reviews, we conclude by drawing what we believe to be the lessons that can be learned from the history of the foreign oil industry over the past quarter-century or so.

THE FOREIGN OIL INDUSTRY: A MODEL FOR ITS ANALYSIS

This economic study of the foreign oil industry utilized the tools of economic theory and statistical inference. A dynamic conceptual model was used in which the *behavior* of the market (measured in price movements, price-cost relations, returns on investment, and technological progress) is determined by the growth of demand, management policies, and the structure of the market. Market *structure*, in turn, is shaped mainly by the technical nature of production, the character of demand, the environment of governmental regulation, and the number and sophistication of buyers. The *market* under study is the foreign non-Communist world market for crude oil and petroleum products, omitting markets in these commodities in Canada and the United States, which have been separated by trade and other barriers.

Competition in this market is viewed as a dynamic multi-vectored process. Its vigor may be measured by trends in the market shares and in the concentration of sales among leading firms, by rates of entry of new firms, by the tendency of price to equal average cost including normal profits, and by the tendency of the rate of return on investment to approach the average for all industries, after adjustment for the level of risk. The hypothesis of this study is that during the postwar period of 1948 through 1972, progressive changes in the determinants of the structure of the foreign oil industry caused the market behavior of the industry to reflect growing competition, and that, by the 1960s, competition was effective.

CHARACTERISTICS OF
THE FOREIGN OIL INDUSTRY

The petroleum industry plays an essential role in the economy of every developed country. In the highly developed U.S. economy, which now produces about two-thirds of the oil it consumes, the industry accounts for over 5 percent of the Gross National Product.

The basic determinants of foreign oil supply include a high level of political and discovery risks of investment, extensive governmental regulation, relatively high barriers to entry, and a need for continuity of operations. Correspondingly, the major features of foreign oil companies are: the use of large-scale plants to achieve operating economies, much multinational diversification, vertical integration into the several divisions of the industry, very intensive use of capital, and long-term planning of investments. These factors tend to make for relatively high concentration in the foreign oil industry. And further, governmental concession policies played an important role in concentrating the industry up to the end of World War II.

THE AMERICAN ENTRY INTO THE
FOREIGN OIL INDUSTRY

World War I created a huge drain on U.S. oil. Fear of inadequate domestic reserves caused the U.S. government to urge its nationals to develop foreign sources and to support them in this effort. But American oil companies were unable to obtain exploration concessions in the

Middle East and other areas because of the political influence of the British, Dutch, and French empires. The United States called for an "open door" policy. Ultimately, after prolonged and stubborn British opposition, an agreement was made in 1928 admitting Exxon, Mobil, Gulf, Atlantic, and Standard Oil of Indiana as participants in the Turkish Petroleum Company (TPC), known after 1929 as Iraq Petroleum Company (IPC), along with Shell, Anglo-Persian, CFP, and Gulbenkian.

The monopoly position of the IPC participants in the Middle East eroded when, in 1932, Socal discovered oil in its Bahrain concession, and in the following year obtained a concession in Saudi Arabia. Gulf joined with B.P. in a concession in Kuwait. Texaco also entered the scene by acquiring, in 1936, a half-interest in Socal's Bahrain and Saudi Arabian concessions; in return, Socal acquired a half-interest in Texaco's Far Eastern marketing facilities and joined with Texaco in forming Caltex. Commercial oil was found in both Saudi Arabia and Kuwait in 1938, and after World War II the vast deposits in these countries drastically changed the world oil situation.

During World War II, the foreign oil industry came under the control of governments; its structure was frozen and there were no important entrants. Military demands for petroleum strained the capacity of the U.S. industry, and at the war's end the oil export potential of the United States had passed its peak; the Caribbean and the Middle East had emerged as the dominant foreign sources. Seven large multinational oil companies, taken together, owned 92 percent of the oil reserves of the foreign non-Communist world and 88 percent of its crude oil production at the end of the war. However, the war terminated British and French domination of the Middle East.

World reconstruction needs dampened United States investment in foreign oil during the immediate postwar years. Only two significant entries occurred in 1948 and 1949: the American Independent Oil Company (Aminoil), a consortium of ten U.S. firms, obtained the concession to

Kuwait's half-interest in the Neutral Zone in 1948; and Getty acquired the concession to the Saudi Arabian interest the next year.

THE POSTWAR EXPLOSION
OF FOREIGN OIL CONSUMPTION

Since World War II, petroleum has been the dynamic element of foreign energy consumption, enlarging its role at the expense of coal. Between 1949 and 1972, oil usage rose from 15 percent to 57 percent of total energy consumption in Western Europe, and from 39 percent to 62 percent in the rest of the foreign non-Communist world.

Over the period from 1948 to 1972, foreign non-Communist world consumption of petroleum grew at the astonishing average compound rate of nearly 11 percent per annum. This was two and one-half times the United States and Canadian growth rate of 4.5 percent a year. In absolute figures, foreign non-Communist world consumption rose steadily from 2.4 million barrels per day in 1948 to 26.2 million barrels per day in 1972. The foreign market accounted for two-thirds of the postwar non-Communist world gain in petroleum usage. This explosive upthrust in the foreign use of oil led existing oil companies to expand their facilities, and it enticed a myriad of new firms into the industry.

There was a huge postwar increase in international movements of petroleum, and major changes in the character of these movements. The United States became a net importer, marking a historic change from its traditional role as an exporter. The flow from the Middle East to other countries swelled from 1.5 million barrels per day in 1950 to 16.7 million barrels per day in 1972. Over the same span of time, the flow of oil from the Caribbean (mainly into North America) rose from 1.2 to 3.5 million barrels per day, from North Africa it rose from a negligible quantity to 3.4 million barrels per day, and Soviet oil shipments to European markets rose to one million barrels per day.

As a result of the location of refineries in countries with large consuming markets, following World War II, rather than in the producing countries, nearly 83 percent of international petroleum trade in 1972 was in crude oil and only 17 percent in products. Before World War II, two-thirds of the movement had been in products.

THE RISING TIDE OF THE FOREIGN OIL SUPPLY

Stimulated by the powerful upsurge in consumption and the influx of new firms, the postwar capacity of the foreign oil industry was built up rapidly. Between 1948 and 1972, foreign non-Communist world proven reserves of crude oil multiplied thirteen times from 41 billion to 522 billion barrels. Crude oil production rates rose tenfold from 3 million to 31 million barrels daily. Refining capacity increased more than twelvefold from 2.8 million to 35 million barrels per day. The tanker fleet octupled its deadweight capacity from 26.2 million deadweight tons in 1949 to 219 million tons in 1972 (most of which was represented by large, fast supertankers). Major trunk pipeline mileage rose from 1,800 to nearly 15,000; and marketing facilities expanded proportionately. All of this was reflected in a nearly twentyfold increase in the amount of gross investment in fixed assets—from $6.9 billion in 1946 to $134 billion in 1972.

The annual compound rates of growth in the foreign oil industry over the period from 1948 to 1972 were exceptionally high: 11 percent for proven reserves; 9.5 percent for tanker tonnage; and 12 percent for gross investment. These rates of growth were matched in the Communist countries, but were three to four times those in the United States and Canada.

The preponderance of the new oil supply came from the Middle East, Venezuela, North Africa, and the Soviet Union, while the bulk of the new refining capacity was built in the major consuming nations of Western Europe and Japan.

Technological developments, such as offshore oil production, new methods of secondary recovery, supertankers, large-diameter pipelines, catalytic reforming, market-oriented refineries, and high-volume retail service stations, created opportunities for new firms and gave them locational and other cost advantages over established companies committed to existing assets.

There was a strong tendency toward aggregate over-investment in foreign oil exploration and development. It arose largely from competitive drives, pressure exerted on oil companies by host governments, the lure of the "big strike," and the subsidized activities of government companies.

As a result of the hectic postwar investment, a large margin of excess capacity had emerged by the late 1950s and persisted through the 1960s in every division of the industry. Proven reserves were sufficient to meet the 1972 rate of non-Communist world consumption for a period of thirty-eight years (ignoring Soviet supplies). Until the 1970s, annual output from existing facilities could have been stepped up quickly by one-fifth, and there were margins of unused capacity of 15–20 percent in marine transportation and refining. United States and European government officials recognized that, after 1957, a buyers' market for petroleum had emerged. In competitive markets, the imbalance between demand and supply led to reduced prices and lower returns on investment.

RISING GOVERNMENTAL INTERVENTION IN THE INDUSTRY

A primary effect of postwar governmental petroleum policies was to increase the number of private oil enterprises and to invigorate competition. In 1972 private enterprises produced about 90 percent of the world's crude oil and petroleum products outside of the Communist bloc. However, governments increasingly intervened in the industry. They nationalized private oil properties, es-

tablished government-owned companies, regulated refining and marketing, imposed higher taxes, and—above all
—began during the 1970s to make strategic crude-oil
pricing and production decisions.

Among the major causes of this rising governmental
intervention were the breakup of colonial empires and the
emergence of more than eighty new nations; rapid advances in popular education, communication, and transportation, which created a drive for early economic
development; the emergence of the Soviet Union as a
powerful exponent of statism; and the grouping of countries into economic blocs such as the European Economic
Community (EEC) formed in 1958, the Organization of
Petroleum Exporting Countries (OPEC) formed in 1960,
and the Organization of Arab Petroleum Exporting Countries (OAPEC) formed in 1968.

The intervention of foreign governments and international bodies affected almost every aspect of the foreign
oil industry after World War II. Most prewar petroleum
concessions by governments to foreign oil companies
were individually negotiated, covered large areas, were of
long duration, and were granted to one or a few firms.
After World War II, most countries enacted general petroleum laws under which smaller and more numerous
concessions of shorter duration were granted to many
firms. In some countries, foreign firms were engaged as
government contractors on a fee basis, rather than
granted concessions to work as principals. These policies
opened the field to new entrants.

Foreign governments enormously increased the royalties and taxes on oil production, and this depressed oil
company profits and returns on investment. With a few
notable exceptions, there was a progressive postwar relaxation of barriers to trade in crude oil and its products, as
exchange controls were generally relaxed and quotas on
imports liberalized. These actions were an exception to
the general drift toward more governmental intervention.
The imposition of oil import quotas in the United States
in 1957 diverted American companies into foreign mar-

keting, augmented foreign oil supplies, and enhanced competition in foreign petroleum markets. And there was a strong revival of competitive market policies in many countries of the non-Communist world, expressed in the passage and enforcement of antimonopoly laws.

After 1959, oil companies had to deal with *organized groups* of nations as well as individual countries. The oil-importing countries of Western Europe moved toward a Common Market energy policy, stressing diversified and secure sources of low-cost energy. The countries accounting for 93 percent of non-Communist crude oil exports and 78 percent of crude oil reserves formed the OPEC with the aim of raising posted oil prices and increasing their revenues. The international oil companies were "ground between the upper and nether millstones" of the opposing pressures exerted by these powerful political blocs. Vulnerable to these pressures, their powers over oil prices were progressively reduced.

THE ENTRANCE OF FIRMS
INTO THE INDUSTRY

During the period from 1953 to 1972, more than three hundred private companies and fifty government companies entered or significantly expanded their activities in the foreign oil industry. By 1972, there were at least fifty new integrated international oil enterprises in operation.

The rush of new entrants was caused by easier conditions of entry, lower apparent risks, and higher apparent profit incentives. Liberalized government policies opened oil-bearing lands to new concessionaires and markets to new refiners and distributors. Technological advances created new opportunities. The rapid growth of petroleum consumption, striking successes in discovering new oil deposits, and favorable tax considerations all reduced the apparent risks of oil enterprise. The high profit rates of the established companies up to the mid-1950s also was an enticement. The slower growth of the U.S. market, combined with domestic production controls and import quotas, diverted attention to foreign markets. Government companies entered the industry to implement national energy policies, to conserve foreign exchange, or to provide a symbol of national sovereignty and prestige.

Collectively, firms other than the "seven largest" (including the Soviet Oil Trust) had, between 1953 and the end of 1972, increased the area of their exploration concessions (from 36 percent to 76 percent of the foreign non-Communist world total); multiplied their ownership of crude oil reserves (from 8 percent to about 33 percent of the total); expanded their production of crude oil (from 13 percent to 29 percent); increased their ownership of tankers (from 71 percent to 81 percent of available capacity); raised their refinery capacity (from 27 percent to 51 percent of the total); and expanded their marketing of petroleum products in major Eastern Hemisphere countries (from 28 percent to 46 percent of total volume).

In 1953 only twenty-eight U.S. firms and fifteen foreign firms—other than the seven largest—had oil exploration rights outside their own countries, and they held no more than 35 percent of concession areas. By the end of 1972, more than 330 other firms had exploration rights in 122 areas of the world and held 69 percent of concession areas.

In 1953 no private oil company (other than the seven largest), and only one government oil company, had foreign reserves of two billion barrels or more. By 1972 thirteen other companies were in this class, and their collective reserves had risen from almost 3.2 billion barrels to nearly 112 billion barrels.

In 1953 no oil company (other than the seven largest) had daily crude oil production of 200,000 barrels or more. By the end of 1972, thirteen of the new companies had passed this level, and their collective production had risen to about 5.2 million barrels per day. Collectively, they accounted for one-sixth of non-Communist world crude oil production in 1953 and nearly one-quarter of the production in 1972.

During the period from 1953 to 1972, 55 percent of all refining capacity was built by firms other than the seven largest. In 1953 no oil company (other than the three largest) had a daily capacity of 250,000 barrels or more. By the end of 1972, seventeen other companies owned at least 250,000 barrels per day or more of refining capacity.

In the marketing of petroleum products, only two companies other than the seven largest (CFP and Petrofina) were substantial international factors in 1953. By 1972 these firms had greatly extended their operations and had been joined by at least a dozen others—plus scores of domestic marketers.

THE REENTRY OF THE SOVIET UNION INTO WESTERN OIL MARKETS

By far the most important single entrant into the foreign oil industry during the 1950s was the oil trust of the Soviet Union. The Soviet Union entered the export market on a significant scale after 1953 and, by 1972, exported 1,035,000 barrels per day into foreign non-Communist world countries, thus accounting for about 4 percent of their petroleum consumption. Soviet entry also reduced the concentration of the industry.

Although the Russian petroleum industry was of great importance historically, revolution and war had interrupted its development, and only after 1950 did the Soviet Union embark upon an ambitious program to expand it. By 1972 Communist bloc output (of which Soviet Union production was 90 percent) was equal to 29 percent of total foreign non-Communist world oil production, and the Soviet Union was then second only to the United States as an oil-producing nation. The USSR contains potential oil-bearing areas larger than those of the United States, and most of this area remains to be explored. Geological factors will not limit USSR production for many years.

The fast expansion of pipelines from the Ural-Volga

fields westward to Baltic ports and the Communist satellite countries, combined with a growing tanker fleet, supports the delivery of more than one million barrels of petroleum per day into non-Communist world countries.

The Soviet Union has sought to expand petroleum exports because of their low cost compared to other Soviet exports. In addition, it has had the political motives of spreading Communist influence in the world and fostering government-to-government trading and public oil enterprise. The Soviet oil trust was sometimes a disruptive factor in Western oil markets because of its unorthodox trading methods, its egregious price discrimination (satellites sometimes paid double the price paid by adjacent non-Communist countries for the same oil), and its acceptance of soft currencies or bartered goods in payment. It diffused the industry by aiding government-owned oil companies in many countries to expand their operations. Soviet oil sales materially increased Western petroleum supplies and contributed to reduced prices and returns on oil investment.

CHANGES IN THE
STRUCTURE OF THE INDUSTRY

The primary impacts of the postwar changes in the worldwide oil industry were to multiply the number of competitors in every division of the foreign oil industry, to reduce its concentration, to diminish the market occupancy of the "seven largest" firms, and to make the industry much more heterogeneous in nature. The established companies were confronted with different groups of new competitors in each division of their business. Competition underwent progressive pluralism.

The average annual compound rates of growth of the seven largest companies combined were high in most divisions of the industry between 1953 and 1972: 9 percent in reserves, 9 percent in production, 8 percent in refining capacity, and 13 percent in product marketing.

But the growth rates of the newcomers as a group were very much higher: 19 percent in reserves, 15 percent in production, 15 percent in refining capacity, and 18 percent in product marketing.

The seven largest companies, taken together, suffered marked declines in their positions in every division of the industry over the period from 1953 to 1972, as has been shown. It was statistically invalid to describe the structure of the foreign oil industry in 1972 in terms of the "seven largest" firms versus "others." Four giants—Exxon, Shell, Texaco, and B.P.—stood high above the others in most activities; but a widening group of newcomers bore increasing strong resemblances in size and economic power to the other three firms among the "seven largest."

Judged by accepted measures, the foreign oil industry passed from a position of very high concentration in ownership of crude oil reserves, daily production, and petroleum sales in 1953 to a position of moderate concentration in 1972. It moved from moderately high to moderately low concentration with respect to refining capacity and product marketing. In ownership of concessions, it moved from moderate to low concentration. And it moved from low concentration in ownership of tanker capacity to a status of very low concentration.

Unsystematic shifts occurred each year, in the market occupancy ratios of individual companies among the "seven largest," in regard to concession areas, reserves, production, refining capacity, or product market sales. These shifts were inconsistent with the existence of any effective overt or tacit scheme of market "sharing" among them.

The plurality of entering companies and the increasing diversity of interests of existing companies, resulting from discoveries of new oil pools and the opening of new markets, greatly increased the heterogeneity of the industry. This widening diversity of interests of existing companies eliminated any real possibility of an effective concert of action among firms in regard to production or pricing policies.

CHANGES IN THE BEHAVIOR
OF THE INDUSTRY

Postwar changes in the structure of the foreign oil industry were accompanied by important changes in its behavior. The movements of prices, the changes in returns on investment, and the pace of technological progress all reflected the presence of growing, effective competition.

Prior to World War II, the supply of foreign crude oil was small in relation to foreign consumption, and foreign oils were priced to meet crude oil from the United States Gulf delivered into foreign markets. This basis of pricing, known as "Gulf-Plus," passed into history in 1948 and 1949, when crude oil prices at ports of origin in the Persian Gulf were sharply reduced (by about 50 cents per barrel) to enable them to undersell Western Hemisphere crude oil in Eastern Hemisphere markets.

As a result of the booming oil demand and curtailed supplies during the Korean War and the Iranian and Suez crises, a strong sellers' market for crude oil prevailed between 1950 and 1957. Prices posted at leading Caribbean and Persian Gulf ports strengthened and rose in 1953 and 1957.

After 1957 surplus oil producing capacity and the advent of U.S. import quotas gave rise to a buyers' market in the foreign non-Communist world. Many new suppliers commenced to sell their foreign crude oils to a growing number of nonintegrated refiners. Posted f.o.b. prices in Persian Gulf and Caribbean ports of origin were cut by about 15 percent in 1959 and 1960, falling to 1953 levels. Because of additional discounts and allowances and reduced transportation charges, average *delivered* prices paid by nonintegrated refiners at ports of entry in major foreign markets fell even more steeply, dropping by 25 to 35 percent, between 1957 and 1962, and continuing in a generally horizontal trend until the early 1970s, when they began rising.

Crude oil prices became essentially market-determined,

rather than supplier-announced, in the major consuming nations. Nonintegrated refiners were able to obtain oil at reduced prices from a growing number of new producers; and nonintegrated marketing firms were able to obtain refined products at reduced prices from many new vendors. Nonintegrated refiners with lower-cost crude oil cut product prices in their national markets, thereby reducing the refining value of crude oil and forcing competing refiners to pay less for crude oil in order to avoid loss. Prices of crude oils thus depended more closely upon the prices of petroleum products in each national market. Imperfect knowledge, intense rivalry among sellers, and shrewd bargaining by buyers led to unsystematic and divergent prices within and between national markets.

The prices of major refined products—gasolines, gas oils, and fuel oils—in the international market behaved like the prices of crude oils. Posted prices rose generally through 1957, after which they declined with the emergence of the buyers' market. Delivered prices dropped by 5 to 45 percent through 1961 and maintained a low level through the 1960s until dollar devaluation and the disappearance of surplus productive capacity caused them to rise in the 1970s.

Competitive market pressures caused managements of foreign oil companies to improve their products and processes, lower costs, and make innovations. Judged by its research and development expenditures, the oil industry's technological progress was excellent.

Postwar returns on investment in the industry reflected a decisive competitive adjustment to changes in supply-demand conditions. For U.S. firms as a group, profits on foreign oil investment reached a peak of 30 percent of average invested capital in 1955, and stayed well above 20 percent through 1957. These high rates of return attracted huge investments and led to proportionate increases in the oil supply. By 1959 the profit rate fell to 13 percent and remained in this neighborhood up to the 1970s. The end of the growth of new capital investment came in 1957 for the seven largest firms and in 1959 for the others.

By basic economic tests, the behavior of the foreign oil industry during the 1950s and 1960s reflected effective competition.

THE WORLD OIL REVOLUTION OF THE 1970s AND THE FUTURE

Between late 1973 and early 1974, the foreign oil industry was subjected to revolutionary economic changes. Crude oil pricing decisions, traditionally initiated by the international oil companies, were taken over by the OPEC members. Oil-exporting nations progressively nationalized private petroleum production properties and acquired majority ownership. The OPEC members quadrupled the price of crude oil, and the OAPEC members cut back production and put an embargo on shipments to the United States for political purposes. These actions set in motion radical changes in national energy policies, in international balances of payments, and in the role of multinational oil companies. The age of inexpensive oil and of market determination of petroleum prices and outputs had passed.

Accelerating worldwide price inflation and the Arab-Israeli war triggered the OPEC's price-raising actions. For years prior to 1973 and 1974, the terms of international trade had moved against the oil-exporting countries, which were trading their low-priced oil for the increasingly expensive manufactured goods and services of the oil-importing nations. The other motive behind the oil price revolution was the rising nationalism, fanned by the Arab-Israeli conflict, of the OAPEC members, who became determined to act in concert to foster their own economic development and political power in the world. A more determined nationalism also lay behind the drive for majority ownership and, perhaps, ultimate 100 percent control of the oil production facilities within their boundaries.

The rocketing price of oil was estimated to add about $60 billion to payments due to the OPEC countries by the oil-deficient nations during 1974. Many countries would need the new credit facilities of the International Monetary Fund (IMF) to meet their obligations. Those OPEC countries whose inflow of funds surpassed their capacity for domestic investment began to invest in foreign assets and to lend money to less-developed countries. The short-term financing problem appeared to be difficult but manageable.

The quadrupling of crude oil prices quickly led to large increases in the prices of coal, natural gas, and nuclear fuels. The rate of energy consumption in general, and especially of oil consumption, dropped significantly. Official estimates of future consumption were revised downward, and the role of oil versus other energy sources was diminished. Foreign oil consumption will continue to grow, although at a much lower rate. Should the OPEC cartel pursue highly restrictive policies in the future, establishing and maintaining, for example, even higher prices per barrel and cutting back production, the annual growth of consumption could be reduced to 4 percent or even much less. Should the OPEC pursue a moderate policy, pricing oil around $8-per-barrel, consumption would probably rise by 4 to 8 percent a year.

The OPEC—and not the amount of hydrocarbons in the earth's crust, or the international oil companies— probably will determine the future foreign oil supply. Factors that would lead the OPEC to pursue a liberal policy include the probability that new large oil fields will be discovered; or that oil will be extracted from shale, tar sands, and coal outside of OPEC control; or the possibility of a world financial breakdown, if the price of crude oil were pushed too high. OPEC members would incline toward a restrictive policy if world price inflation continued, or if its members were unable to find acceptable investments for their surplus funds. The balance of considerations appears to lie in the direction of a moderate petroleum policy by the OPEC. This assumes, however, that the OECD countries act vigorously to reduce inflation and facilitate long-term foreign investments by the OPEC members, and that the OPEC countries rationally assess their long-term interests.

The strategic decisions in pricing and producing foreign oil having passed—for good or for evil—into the hands of the OPEC governments, the relevant issue now is to determine what kind of institution and process is needed to formulate petroleum policies beneficial to the world. Clearly, such policies will not in the long run be left to the unilateral determination of a cartel of oil-exporting countries representing only producer interests. An oligopsony of the oil-importing nations, bargaining collectively with the OPEC bloc and countervailing its power, does not appear attractive because of the frictions it would generate and the danger of an impasse.

Nor would a consortium of multinational oil companies, formed with the cooperation of the governments of the oil-importing countries and acting as their "chosen instrument" for collective bargaining, be satisfactory. This course of action is open to the same objections that can be urged against an international monopsony, plus the drawbacks of possibly impairing competitive drives and of being less effective than government-to-government bargaining.

An international commodity agreement, reached by negotiation within a world petroleum policy organization representing the OPEC and OECD countries and the multinational oil companies, appears to be the best means of stabilizing the supply of crude oil at a reasonable price level. Such an agreement could fix, for several years ahead, the *ranges* of taxes and royalties to be charged by the OPEC governments, of the prices they would charge for oil, and of aggregate production to be maintained. Within this framework, market competition among oil enterprises would continue to determine actual prices and to allocate petroleum supplies throughout the world. Although the obstacles to the establishment of a global oil policy body are formidable, the probability of recurrent energy crises in its absence and the common interests of most countries in an ample price for crude oil give hope of ultimate success.

Multinational oil companies will continue to perform vital economic functions in the new world petroleum order, as buyers of crude oil from governments and as refiners and marketers of petroleum products. Their exploration, production, refining, and marketing expertise are indispensable to the OPEC members—and about three-quarters of their assets are outside of the OPEC countries. A foreign oil industry consisting mainly of private multinational companies competing in open markets has unique values to the Western World. Profit-motivated firms have proven to be better adapted to accept long-term risks and to allocate investment multinationally than have politically motivated governmental agencies. Furthermore, taking a world view of consumers' requirements, multinational corporations tend to promote freedom of trade and to moderate extreme nationalism.

LESSONS FROM
THE POSTWAR HISTORY
OF THE FOREIGN OIL INDUSTRY

We may conclude by paraphrasing Santayana: those who cannot learn from history are condemned to repeat it. An economic analysis of the postwar evolution of the foreign oil industry teaches some lessons of value to makers of contemporary public policy. Some of the insights helpful in dealing with current energy issues are these:

1. The system of market competition among oil enterprises that prevailed during the postwar era did, on the whole, serve the world's consumers of petroleum products well. It met the exploding demands with remarkably little disruption; and it did so at returns to investors that were

modest in relation to the risks assumed. Because the competitive market has proved its worth, the burden of proof that consumers of petroleum products would be better served by public enterprises or by governmental regulation of oil prices, profits, and investment returns, is surely upon him who makes such proposals. The future world oil order should retain a maximum role for market competition among enterprises.

2. Nation-states have always dominated the structure of the petroleum industry in one way or another. The influence of governments has pervaded the industry from its beginning, having been expressed in national energy policies, concession policies, refining policies, trade barriers, and so on. In the end, governments determine the number of firms in the industry and how vigorously they compete. Nations have gotten as much or as little competition as they permitted!

3. National sovereignty has prevailed over corporate power, notwithstanding the popular belief to the contrary. The largest multinational oil company has bent to the will of the governments with which it dealt. Even a giant like Exxon has had to accede to demands for higher taxes or the nationalization of its properties made by the governments of comparatively small and weak nations, such as Libya. This imbalance of power is likely to continue.

4. The multinational oil companies vigorously and tenaciously—but unsuccessfully—opposed the actions of the OPEC members to raise oil prices and to restrict production during 1973 and 1974. The record refutes the notion that they conspired with the OPEC governments to cut back production, raise prices, and extort profits from consumers.[1] Company profits did rise sharply as a result of dollar devaluation and temporary shortages; and the coincidence of this event with a vast increase in the revenues of the OPEC countries no doubt lent credibility to a theory of conspiracy. But the growing surplus of crude oil at the prices that prevailed in mid–1974 appeared likely to reduce oil company profits substantially,

although the bonanza enjoyed by the OPEC members could continue indefinitely. Temporary bulges in company profits should no more justify higher income taxation—which would cripple the ability of firms to meet public energy demands—than temporary losses should become the occasion for public subsidies.

5. Monopolistic behavior by the largest firms is highly improbable in a dynamic industry with a fast-growing market open to entrants. Under these conditions, it is simply too difficult to maintain any "understanding" for restricting output, holding up prices, or dividing up markets, that will optimize the interests of all companies in the industry.

6. The structural and behavioral *dynamics* of an industry should be intensively assessed before any broadside antitrust action is launched against its member firms. Had such an analysis been made of the foreign oil industry before the International Oil Cartel suit was commenced in 1953, it would have been found that foreign governmental policies and market growth were eroding the basic premises upon which the suit was based, and large resources of both the U.S. government and of the oil industry could have been saved. Nevertheless, the governments of some countries have recently filed antitrust charges against multinational oil companies in an effort to make them responsible for the rise in the prices of petroleum products. The real cause is, of course, the OPEC cartel.

7. Because the international petroleum trade constitutes the outstanding case of international economic interdependence in the world today, the political capabilities of nations for cooperation will be tested sooner, and more rigorously, in dealing with world oil than with any other matter.[2] The absolute necessity of cooperative action among the major oil-importing nations, and between them and the OPEC countries, in formulating strategic petroleum policies, has become apparent to all thoughtful observers.[3]

NOTES

1. The Subcommittee on Multinational Corporations of the Committee on Foreign Relations of the U.S. Senate held hearings on the actions of American multinational oil companies during the Arab oil embargo. Senator Church, Chairman of the Subcommittee, stated that charges that ARAMCO encouraged the Saudi Arabian government to increase the posted price of crude oil "were not substantiated." See *Platt's Oilgram News Service*, August 7, 1974, p. 3. Senator Henry Jackson, who also presided over a senatorial investigation of the oil embargo and the multinational oil companies, stated that his probe had "not turned up any hard evidence that the major oil companies deliberately created the crisis, either in parallel or in concert. . . . I have found no reason to believe that the companies set about knowingly to create it [the oil shortage]." See *Oil Daily*, January 24, 1974, p. 1.

2. See, for example, "Cooperative Solutions," *The Petroleum Economist*, vol. 41, no. 5 (May 1974), p. 162.

3. See Sam H. Schurr and Paul T. Homan, *Middle Eastern Oil and the Western World* (New York: American Elsevier Publishing Company, Inc., 1971), p. 14.

Index

Studies of the Modern Corporation
Columbia University Graduate School of Business